CW01632452

ALL OUR YESTERDAYS

Kevin Sinclair

A HISTORY OF SUNDERLAND AFC

1945 - 2025

Back Cover photography by Malcolm Richardson

First published in 2023
Second edition 2024
Third edition 2025

lou56903@gmail.com

ISBN: 978 1 7384484 2 5

Printed by Penny Print, Unit 1 Halifax Road, Dunston,
Tyne and Wear, NE11 9JW.

CONTENTS

ACKNOWLEDGEMENTS

I convey warm thanks to Stephen Murdoch who has taken great time in proofreading, editing and formatting.

Kevin Sinclair

FOREWORD

I have supported Sunderland from the age of seven. My late father Gordon took me to my first game, a late summer's evening fixture against Southampton in 1966, which our team won 2-0.

Back in those days, other than in newspapers and the match day programme, very little was written about the club's history; also, those publications were not as lavish and in-depth as today's counterparts. I relied on stories told to me by an older generation; stories I suspected that were exaggerated, stories that always seemed to include the name of Len Shackleton and a recurring theme of huge crowds and glorious failures. I soaked up the colourful prose of Len Hetherington in the Evening Chronicle and avidly read Arthur Appleton's fascinating, but in the style of the times, rather dryly written book, 'The Hotbed of Soccer'. It was not until 1979 that I was able to separate fact from fiction and form a definitive grasp of where the club stood in the game. That was when Appleton, whom I believe to have been the finest writer in bringing to life Sunderland's early history, produced a superbly written and researched Centenary booklet, with the assistance of Billy Simmons.

Since my retirement I determined to write my own history of the football club. There are now numerous publications regarding Sunderland, some remarkably informative, covering a wide range of topics. I trust that this book succeeds as a favourable alternative in providing a complete, accurate, and indeed unbiased view of the club over such a long period.

I have principally used archived newspaper material, my collection of battered memorabilia and a wealth of football books, in particular those including the autobiographies of past players and managers. Most importantly, I have provided personal recollections in an attempt to place the reader at the heart of events.

Kevin Sinclair

INTRODUCTION

This is a true story of agony and ecstasy, right and wrong, hope and despair, good and bad. A microcosm of life. Sunderland recently languished in League One and are now back in the Premier League. Yet, it is the achievements in years gone by, if not quite in time immemorial, that will guarantee the red and whites a position firmly at the centre of the game's rich heritage. Until 1958 they were the only club in England to have experienced nothing other than the top-flight. Before the accession of King Charles III, they were the only club to have won one of the main domestic honours available under every monarch since Victorian times. In total there have been six English titles, no less than nineteen finishes in the first three and two FA Cup triumphs.

Most of the post-war period is distinguished by a meagre rationing of moving between the top two divisions, initially at an increasingly dated Roker Park and then at a once opulent Stadium of Light. Only rarely has the fanaticism and never-ending faith of the Sunderland followers been rewarded. Without warning, suddenly and startlingly, there was in 1973 an FA Cup win to wonder at in disbelief. The great and original Sunderland historian Arthur Appleton was not wrong when he deemed it, 'A gift from the gods'. However, that victory over Leeds United did not signpost a return to eminence. The fabled upturn never materialised. Now there has been another wondrous episode, almost as unexpected and with enough incredibility to elevate it within an echo of that never to be repeated '73 fairy tale. Sunderland, after an eight-year absence, are back in the Premier League. That is a remarkable achievement for a club that has relied almost exclusively on their academy to develop players. The drama from the play-off games against Coventry and Sheffield United will be long remembered, not the previous 46-game slog.

Football supporters have selective memories. There is a tendency to recall with fondness the first, or probably, only period of success he or she has witnessed over the many years of watching their team and wonder why this cannot be the default position. If that success should coincide with the impressionable years of youth that feeling is heightened; how many Nottingham Forest fans who cut their City Ground teeth on the European Cup glories of the Clough-Taylor era remain convinced their team is merely marking time before a return to former glories? Quite a few I suspect.

INTRODUCTION

My father's generation that experienced its first awakening of interest in the game during the immediate pre- or post-war years was hooked for life by the devastatingly intelligent, skilful inside forward play of Raich Carter or the sorcery of Len Shackleton. The following years of mediocrity were sugar-coated by an unshakeable belief that at the very least, success comes in cycles and that, in due course, the club would rise again.

The immediate post-war Sunderland teams were overshadowed by the greats of the past. When competitive football commenced after the war a population starved of entertainment and freedom flocked to grounds. Roker Park was busier than it had ever been. The public however remained in awe of the late thirties' team that had ended Arsenal's run of three consecutive championships. The coruscating trio of Gurney, Burbanks and Carter contributed 78 goals from a grand total of 109 during that famous title-winning 1935-36 season. This placed Sunderland on a historical league-winning par with Aston Villa and above everyone else. The following year at Wembley a first FA Cup triumph followed.

Arsenal, resplendent within Highbury's marble opulence, were the original Bank of England team and proof that success could be bought. Their acquisitions of David Jack and Bryn Jones had smashed the British transfer record. As the fifties dawned a Sunderland board of directors headed by their charismatic chairman Ted Ditchburn attempted to emulate them. Ditchburn, a lifetime fanatic, could recall the Victorian 'Team of All The Talents' and was present at Crystal Palace in 1913 when a 1-0 Cup final defeat from Villa deprived his first love of the famous double. That side included Charles Buchan, the club's all-time record league scorer.

The Stadium of Light contrasts sharply with Roker Park. The feature binding the old with the new is a unique, timeless roar that crystallises on those rare occasions when something special is stirring. It was heard at the stadium for the Coventry game; it was transported to Wembley for the Sheffield United game. Is it enough to give Sunderland a sporting chance to overcome those clubs based in the fashionable parts of the country or who have obscenely wealthy owners? Anyone who remembers the romantic events of 1973, whether a die-hard supporter or corporate box holder, can be forgiven for thinking that dreams can come true, and the very recent events from May 2025 has given contemporary followers a tantalising hope that their dreams also, can become reality.

1

DITCHBURN'S DREAM

1945-46 to 1948-49

When football returned after the Second World War there was a transitional season with only the return of the FA Cup, albeit in a two-legged format, providing genuine excitement. The old wartime regionalised leagues survived for another season. From August '45 Sunderland competed in a Football League North finishing eighteenth with a return of 35 points from 42 matches. This comprised a mixture of the geographically-based northern First and Second Division clubs remaining from the short-lived three game 1939-40 season. The FA Cup reverted to a single knockout game at the semi-final stage. Birmingham eliminated the Wearsiders in the fifth round, 3-1 on aggregate. The first leg, which Sunderland won 1-0, was played with spectators excluded from a bomb-damaged Roker End and attracted a crowd of almost 45,000. Some in the crushed three-sided ground who spilled onto the pitch were forced to hastily relocate to the empty, out-of-bounds terracing. Sadly, the fans who overfilled Burnden Park for the Bolton v Stoke encounter in the following round had no such choice. Thirty-three were killed.

It was obvious that Cup fever had survived the six-year hiatus. When league football resumed the following year it underwent a boom so great that it sometimes proved beyond the scope of administrators to keep pace. Players remained tied to archaic terms of employment. Stadiums were not fit for purpose; they were often dangerous and ramshackle. That seemed of the least concern to a British public that filled open terracing in all weathers. It would not have been lost on Sunderland fans that Raich Carter from Hendon, one of their very own who had lifted his hometown team's only Wembley trophy in 1937, was now the owner of another FA Cup medal after signing for Derby County in December '45. His transfer was registered in time for Cup eligibility with only one hour to spare thanks to a desperate seventy-mile taxi dash from

York to Sunderland's Grand Hotel. Carter had spent the wartime period initially as a fireman and then a Physical Training instructor with the RAF at Loughborough. His wife, suffering from bad health after the birth of a daughter, had moved to live with her parents in Derby and Carter, wishing to follow her, was keen to sign for the Midlanders after Sunderland had refused his request for a ten-year contract which, crucially, would have guaranteed him extra benefit payments. This was surprising given that, in the words of Edward William Ditchburn, the Sunderland board envisaged Carter as 'a priceless asset in helping comparatively inexperienced players. We expected a number of years' service from Carter'.

The reality of losing Carter came all too quickly when the 32-year-old brought his new club Derby up to Roker to kick off the new era of League football in August '46. He was in opposition that day to his former '37 team-mates of Johnny Mapson, Len Duns and Eddie Burbanks. It was in fact Burbanks who set Sunderland on their way to a 3-2 victory with a penalty in front of 48,466. Making their debuts in that game were the imposing centre half Fred Hall and skilful inside forward Willie Watson; the latter gained four England caps during his time with Sunderland, also establishing himself as a test match cricketing all-rounder by winning selection against Australia. Tommy Reynolds, a forceful left winger from Felling, and goal poacher Dickie Davis also appeared for the first time in the campaign. That quartet played a big part in the immediate post-war sides. In the return fixture at the Baseball Ground, Carter scored twice leading Derby to a 5-1 win. Chesterfield of the Second Division ended Cup interest in the third round and in a season marred by a bitterly cold winter Sunderland, after an encouraging beginning, finished mid-table. The average league crowd of 35,301 was an improvement of 5,000 on the previous best. Only two points separated the top four placings with Stoke deprived of an unlikely title success when Sheffield United defeated them in their last game.

Sunderland were soon flexing their financial might. The following season the club were involved in a late relegation scare finishing third from bottom. Gates however were up again with an average in excess of 42,000; end-of-season matches against Wolverhampton Wanderers and Blackpool set new league attendance records. Ronnie Turnbull marked his first game with all four goals in a 4-1 win over Portsmouth after a substantial fee had been paid to Dundee. A couple of months later in February '48, Len Shackleton, an outrageously gifted inside forward who often prioritised the entertainment of the crowd over the business of prising open defences, was desperate to leave Newcastle and Sunderland obliged him. So star-struck were the Wearsiders, that to win a sealed ballot they added an odd fifty pounds to their British record bid of £20,000. Shackleton, on his debut for Newcastle after moving from Bradford Park Avenue, scored six goals in a 13-0 win over Newport but never settled at St. James' Park where he claimed the directors had reneged on a gentleman's agreement to hand him a generous signing on fee. The arrival of 'Shack the showman' did not immediately bring an upturn in fortunes as his debut coincided with another 5-1 defeat at Derby, a game in which Carter again sparkled, scoring four times. Sometimes his ceaseless craving to entertain was counterproductive; his superior ball skills may have embarrassed an immediate opponent but not always influenced the outcome of the match. His presence eventually lifted Sunderland away from the relegation zone and sparked a stampede to witness his extravagance. The ambition of Ted Ditchburn was not merely rhetorical; he handed manager Bill Murray a clear remit to get the best players money could buy. Sunderland were now the acknowledged 'Bank of England' team.

Ditchburn, a former Mayor of Sunderland, noted for his successful nationwide furniture empire, vowed to take his beloved club to the very top of the English game. He became a director of the club around 1930, succeeding Colonel Joe Prior as Chairman in November '49. Prior, owner of a thriving haulage business and a larger than life, flamboyantly dressed, eccentric old school Edwardian figure, beamed down in benevolent fashion from the directors' box. Ditchburn, despite his distinctive pink and mauve Rolls Royce, was of the people. A self-made man, he possessed few airs and graces. Although he ruffled feathers when necessary, he was tremendously well liked. There was wealth in his thriving industrial town. Almost a third of all merchant ships built in Britain during the war were launched on the Wear. Today, a National Glass Centre on the banks of the river bears witness to a proud legacy of commercial glassmaking. Board members with deep pockets included Jack Parker, a building contractor, and Bill Martin, owner of a chain of garages.

Although the game was not contaminated by mass media coverage, coarse commercialism and conspicuous foreign investment, the era was far from innocent. A club was often the fiefdom of a powerful individual, invariably a local businessman, attracted more by prestige than altruism. The post-war masses that thronged the spartan terracing were sometimes not rewarded for their fanaticism. Because footballers were paid a pittance in comparison to the money in the game, well-supported clubs without aspiration were able to tread water and still generate a large enough profit for distribution to shareholders. The curse of the game was the imposition of the maximum wage alongside the transfer and retention system. A wage cap set by the Football Association that the clubs were not allowed, or even not inclined, to breach ensured an unfair distribution between master and servant. In addition, a club was able to retain indefinitely a player's registration to the point where it resembled a form of modern slavery or restraint of trade depending which viewpoint was adopted. Abolished in 1961, it created a situation whereby

Stanley Matthews was no better off than a team-mate of average ability. Extremely iniquitous was a uniform £10 signing-on fee, a derisory amount that had remained unchanged from 1901. Little wonder that players often demanded and were given a hefty backhander as an inducement to switch clubs.

Few complained. Wilf Mannion, his skill and positional play arguably unsurpassed by any post-war English international inside forward, was an exception. When Middlesbrough denied him a transfer he refused to play. The Boro directors, not noted for generosity, should have at least compensated his considerable talents with the usual under-the-counter payments prevalent in that era. It wasn't until he had accumulated almost twenty years' service on Teesside, by which time he resembled a mere mortal, that he was able to escape and appear a dozen or so times for Hull City. The continued reluctance of Middlesbrough to release him denied Mannion the opportunity to win domestic honours and be handsomely rewarded for doing so. After Boothferry Park, the inevitable non-league terminus led to a sad conclusion in the early seventies, when the one-time golden boy was employed as a labourer on the massive ICI Teesside plant. I recall my father, at that time sub-contracting within the complex, relating the story of how Mannion, an all-time great, had been reduced to the status of a glorified tea boy. I had not heard of Mannion. The current heroes of the game who unexpectedly fall on hard times, sometimes through an overindulgence in the easy trappings of modern life, now possess the safety net of exploiting the ever-widening opportunities that the football industry presents. They remain in the public eye thanks to the public's insatiable demand for nostalgia.

Nevertheless in the fifties a footballer, even without the possibility of further payments from a sinecure, enjoyed an enhanced standard of living. In 1953 the maximum wage for a top-flight player was £15; this was subsequently increased to £17 in 1957 and then £20 in 1958. In the close season it was slightly less, and footballers who played cricket for a local village side earned a comparable amount. In addition to a weekly wage, they were eligible for bonuses and a discretionary payment that rewarded loyal service. In 1955 a First Division player could receive an additional £750 lump sum every 5 years. Factoring in the statutory £1 a point bonus meant that a player would earn somewhere in the region of £20 per week at a time when the average wage within the UK was £8. Players in the lower divisions did not receive significantly less. Furthermore, commencing from 1950, on retirement each player received a tax-free lump sum equivalent to 9% of all the money paid to him over his career from a club; crucially the cost of accumulating that substantial amount was fully borne by the club and did not take the form of weekly deductions. The bulk of the population were employed in hard, dangerous occupations within coal mines, shipyards and factories with a working week of five and a half days. Many players considered themselves fortunate to be relatively well paid for a game they loved.

The true stars of the game such as Shackleton and Matthews, riled at the unfairness of having their talents valued the same as the countless journeymen with whom they shared a dressing room. Especially when Matthews, the focus of 134,000 at Hampden Park, was expected to travel home in a second class rail carriage. The £50 appearance fee that accompanied the award of an international cap was scant reward. Charles Buchan, now a football correspondent, wrote, 'I am convinced that the modern player, on the whole, is well rewarded for his labours' but acknowledged that 'stars like John Charles, Jimmy Dickinson and Billy Wright are worth much more than the maximum wage'. Tommy Lawton, a great Everton forward who lost the first stage of his career to the war, thought differently. He justified the wages of less gifted colleagues on the basis that football was essentially a team game and he mentioned the 'unlimited wage system' of American baseball as something he thought would not be viable in football. What Lawton and everyone agreed on however, was the travesty of a club being able to hold a player's registration, even after his contract had expired. As Mannion discovered, a player refusing to sign a fresh contract, could have his wages stopped. An impasse would invariably be resolved by a reluctant employee signing on for another year, or taking an escape route into non-league, outside the jurisdiction of the authorities and where, ironically, the money was often better.

Shackleton and Matthews knew their worth. At away grounds the locals, having glimpsed them intermittently on British Pathé newsreels, turned up in huge numbers to see the shadows of their flickering frames transformed into real life 5'8" giants. Each team boasted a local lad made good whose ambition and ability sometimes outgrew the modest aspirations of the club he performed for. Trapped indefinitely at the whim of management in the stultifying atmosphere of a small provincial town, such players were spread evenly throughout the leagues, therefore ensuring less of a gulf between the stronger and weaker teams. Of the eleven players England fielded against Belgium at their opening 1954 World Cup tournament game hosted by Switzerland, no less than ten were drawn from different clubs: none from London. A side in the maximum wage era therefore found it difficult to dominate for any length of time, unless they resorted to offering illegal payments to potential signings, had an exceptional youth system for developing homegrown talent or were able to bribe the parents of budding offspring with cash, a holiday or consumer goods. Sunderland in the fifties, like many others, specialised in illegal payments. The practice was so widespread that in 1950 the chairman of Manchester City, Robert Smith, suggested an overall amnesty but was rejected out of hand.

Attention often centred on the box-office appeal of a visiting player rather than the league placing of the opposition. The floating London soccer public came in droves to watch Shackleton at Highbury. Rejected by Arsenal as a youngster, he suffered the indignity of having his thrifty, bohemian working-class northern upbringing queried by what he perceived as a superior suburban attitude. To young Shackleton the revered bust of Herbert Chapman was a long way from the mill chimneys and soot of homely Bradford. When the war broke out it would seem even further removed when he was underground, working as a Bevin Boy in a Castleford colliery. At Roker Park, a major draw was Stanley Matthews in the tangerine of Blackpool. Disregarding Newcastle, Middlesbrough and Cup matches, and including a Second Division match he was forced to miss when playing for Stoke, he is responsible for no less than four of the seven highest league crowds ever seen on Wearside. All told, Sunderland have hosted 16 post-war league and Cup matches that attracted crowds in excess of 60,000. The three pre-war matches comprising attendances in excess of 60,000 were all Cup ties.

The 1948-49 season brought an improvement. Sunderland lost only one of their first nine games and none of the last eleven. It was the middle that was prohibitive and indeed catastrophic if the FA Cup is included. Fourth round opponents Yeovil were to finish eighth in the Southern League, a couple of places ahead of Exeter City Reserves. They had knocked Second Division Bury out of the competition in the third round to earn a home tie against the Wearsiders. Player-manager Alec Stock, despite his tender years, was well schooled in the dark art of infantry tactics having served as a tank commander in the war. He spent the week leading up to the biggest sporting event in Somerset's history employing mind games that would have earned approval from José Mourinho. He exaggerated the famous slope on the Huish pitch. He posed with a spirit level on the halfway line. In reality the drop was eight feet and that was from one side to another, not from goal to goal. He arranged for a brewery to deliver beer barrels to enable more spectators to crowd the ground, thereby making the touchlines tight. He did not allow the visiting Northeast outfit to set foot on the surface until the very game commenced. For a team fielding Shackleton, Hall, Watson, Duns and Arthur Wright it should not have mattered. Furthermore, Stan Hall the regular Yeovil goalkeeper, suffered a freak accident when he hurt his knee on a bottle top whilst posing for photographers a day before the big occasion. Dickie Dyke, a solicitor's clerk, with only a single appearance to his name, replaced him. Sunderland however were humbled 2-1 in front of 17,500. Stock, picking up the pieces from a free kick put Yeovil ahead in the first half. Sunderland equalised through Jackie Robinson, who coincidentally had put the West Country side out of the competition with a goal when sporting the Sheffield Wednesday colours in 1939. Yeovil scored a winner in extra time as an unexpected fog closed in. The 30 minutes was added to prevent a replay, in order to assist the post-war countrywide economy drive. When a home defender kicked the ball out of the ground to waste time, Shackleton turning to Stock said, 'Don't spoil a good game' only to receive the riposte, 'A game? This is life and death to us'. If only it had been life and death for Sunderland; not just on that harrowing afternoon but on those future occasions in the fifties that would leave supporters bewitched but, more often than not when it mattered, bewildered. In the fifth round, 81,565 spectators packed Maine Road, instead of a bomb-damaged Old Trafford, to see Yeovil beaten 8-0 by Manchester United. The gates were shut twenty minutes before kick-off.

Days after the Cup dismissal, it took Sunderland a remarkable fee of £19,000 to win an intense bidding war with Preston, Blackburn and Manchester City for the signature of the 26-year-old player-manager Ivor Broadis from Third Division North Carlisle United. A director at the Brunton Park club commented, 'the figures offered took the wind out of my sails'. The influential inside forward remains the youngest ever to combine both roles. There was no bounce-back from the Yeovil debacle when Broadis debuted as Sunderland lost 5-0 at Arsenal. Handed down over the years is a belief that Len Shackleton always reserved his best for a game at Highbury, striving for revenge over the club that considered him too small for the rigours of the professional game. Whether or not he honed his repertoire of tricks in the days leading up to an Arsenal match is open to conjecture, but on this afternoon he was well below par. 'Argus' in the Sunderland Echo wrote critically of Shackleton, 'The lack of form of the latter is rather amazing. He sometimes gets himself tied up and then seems to toe-end the ball anywhere'. On one occasion at Highbury he took pity on their new forward Derek Tapscott who was having difficulty in crossing the ball. To the amazement of 60,000 spectators and with the game in progress, Shackleton gave the young Welshman an impromptu lesson in how to curl his foot around the ball to prevent him overhitting it into the crowd.

2

NO POST-WAR RATIONING AT ROKER

1949-50 to 1952-53

At the end of the 1949-50 season four points separated the top seven teams. Len Shackleton, at the peak of his game, was in his element striking a wonderful understanding with one of his favourites, Dickie Davis. The centre forward, benefitting from a constant supply of inch-perfect passes, had fans speculating as to his true worth without Shack at his shoulder. Ted Ditchburn later damned him with the faint praise of being a 'great trier' but nevertheless, a haul of 25 goals from 34 games made the unassuming Brummie the leading scorer of the division and was the reason Sunderland topped the charts with 83 goals.

Perhaps they should have won the league or, perhaps not, considering Bill Murray's romantic notion of how the game should be played. Murray, during the early fifties, wrote 'There is not enough football played just for the fun of it, the type of football which produced the natural player, not the robot who is the product of an over-coaching system, in which players are lectured to satiation point on tactics until they are blinded by their own science'. By throwing caution to the wind more goals were conceded than anyone else in the top half of the table. The interest in Sunderland continued to grow. Although only one point had been taken from the two opening fixtures, both played away, the first home match, a 4-2 win over Arsenal featuring two goals from Len Shackleton was watched by 56,504. Before the introduction of floodlights, evening matches started earlier and were only contested on the lighter nights. On the following Wednesday, Sunderland defeated Burnley 2-1 in a match that kicked off at 6.30 pm. The attendance of 53,032 seems remarkable for a midweek match starting at that time, even allowing for the widespread policy then of all shops having a half-day closure on a Wednesday. A noticeably settled side finally climbed to pole position on Easter Saturday following a 3-0 victory at Fulham that concluded an unbeaten sequence of thirteen matches. With a consistent full back pairing of Jack Stelling and Arthur Hudgell alongside Fred Hall, complete with Arthur Wright, a half back considered unlucky not to be capped by England, the future looked assured provided the side could rein in their attacking instincts.

During the run of form that hoisted Sunderland from ninth to first, there were consecutive home crowds of 62,413, 63,251 and 68,004. The latter figure, for a Newcastle derby, remains the highest post-war at Roker. Argus remarked in the Sunderland Echo in understated fashion, 'The gate of 68,004, a League record, surprised me. How many did not get in before the gates closed I could not even guess at: how many who were in and only saw patches of the play, makes your guess as good as mine'. The ground was able to accommodate 68,000 because with the exception of the grandstand upper tier that comprised 5,875 seats, everywhere was standing room only. Shortly seats were added to an area beneath this but it was much later, before the onset of the 1966 World Cup, when the introduction of 3,600 seats at the rear of the Clock Stand reduced capacity further to 56,000. The all-time record attendance at Roker is 75,118 for a Cup match with Derby in 1933. Raich Carter, in his autobiography entitled 'Footballer's Progress' recalls, 'wingers had to burrow a passage through the crowd before they could take corner-kicks, and half backs had to throw in with spectators sitting round their ankles'. A faded contemporary photograph depicts a crush of spectators three or four deep, touching the byline beyond the Roker End terracing. Allowing for the crowded perimeter track and pre-war design of the ground it is possible to comprehend such a crowd. For someone spectating in today's sanitised all-seater environment it would, nevertheless, be impossible to imagine the ordeal of a young Arthur Appleton who in his seminal book 'Hotbed of Soccer' wrote, 'I made my way in high up at the Roker End and, after a frightening descent, finished an inch or so from the touchline'.

On Easter Monday Middlesbrough stalled Sunderland's momentum with a 2-0 win as 44,000 packed Ayresome Park. With four games remaining and three of those at Roker, Manchester City bottom of the table without an away win, visited Wearside. Even after their Teesside setback, the red and whites remained favourites to win a seventh league title. They were in second position with the same number of points as leaders Manchester United but despite an inferior goal average had played a game less and were going pell-mell for glory. The thickness of a cigarette paper separated the chasing pack. The gods were not kind. Injured Dickie Davis missed his third match in a row. Willie Watson, the influential captain, was on international duty with England; ironically, he travelled in vain to Hampden Park as he was merely reserve cover. At Roker it was a truly horrible afternoon. Argus wrote, 'In no game this season have I seen such a poor display of football as I saw on Saturday and Shackleton was just as poor as the rest … so often when meeting a poor side Sunderland go down to the level of the opposition'. He uncharitably described Watson's replacement Reg Scotson as 'just a plodder'. City, who would be relegated, went two up on the hour before Jack Stelling quickly reduced the arrears with a penalty. Bert Trautmann was not beaten again. He saved a second Stelling penalty; this after the referee ordered a retake. City, a game in hand, actually moved to within one point of safety with that victory, their third in four games. They seemed destined to stay up but then faltered. Stelling, the local lad from Washington who gave Sunderland ten years sterling service, was forever associated with that first post-war failure. The challenge died at Huddersfield the following week. With the pressure off, two wins secured third place with only a solitary point and worse goal average separating the deflated Wearsiders from champions Portsmouth. Davis returned for the final match scoring twice but only 21,000 were present. The average gate was 47,785 but before the final pair of home games had been 50,442. Only promotion-winning Tottenham and neighbouring Arsenal exceeded those numbers. Ditchburn always inferred that allowing Raich Carter to leave in 1945 was a mistake, stating, 'When I am asked to account for Sunderland's post-war playing failures I always begin by saying that the missing link Carter was the primary cause'. He might have added that Sunderland themselves were the architects of their own downfall.

An underwhelming beginning to the 1950-51 season, comprising three wins from 13 games that yielded only 15 goals, prompted an appearance of the chequebook again. Trevor Ford, a powerful, dreadnought of a striker was sensationally signed from Aston Villa for a British and world record fee of £30,000. In 1999, he received recognition from the Football League as one of a select 100 players to mark the commencement of its one hundredth season, distinguished for 'their individual contribution to the game' as stated by Chief Executive Richard Scudamore. Shackleton, despite a series of snubs over his career from the England international selectors, also appears within that list of football royalty. One is forgiven for presuming that 'Shack' and his new partner at Roker would have had a ball of a time.

Ford was controversial both on and off the field. Chelsea's offer of extra part-time work was handsomely bettered with an inducement of £1,000 per annum to be employed as a car salesman with the potential of progressing to a directorship. This practice was not illegal but the Football Association, later acting upon suspicion from Chelsea that Ford had asked for and received from Sunderland a substantial signing-on fee well in excess of the statutory £10 per week, hauled the striker before a joint eight-man FA and Football League deputation. A humiliated Ford, although he denied such allegations and no proof existed, received a £100 fine. Within hours he was contacted by a London-based reporter who offered £100 for his side of the story. He then received an envelope containing £100 through his letterbox, signed 'Exiled Welsh Fan'. Despite the constraints imposed by the authorities, Sunderland went above and beyond in looking after their players. Nothing was overlooked. In exchange for a peppercorn rent, Ford was given a newly decorated semi-detached house in a sought-after location of town. During away trips to the capital, a taxi took players to the theatre where the best seats were made available. The Director Bill Martin made it his business to take on Ford at snooker, with Ray Daniel, a fellow Welshman and later signing, joining in. The notes on the table were not liable to end in Martin's pocket.

Sunderland were third from bottom, when Ford made a sensational home debut against Sheffield Wednesday, scoring a second half hat-trick in a game won 5-1. For his third, Ford's determination bludgeoned both ball and the Wednesday keeper into the net whilst exerting a force that dislodged a goalpost. He had already broken the jaw of the centre half in a heading duel. The following week Sunderland lost 5-1 at Arsenal. In December Murray's entertaining, if sometimes whimsical, side were edged out 6-5 at Derby. It equalled the highest aggregate of goals in a league match featuring Sunderland. A treacherous snow-covered pitch, frozen solid underneath, proved instrumental.

On Christmas Day morning, the Northeast justified its billing as the hotbed of soccer. After 23 matches Middlesbrough, buoyed by Mannion, who else, were two points ahead at the top of the First Division with Newcastle lying fourth. Sunderland, minus an injured Shackleton, prepared for two games in 24 hours against a Manchester United side who were again in title contention, aiming to improve on three consecutive runners-up finishes and a fourth position in the season gone. Both festive matches were won. For the Old Trafford visit, the second of the double-header, Murray, without the services of Ford and Shackleton, reintroduced the out-of-favour Ivor Broadis. Despite the money spent, despite the high hopes, it would soon become obvious that the three most sought after names in British football were never likely to bond. Manchester offered a clue when Broadis, freed from the unpredictable Ford-Shackleton axis, netted a hat-trick whilst Bingham and Davis were the other contributors as Sunderland belied their lowly position with an emphatic 5-3 victory. In April, a visit to Fratton Park elicited the following words in the Portsmouth programme, 'The Sunderland club seem to have a flair for creating sensations in the football world. They staggered the football fraternity in February 1905, by accepting the amazingly high price (in those days) of £1,000 for Alf Common! The Edwardian verdict then was – football has gone crazy – and now, almost fifty years later, they are reputed to have paid thirty times that for Trevor Ford ... This season, however, has caused them great anxiety, for they have been struggling in the relegation zone, in spite of the fact that they possess some of the most outstanding players in present day football'. Such were Sunderland in that deceptive decade.

Ford, by virtue of his first appearance at Roker Park, had captured the hearts of a partisan, ever demanding crowd in a way that was beyond the cerebral Broadis. They also took an instant liking to the unassuming Irishman Billy Bingham. A relatively modest £8,000 purchase from Glentoran, the talented right winger always gave 100%. Sunderland finished with a modest forty points but it was a long overdue FA Cup run that created excitement for those followers who had memories of the unemployment queues of the thirties, the horrors of war or stultifying tedium of National Service. Home ties with Southampton, Norwich City and Wolverhampton Wanderers pulled in 60,000-plus crowds before Sunderland were dismissed from the competition in a Molineux quarter-final replay. Intriguingly, had Sunderland progressed, the semi-final would have featured a Tyne-Wear derby. The visit of Third Division Norwich attracted 65,125. The squeeze at the back of the all-standing Clock Stand was unrelenting. At the Annual General Meeting of the Football League a proposal from Sunderland to increase the maximum wage from £12 to £14 received the required majority support.

Great expectations for the coming 1951-52 season were dashed when Sunderland flattered to deceive. Ironically, although Ford and Shackleton scored twenty-two league goals apiece, the latter's haul by far the best in his time at Roker, it was a campaign without much else of note. It might or might not be somewhat apocryphal to assert that each of those great talents was intent on outsmarting the other. Unrest surfaced during an early season 3-1 home defeat by Aston Villa, an occasion that signalled the end for a constantly barracked Broadis. He returned to the dressing room in a distressed state, vowing never again to kick a ball for Sunderland and was quickly transferred to Manchester City. That there was no determination from management in persevering with a player of the talent of Ivor Broadis, especially in such an unpredictable side, amounted to nothing less than sacrilege. Almost as a parable of his time at Roker, he would go on to gain 14 England caps in the remainder of his career. The £20,000 received from Manchester City was spent in November on half back George Aitken from Third Lanark. It was said of Aitken, who made over 200 appearances for Sunderland, that he was often the only player in the team who was a better tackler than he was a ball-player. His new club languished in twentieth position. There was an improvement to mid-table. On Good Friday Shackleton and Ford scored twice in a 7-1 rout of Huddersfield before 34,640 at Roker. It equalled the most goals for Sunderland in a match since their '36 title winning vintage. Ford's robust style was again evident. On the hour, he twice clashed with the visiting goalkeeper Mills who was forced off hurt, to leave the visitors one man down.

A simmering tension between Shackleton and Ford was of concern. The 'Clown Prince' perhaps resented the matinee-idol looks and charisma of the muscular Ford, whilst the Welshman, although in thrall to Shackleton's genius, felt he was not getting the service he deserved from a player who could do no wrong in the eyes of many supporters. This was showcased in May '52 during an end-of-term tour when a Dutch B team were in opposition. Sunderland won 7-3 in a canter. Shackleton, displaying his full repertoire, bamboozled their whole defence before stopping dead in front of an unguarded net and rolling the ball back to Ford with the riposte of 'Here. Don't say I never give you a pass'. The astute Bingham, forever diplomatic, reckoned that Ford's positional awareness was not on a par with his other attributes. That they were disparate talents and personalities was not in doubt. To what extent Ford failed to read passes from the 'Clown Prince' or frustratingly found them sometimes a stride away from him is a matter of conjecture, but within months of their partnership there was discord. The two most expensive players in the British game were cancelling each other out. Shackleton's eagerness to put his foot on the ball, dummy his marker or flummox a player with his bag of tricks was in contrast to the direct, no-nonsense Ford who craved a quick pass or cross to capitalise on his natural strength and ability to lead the line. Ford, like his colleagues, was in awe of Shackleton's capabilities but was annoyed by his constant tendency to indulge himself. Colin Malam's excellent book 'Clown Prince of Soccer?' attributes the abnormally long toes of Shackleton as an important factor in his ball control.

Stan Anderson, an 18-year-old defensive midfielder from Horden Colliery debuted against Portsmouth in October '52. Johnny Mapson, the 1937 Cup-winning goalkeeper, made a final appearance that season but not before Anderson was able to twice share a dressing room with Mapson, his boyhood idol. Years later, fully established as a regular, Anderson was present when Jimmy Montgomery made his first appearance in a League Cup tie with Walsall. Anderson therefore has the unique distinction of being the only individual to line up alongside a Sunderland player from each of the 1937 and 1973 Wembley finals. The first time Mapson and Anderson featured together was in a resurgent Sunderland eleven, minus an injured Shackleton, who convincingly overcame leaders Wolverhampton 5-2, with doubles from Davis and Bingham. The second time was the following game, also at Roker Park, when the spoils were shared with Aston Villa on New Year's Day. A third consecutive home fixture saw Sunderland, watched by 55,000, storm to the top of the division with a 3-1 victory over fourth placed Arsenal. Shackleton, unrestrained by slushy conditions, wrong-footed four opponents to create a final goal for Bingham. In January '53 a third round tie at Roker with Scunthorpe beckoned. The 56,507 present expected a procession but the visitors forced a replay. Worse followed in Lincolnshire despite progress to the last 32. Trevor Ford broke an ankle, played on bravely and managed to score a winning goal. Sunderland however paid for the 2-1 victory as Ford was ruled out for eight games.

During that desultory time only four points were gathered alongside a Cup exit at Burnley when 53,000 squeezed into Turf Moor. The poor run continued after Ford's return with consecutive five-goal away defeats contributing to the third worst defensive record in the division, and this for a side who were expected to challenge. For a third time in a row, a season meandered to mid-table and when the curtain came down only 7,469 were sprinkled around Roker Park on a Monday evening of monsoon proportions to witness a meaningless 4-2 victory over Cardiff City. The game had been brought forward to avoid the usual Saturday clash with the FA Cup final, which up to that time was not broadcast live on the BBC. The average attendance for the first fourteen games had been 46,563. Crowds melted away when the title challenge died; an average of 26,173 watched the remaining third of the season. When the need or mood arose, 'Shack' single-handedly dominated a game. At Wembley in 1954, he inspired England to victory over the World Cup holders Germany with a marvellous goal. His highlight was a jinking dribble, when he beat half the opposition before unfortunately running the ball out of play. Shackleton only represented his country on five occasions. Explaining this, a national selector was alleged to have said, 'We play at Wembley, not the London Palladium'.

3

THE CUP THAT DOES NOT CHEER

1953-54 to 1955-56

Ted Ditchburn did not want another disappointment. The stakes were raised; even by Sunderland's standard the June '53 splurge of over £60,000 was exceptional. For that the club purchased Ray Daniel, Billy Elliott and Jimmy Cowan from Arsenal, Burnley and Morton respectively. Centre half Daniel left Highbury after his 41 league appearances helped them take the championship. For a fee of £27,500, a record for a defender, he was expected to be a worthy successor to Fred Hall. Elliott, a left winger costing £26,000, whose callous streak was hitched to a short fuse, quickly became a terrace favourite. He eventually performed with distinction at left half and left back. Shackleton rated him as one of Sunderland's finest and much later bracketed him the equal of Roy Keane. The goalkeeper Cowan came highly rated. He made his name in the 1949 'Auld Enemy' clash, inspiring his fellow Scots to a 3-1 win at Wembley. John Moynihan wrote in his acclaimed book The Soccer Syndrome, 'Cowan, in his yellow jersey, was a piece of elastic that afternoon against Mortensen, Pearson, Milburn, Finney and Matthews'. However, on Wearside he proved an inadequate replacement for Mapson. For perspective, the £34,500 Sheffield Wednesday paid to secure Jackie Sewell was now the British transfer record.

Uniquely the campaign commenced on a Wednesday evening. It was the first season the FA Cup final was broadcast live and when the Football League gave the BBC their consent, the dates for the new season had already been arranged. The League, concerned at the impact a live transmission would have on attendances, hastily switched all the end-of-season fixtures to a midweek berth in August. Murray's expensive ensemble therefore started at Charlton Athletic with a night match in front of over 49,000. It was an eventful encounter at a not so happy Valley, as after Ford scored twice to bring Sunderland level Charlton ran out 5-3 winners. Four of the first six games were lost with seventeen goals conceded. This was hardly surprising in the view of Billy Bingham, who wondered why an essentially adventurous centre half such as Daniel was bought for a team who were already attack minded. How Sunderland could have done with a younger version of Hall, now 34 years old, who was thought by Trevor Ford to be one of the 'greatest generals' on a football field. Hall, like so many of his generation, lost the best years of his career to the Second World War.

It was becoming apparent to those sharing their dressing room that Shackleton and Ford were opposites who did not attract. Following this diabolical start, a visit from his nemesis Arsenal inspired the 'Clown Prince' to temporarily bury the hatchet. Ford cashed in with a hat-trick as Sunderland raced to a 7-1 victory over the reigning champions leaving 59,784 observers questioning why they could not repeat that performance most weeks. The answer arrived soon. Two days later Aston Villa defeated Sunderland 3-1. A thoroughly dispirited Ford, unable to raise a gallop, handed in a transfer request and asked to be omitted from the trip to Portsmouth. Sunderland were fortunate not to lose by a higher margin than 4-1. Daniel, the expensive buy from Arsenal, was made to look ordinary by Pompey's veteran centre forward Charlie Vaughan. When he starred for the Gunners, before Murray bought him, he had benefitted immensely from a very disciplined, defensive formation that atoned for his adventurous instincts. Ditchburn, chastened as his dream-team imploded said, 'There is no chance of Trevor Ford leaving Sunderland. We will not consider parting with him and any suggestion we will is nonsense'. Thereafter followed a farce. Shackleton gave way to the returning Ford whose two goals defeated Blackpool in front of a 60,998 crowd, all eager to glimpse Stanley Matthews. Ford was then replaced by Shackleton, who in turn then stepped down for Ford. Unsettled Sunderland, fielding Ford, were drubbed 6-2 at Preston before overcoming Tottenham 4-3. Shackleton then replaced the Welshman; Sunderland lost at West Bromwich Albion. Over a period of eight matches both appeared four times, although never together. Various reports claimed that Shackleton was nursing an injury and Ford was suffering from a damaged shoulder. On 14th November, with Sunderland stuck at the bottom of the table, an uneasy truce was brokered in desperation when the two protagonists were paired together. Despite the visiting Liverpool centre half Lawrie Hughes pulling a muscle and being forced to occupy most of the afternoon isolated on the wing, Trevor Ford was of little or no threat. This was his last game for Sunderland. It was the spirited Billy Elliott who pulled the points out of the fire with two goals on 74 and 77 minutes as the Roker side, trailing 1-2, came back to win 3-2. The Liverpool Echo reported, 'The present Sunderland side must have cost ten times as much in transfer fees as the Liverpool team as constituted, yet they were not one bit better than the Anfielders in football ability. No wonder the folks up north are asking what is wrong'. A recurrence of his shoulder problem was given as the reason for Ford missing the following game at Hillsborough but that was evidently not the main reason, as on the very same Saturday he was with Ditchburn negotiating a transfer to Cardiff City. Sunderland, not in a position to haggle, at least managed to get back the fee of £30,000 they had originally paid to Villa. The Welshman had scored 67 league goals in 108 appearances. His departure may have split fans but it left Shackleton as the undisputed number one. Shortly afterwards, Dickie Davis, who never recaptured the form of his season leading the scoring charts and struggling to attain a regular run in the starting eleven, played in his last game for Sunderland at Burnley, a 5-1 defeat that returned the club to the bottom of the First Division. Exactly a year previously they were on the brink of going top. Davis, enduring many a frustrating afternoon turning out for the second string in the North Eastern League, still managed an impressive haul of 73 league goals in 144 appearances over eight seasons.

As Sunderland struggled they were fortunate that Tommy Wright, normally a right winger but versatile when the occasion warranted, was in decent goalscoring form. An invaluable supporting cast member of the era, he often competed with Bingham for a regular berth and found the net 14 times in the first 18 games of that unsettling season. As usual, the answer to Sunderland's tribulations was a return to the market. The money, burning a hole after Ford's goodbye was spent on Ken Chisholm and Ted Purdon, who arrived within days of each other for a combined £30,000. Purdon made an instant impact. Two goals on his debut in a 5-0 win over Cardiff, a hat-trick at Highbury and a further strike against Portsmouth formed the basis of three consecutive victories that removed the Wearsiders from immediate danger. An aggregate of 11-2 over reigning league champions Arsenal underlined the capabilities of Murray's team and made their inconsistency all the more frustrating for supporters unhappy with the loss of Ford. Four consecutive defeats plunged them back in trouble. Goalkeeper Willie Fraser, signed for a modest fee from Airdrie and replacing the disappointing Cowan, made his debut at Tottenham on 20th March where a 3-0 win heralded a run that banished relegation worries. The indefatigable and erudite famous reporter John Macadam, now writing for the Daily Sketch, remarked of Fraser, 'The confidence with which he handled the ball on Saturday marked him as one of the great ones of his day'. The game provided a rare glimpse of what they could produce when together as a unit and this was acknowledged by Macadam, 'Most heartening thing from manager Bill Murray's point of view is that Sunderland have at last got a team that plays as a team, and not as a bunch of individuals'. Shackleton of course remained Shackleton, a mixture of everything as Macadam's report illustrated, 'His genius was demonstrated very clearly twice … once when he took a free kick for the up-ending of Chisholm, cleaned the ball with some finicking on his shirt and then, choosing a gap in the Spurs phalanx, whammed it high into the corner of the net. The other time was when he came back in defence and, faced by an attacking Spurs man, fondled the ball on his instep at least five times without letting it touch the ground and then, when he was ready – and not before – moved off with it on the ground'. This type of report now seems old-fashioned but for its time was considered cutting-edge. Gone were the oblique terms that had been the preserve of an earlier generation of writers: the ball was no longer referred to as a spheroid, the net as rigging, the goal as the citadel, the goalkeeper as a custodian and, one more example, a series of fouls no longer dubbed as dubious tactics. Golfer Dai Rees, three times runner-up in The Open Championship, who was sitting in White Hart Lane, referred to Shackleton, 'How can England ever leave a ball-player like that out?' The final position of eighteenth was a mere six points above relegated Middlesbrough.

Despite another year without silverware, hope as ever sprang eternal. In August '54 nearly 57,000 were present to witness a 4-2 success over the previous season's runners-up West Bromwich Albion. After good away results at Aston Villa and Tottenham the 50,000 figure was exceeded in the next two home matches, one of which was a midweek game. Sunderland, without the injured Shackleton and Purdon, were forced to improvise for the mid-September visit of reigning champions Wolverhampton Wanderers. Daniel relished his temporary role at centre forward but, according to a report, 'All that was lacking was the finishing touches for some storming raids which had the visitors really groggy at times. Ray Daniel … must still be scratching his head and wondering how he missed getting the winner in the closing minutes'. His replacement Fred Hall made the last of more than 200 appearances. The early months had gone well. After twelve matches the club defeated Newcastle 4-1 to go top in front of 66,654 at Roker. The new strike force of Chisholm and Purdon were amongst the goals that afternoon with the ever-dependable Bingham scoring twice. Points were then dropped but a further run of 9 matches comprising 3 wins and 6 draws put Sunderland back in the driving seat. A 3-2 success over Manchester City was distinguished by two Shackleton goals in 45 minutes, both worthy of his ability. Neville Holtham waxed lyrical in The Journal: 'The first half brought most of Shackleton's golden moments … But oh that first half. From a pass by Aitken, he weaved and swerved past two men in a small space for his first goal. Then with the gale to help him, he thundered in a 20-yard shot to which Trautmann responded with a bone shuddering save of the match'. The reporter made reference to a Shackleton 'party piece' when he sent all the City defence moving the wrong way before losing his balance with the goal at his mercy.

City were allowed back in the match with two second half goals. By then Shackleton felt he had done enough to justify his £15 basic wage. Nevertheless, it seemed peace had broken out in the camp. A togetherness of purpose prevailed; on the horizon was the siren call of the FA Cup. Compared with the alarming loss of 89 goals in the previous campaign the defence was relatively watertight and the 54 goals conceded would prove the best performance in any of Murray's eleven full seasons in charge. Fraser excelled and earned caps for Scotland. Murray curbed the habit of Ray Daniel to charge out of defence. In addition, a remarkably settled defence contributed. Hedley, McDonald, Anderson, Daniel and Aitken between them only missed twelve league games.

Days after defeating Preston in a fourth round replay, a point at Blackpool returned Sunderland to the First Division summit. Forward Charlie Fleming made a debut having arrived from East Fife for £20,000, the bulk of which was contributed by the part-exchange of Wright, who was allowed to depart given the excellent form of Bingham. Unusually, fifteen out of twenty-eight league games had been drawn. Talk of a domestic double seemed optimistic as it had only ever been achieved twice. In the late nineteenth-century Preston and Aston Villa lifted both trophies but because the sport was in its infancy they only played 27 and 35 matches respectively. There was a feeling within the game, and not only at Roker, that the quest for both would prove a challenge too far. Charles Buchan disclosed in his 1955 book entitled 'A Lifetime In Football', 'In present-day soccer the pace has increased to such an extent that I think it is almost impossible to bring off the League and Cup double. It is too great a strain on the players'. The prospect of instant glory at the Holy Grail of football was, in any case, preferable to most footballers than that of the long slog for a championship medal. Stan Anderson was in a dissenting minority. In his autobiography 'Captain of the North' he acknowledged that 'in those days the FA Cup was "the" tournament, bigger than the league and the World Cup … playing well in the final could bring footballing immortality', but stressed that for him, personally, winning the title was the ultimate achievement. The glory aside, there was certainly little financial reward for the players. FA regulations stipulated a payment of £20 to each member of a Cup-winning side, a mere increase of £5 on a successful semi-final passage. A sharp downturn in league form once the fifth round was reached betrayed where loyalties lay in the Roker Park dressing room. Having climbed to pole position at Bloomfield Road, a string of deplorable league performances followed, markedly at odds with the effort expended on a stirring Cup run. One game was won in eight and that was the Tyne-Wear derby with local pride at stake. Wolverhampton Wanderers were first and Sunderland second when they met in a quarter-final at Roker. Leading up to this, the Wearsiders forfeited the opportunity of returning to the top of the table when they surrendered 3-0 at struggling Bolton and then failed to overcome a moderate Cardiff. Early in proceedings, the Cup visitors were reduced to ten men when left back Shorthouse was stretchered off with concussion. On the hour, Purdon finally ended the resistance of the ten men with a low shot from 18 yards and then added a second in the closing minutes to cheer the 55,000. Arthur Ellis, who earned national recognition a decade later refereeing the BBC game show 'It's a Knockout', sounded the final whistle. Straw used to protect the pitch from frost was piled up on the ash track and obscured the perimeter.

The last four included Third Division York, Manchester City and Newcastle United. When it came down to a one-off game the Geordies were a team with fire in their bellies, the sum of which was greater than the parts. Jackie Milburn aside, how else could one explain Wembley triumphs of '51 and '52? Luck, or rather the capricious nature of sudden death football, is a fair estimation. They never seriously challenged for the league. On four occasions United lost a final at the old Crystal Palace back in the Edwardian era. Perhaps the pendulum of fortune was swinging their way. They were drawn against York. The Northeast buzzed with the prospect of a derby day at the Twin Towers. The immediate task for Sunderland was an unglamorous midweek shuffle to Bramall Lane but one which could put them, if they were so inclined, in the driving seat for the elusive double. They were not so inclined. With Shackleton and Bingham left out, a weakened side lost 1-0 in front of a sparse Sheffield United crowd of 14,000. The next game was lost also. It was the Cup or bust.

Early morning on semi-final day the heavens opened. The Sunderland team, inching their way through flooded roads to Villa Park from their base in Leamington Spa, were convinced the game would be postponed. Both teams were reluctant to play on a waterlogged surface but the authorities deemed it too late for a cancellation, given the huge number of travelling supporters. The field resembled a sticky mud pudding as much as a lake. Shackleton, brought back to the side after an ankle injury, was clattered early on but remained determined and dispensed with his usual theatrics. He considered his performance to be the best that the conditions would allow, even though the clogged pitch mocked his promptings. To accommodate the maestro, Murray had surprisingly omitted the dangerous Ken Chisholm, whose presence would surely have been an asset in the conditions. Sunderland, their followers covered in 'pac-a-macs', were drowned in more than sorrow as their team, despite the lion's share of pressure, failed to cancel a second half Manchester City goal from Roy Clarke. Despair hung heavier than any cloud over Birmingham that gloomy unlit afternoon. It took Newcastle a replay at Roker Park to overcome dogged York. They progressed to defeat City and claim a third Wembley triumph inside five seasons. In the '51 final their opponents

Arsenal were reduced to ten men after only fifteen minutes when right back Barnes twisted a knee. In '55, fate intervened favourably again when City, for most of the final, lost right back Meadows with torn knee ligaments. As Sunderland rued their misfortune over missed opportunities, never was the saying 'you make your own luck' more relevant. They finished fourth in the league, level on points with runners-up Wolves and a mere four behind Chelsea. The Pensioners as they were nicknamed, managed by the laid-back Ted Drake, defied their stereotype as the poor relations of London in achieving a first ever honour. They succeeded with a joint record low of 52 points. Galling for Sunderland were the points thrown away to moderate opposition and in particular a total of eighteen draws, a number that only one club had previously surpassed in the top division.

Sunderland, bristling with intent, and invoking memories of the Carter era, made another title-challenging beginning to the 1955-56 season. After 12 games, Charlie Fleming and Ken Chisholm were responsible for eighteen of the thirty goals scored as eighteen points took the side top of the table and ahead of Manchester United on goal average, who in addition had played a game more. Against Aston Villa, the 33,761 present at Roker for the first home game, following an opening day defeat at Cardiff, was considered a poor attendance. There was a suggestion that this turnout, when viewed alongside a disappointing opening day figure at Newcastle, was part of a continuing national drop that signalled an end to the post-war boom. The season's eventual aggregate First Division figure of 14,108,961, at an average of 30,539, compared poorly with the 1948-49 high of 38,776. Sunderland however convincingly beat Villa 5-1 to commence a series of high scoring games. The missing thousands returned. A 7-3 defeat at Blackpool was excused by losing left back McDonald early in proceedings. In the midst of that sequence, goals from Shackleton, Fleming and Chisholm dismantled Bolton at Burnden Park. The Manchester Evening News correspondent Ronald Haines did not hold back: 'Sunderland must be strong favourites for the First Division championship this season, and judging from the way in which they disposed of Bolton Wanderers they can be supported strongly for the Cup. They have everything and Shackleton. Wanderers were bulldozed to defeat after the opening ten minutes. When Len Shackleton hitched up his shorts it was the signal for a stream of body punches which had Bolton's defenders reeling and breathless before the final whistle'.

It was no great surprise when the FA invited the crack Russian side Moscow Dynamo to Roker Park in November. Bill Murray was delighted, having waited ten years for such a moment. In 1945, the year of their only other tour, they were sensationally received by the British public. A match at Stamford Bridge against Chelsea attracted an estimated crowd of 100,000. They finished with a game at Ibrox when Murray, in Glasgow hoping to persuade them south to Roker at short notice, received an official refusal in person from their interpreter Mme Aleksandra Elliseyeva, a teacher of English at Moscow University. She relayed the news dabbing her nose with a handkerchief, drawing an apology from Murray who presumed the Scotch mist was responsible. She told him it was the 'awful London fog', a legacy of their visit to the capital.

Before European competition was established, the continentals were invited to compete against the leading sides of the era. In 1954 Wolves hosted Honved. The Hungarians paraded six of their national side who had famously embarrassed England twice to end the superiority complex of a country who invented the game. Foreign football was ahead in tactics; our domestic game remained rooted to a rigid, attack-minded 2-3-5 system. Defences were wide open, with end-to-end exchanges devaluing the currency of goals. Even by that measure, the aforementioned start Sunderland made to the campaign was a marked antidote to the anticlimax of the previous one.

When Dynamo ran out at an all-ticket Roker they faced 55,000 expectant faces glowing under the primitive lighting and a team wearing fluorescent cherry red tops. In comparison to the night when Wolves defeated Honved by employing quick, direct football better suited to a heavy Molineux pitch, there were few thrills on Wearside. Bingham hit the bar whilst 'Shack' shimmied and weaved between the shadows to no great effect, before Dynamo scored a decisive goal in the closing moments. The great disappointment Murray and everyone felt from this signature occasion carried over to an unfathomable 8-2 defeat at Luton on the Saturday. If anything, the visitors created the greater of the chances but gifted Luton the lead when goalkeeper Willie Fraser needlessly gave away a penalty. A determined Sunderland came out after the interval 4-0 down but despite a spell of incessant attacking were undone by two unfortunate incidents. A fifth was conceded when Fraser lost his footing on the mud-covered surface whilst attempting to collect a back pass and number six resulted from a penalty when the ball brushed Daniel's arm. On the same day, Crook Town at Millfield, before 9,818 spectators who paid £970 and eight shillings, held Third Division North Derby County 2-2 in the first round of the FA Cup. The visit of Dynamo witnessed the high-water mark of the decade.

The club's controversial policy of big spending began to unravel. If the Luton escapade was an exception, the Christmas double-header with Newcastle of two defeats, one by a 6-1 margin at Roker, certainly was no aberration. The 95 goals Sunderland eventually conceded, the worst by a country mile in the division, can only be described as terrible for a side who eventually finished ninth. The championship challenge was over.

January delivered football's most illustrious competition to sharpen focus. Third Division Norwich and York were ousted in front of 46,380 and

43,928 before a replay victory over Sheffield United set up an onerous task at holders Newcastle, who included Stokoe and Milburn. The almost obligatory collapse in league form and a sense that time was not on the side of an ageing team, now endowed the pursuit of Wembley glory with a mystical quality. Sunderland were inspired; two Bill Holden goals knocked out United. A semi-final with Birmingham beckoned. Sunderland were sixth in the table on the morning of the match, whilst Birmingham, although three places below were a team in form, not having lost in nine matches. Manchester City, two points ahead of the Wearsiders, faced struggling Tottenham. The field was wide open but Shackleton did not envisage more heartbreak. He promised his eldest son Graham a trip to Wembley where he would see the Queen. At Hillsborough, before 65,103, Birmingham edged ahead on nine minutes when full back Joe McDonald, who otherwise had an excellent game, put through his own goal. Try as they might, Sunderland were unable to prise open a durable defence and chasing the game conceded twice in the second half to subside 3-0. A devastated 'Shack' hid behind gallows humour, 'If we get past the sixth round next year I think they'll have to give us a bye'. A month later Birmingham were defeated at Roker in front of less than 15,000. Sunderland finished with 43 points. The average gate fell to a post-war low of 35,888. Manchester United took the league by a record margin of 11 points.

Fleming's final tally of 28 goals was second only to Nat Lofthouse in the First Division scoring chart. He was already 27 when moving to Roker, having spent all his career at East Fife, where he won a solitary international cap at a club ranked below Glasgow and Edinburgh's elite. Far from being a 'big name' in the game, he more than matched the achievements of his contemporaries on Wearside and by so doing he strengthened the argument that Sunderland would have won honours had they employed a more judicious approach to the transfer market. Fleming's impact in England also underlined the rude health of football north of the border; until darkness descended the flower of Scotland's youth honed their skill by kicking a tennis ball about in the backyards of communal slum tenements, in an era that shaped the genesis and genius of Baxter, Johnstone, Law and Gilzean.

4

BROWN'S PURGE

1956-57 to 1957-58

Within weeks of an opening day 6-2 defeat at Luton on 18 August '56, there had been home victories by margins of 8-1 and 5-2. Fleming, living up to his nickname of 'Cannonball', was responsible for the majority of Sunderland goals but a porous defence continued to handicap the team. On 3rd November the season deteriorated with a 6-0 reverse at Preston with five goals conceded by half-time. In less than 24 hours a bombshell news story reduced the Deepdale debacle to a mere footnote. The much-awaited serialisation of the Trevor Ford autobiography 'I Lead the Attack' received an airing in the Sunday Express. Cardiff immediately dropped him. Never picked again, he eventually resumed his career abroad. Ford, unwilling to forget the £100 FA fine he received when leaving Villa for Sunderland, pulled no punches in print. He was reported to have received the then huge sum of £6,000 from the Express, which was even less than that received from the publishing house when the book was released in January '57. In reality, Ford did not name names or reveal specific details of the under-the-counter payments prevalent within clubs. He aired a series of grievances regarding all aspects of the game with some of his criticism highly constructive. He compared the remuneration of footballers with cricketers stating that a cricketer, enjoying a potentially lucrative benefit season, was not taxed on his earnings and quoted the example of Lancashire's Cyril Washbrook who received £14,000. Provided he stayed with the same club, a footballer was eligible every five years to a taxable loyalty payment up to a maximum of £750. The amount paid was solely at the discretion of the employer. Within a month, an FA investigation found that Mansfield Town were guilty of illegal payments; the Third Division North club were fined £500. Officials and players from the past and present were either fined, censured or suspended.

It was little secret that at all levels, illegal payments were common. Sunderland however, having broken the British transfer record twice and encountered no difficulty in attracting some of the biggest names in the game, were constantly subject to whisper and rumour. As a desperate relegation battle was fought during 1956-57, the vainglorious project of emulating Carter, Burbanks and Gurney seemed further from fruition than ever. A wind of change was blowing through the game. Manchester United and Wolverhampton Wanderers, who were managed by Matt Busby and Stan Cullis respectively, fielding at least half a dozen teams from senior to junior levels, were part of an enlightened movement to produce their own talent. The FA Youth Cup, inaugurated in 1952, was won in the first five seasons by the famous Manchester United Busby babes. They defeated the Cullis cubs in the first two of those finals before the famous old gold colours of the Midland side themselves lifted the trophy to break their monopoly. As Sunderland struggled through the winter, United were on their way to a second consecutive championship title. Wolves, having tasted their first ever title success in 1953-54, proceeded to take the last two of the decade. There was an additional dividend from producing homegrown talent, particularly as transfer fees were spiralling. The surplus of players unable to command a first team place or past their best proved a lucrative source of finance. United, remarkably, did not make a single foray into the transfer market between March '53 and November '57. Stan Anderson, a local lad rubbing shoulders with the expensive imports, was a rarity at Roker. Bill Murray, born six weeks after Queen Victoria's death in 1901, was set in his ways. That was evident in an article he had written for 'Charles Buchan's Football Monthly', coincidentally during the same year as the Youth Cup's emergence. 'What produced the Buchans, Mordues, Penningtons, Seeds, Jacks and their contemporaries? Certainly it was not the lecture room. No, they graduated through the school of experience … Are we trying to be too clever in turning football into a science, with all this streamlining and finesse.' Sunderland were behind the curve.

Within a week of Ford's disclosures Sunderland signed the 29-year-old Don Revie from Manchester City for £24,000. Revie, a creative player and tactically astute, had inspired Manchester City to their Cup final win by ordering his team-mates when the game was in progress to discard the instructions of the manager Les McDowall. Around the time of Revie's arrival on Wearside, the debuts of local products Alan O'Neill and Jack Malty hinted at a change in direction for the big spenders. Sunderland remained in the doldrums. They were rooted to the bottom in December. The prolific Fleming scored in consecutive wins before Christmas but his brace at St. James' Park was in vain as Newcastle prevailed by a large margin. Colin Grainger, a fine left winger, was signed from Sheffield United and shortly afterwards received a seventh and final full England cap. Given the constraints of the maximum wage, a footballer discussing terms would sometimes ask 'What's in it for me?' Grainger was different in that respect; he was a well-established singer and contracted to the HMV record label, therefore earning considerably more outside the game. Regardless, by then Sunderland were subject to an FA enquiry and a demand for extra would have been refused. The Wearsiders surrendered 5-2 at White Hart Lane during Grainger's debut but relegation fears eased when Revie, returning from injury, was paired with the newcomer. They came together against Sheffield Wednesday in Grainger's first home outing. Interest was piqued. Over 44,000 were present, an increase of 13,000 on the previous figure. Sunderland came from 2-1 behind with Fleming scoring twice, in a match that featured Shackleton's final goal for his adopted favourite club. A 56,551 Good Friday crowd for the final home game against Leeds was relieved when Anderson and Fleming secured a fourth victory in seven unbeaten matches, which granted breathing space before three away outings. All were lost but it did not matter as Cardiff, ironically without Ford who was now playing in Holland, ended their season with three straight home defeats to finish twenty-first, three points adrift of Sunderland and safety. The second of those away matches featured the return of the double-header Easter fixture with Leeds. Elland Road bade a farewell to their 'gentle giant' John Charles who was joining Juventus for a fee slightly less than the prevailing world record of £75,000. An astronomical signing-on fee of £10,000 was spread over his two-year contract with a win bonus of £40 per game. Had Ford delayed publication a few months that detail would have provided more grist to the mill.

Action on the pitch had become far from the main story. The Ford revelations encouraged a certain Mr. Smith, the identity of whom has forever remained anonymous, to send two letters to the Football League. He effectively named names and detailed the illegal payments to players that Sunderland had made over a number of years. Without proof of wrongdoing, the newly installed League secretary Alan Hardaker decided to examine the financial records at Roker. Within the accounts there was a figure of £3,000 relating to a purchase of straw that some clubs used to protect their pitch from frost. Hardaker telephoned his brother, chairman of Hull Rugby League Club, who advised him that in a normal winter the amount of straw used would only be a tiny fraction of that. In addition, payments in excess of work done had been made to contractors. The deliberate overcharge that totalled £5,427 had been refunded to the club by way of normal pound notes that were then secreted in brown envelopes. This evidence was presented to an FA and League joint commission, attended by the Sunderland board, manager, secretary and accountant. A week later on 6th April the commission convened again, concluding they had conclusive proof that the above amount formed the basis of the illegal payments. The club were sensationally fined a record

£5,000. Newcastle had incurred the previous highest of £750 back in 1924. Ted Ditchburn, the Sunderland chairman, received an eternal ban from the game he was devoted to. Interviewed some days afterwards and with time to reflect he said, 'I intend to take every action that is possible to protect myself and the club in particular, as I think the FA rules are antiquated and out-of-date, taken out as inquisitor, jury, judge and hangman. Even a criminal is entitled to a Court of Appeal, but for the Football Association, no'. Martin, the snooker-playing accomplice of Ford and Daniel, met a similar fate. The remaining board members received an indefinite ban from the game or were severely censured. It was apparent they may have been unaware of the illegalities and that, in addition to the collusion with contractors and farmers, Ditchburn was giving players favour from his personal wealth. Jimmy Hill had only just been appointed chairman of the Players' Union and seized the developing crisis as an opportunity to advance his campaign for better treatment of his members. He called the situation 'one of the biggest battles' in the history of the union. He firmly believed that 'these payments were widespread and that the players at Sunderland were no more guilty than almost any other professional player'. Hill wanted as many members as possible, from all clubs and divisions, who had been paid a penny over enforced maximums, to come forward and therefore render the commission findings farcical. As his clarion call was issued with only a week remaining of the season, time was against him. In the event, the gathering of at least 250 signatures on his document, following a mad dash around the country, could be seen as a positive result, especially considering that 95% of players approached admitted to under-the-counter payments.

As Hill rode to the rescue, he was made aware of a legal technicality that would eventually deem the commission penalties unlawful. The Players' Union decided to bide their time and allowed the FA to summon six past and present Sunderland players to answer allegations. Ford was not present as he had left Cardiff for football abroad but Chisholm, Daniel, Elliott, Fraser and Hannigan were. On advice of remaining silent, they were banned sine die; Fraser, Daniel and Elliott were removed from the side for the last fixture of the season. On 17th May a final commission dealing with manager and players took place. On this occasion confessions were made; the bans were lifted but part of the future five-year benefit lump sum was to be forfeited. It was hardly a severe punishment although Ford, who denied receiving a £250 lump sum when he signed in 1950 was banned from playing in England for three years. Murray, who had not taken payments and was acting on behalf of Ditchburn, was harshly fined £200. Ken Chisholm disclosed he had taken £750 when signed in 1954. The larger-than-life forward adopted the maxim of 'shy bairns get nowt' during a widely travelled career of big moves. His small fortune would have purchased a family car then or a modest property. No action whatsoever was taken against secretary George Crow.

The football authorities had in fact bungled the whole investigation. They did not possess the legal right to suspend anyone sine die; only the clubs were able to do that. Furthermore, the powers of the joint commissions were confined to merely establishing the facts rather than pass sentence. Any such latter action could only be taken by a fresh deputation comprising different persons. And so the decisions were eventually nullified in time for the new season, with financial recompense granted to the players. Sadly, it was all too late for Ditchburn, a broken man; it was not until 1962 that he received exoneration. By then a new board had been formed, Syd Collings was Chairman and the clamour for his return had subsided.

The so called 'illegal payments' scandal' at Sunderland helped to pave the way for an abolition of the maximum wage in 1961 but not before Orient had received a fine of £2,000. The ultimate hypocrisy was that some of the individuals appointed to the investigation on behalf of the FA and League, were the very same persons aware of and instrumental in making the payments that were deemed illegal.

The Aberdeen-born Bill Murray ended a long association with Sunderland when he relinquished his managerial post in June '57. He had been appointed months prior to the commencement of the Second World War. His previous ten-year playing career stretched to over 300 games at Roker, including 21 appearances for the 1936 title-winners. Also departed was trainer Bert Johnston, likewise a long servant, whose fondest moment as a player was winning a Cup winner's medal in 1937. It is questionable whether anyone other than Murray could have employed more tact and diplomacy in smoothing the difficulties of blending a moveable feast of larger-than-life personalities and egos. He stretched like elastic to accommodate the whim of player and director alike. It was no easy task. The Sunderland cast of the mid-fifties sometimes played harder off the field than on it. According to Bingham in his autobiography 'Soccer with the Stars', Ken Chisholm's social gatherings, often attended by the chorus line of the Sunderland Empire, were the talk of the town. In Daniel and Purdon he had willing accomplices. That all changed when Murray's successor Alan Brown, a stickler for discipline, took his first training session. In contrast to Murray, a shirt and tie man, he stood bare-chested, wearing only shorts and plimsolls as he addressed the full playing staff. Daniel, Elliott, Revie and Shackleton were ordered to collect the practice balls as the apprentices looked on shocked. Ray Daniel, who never made secret of his hatred of fitness work, was the first to have his card marked; he was never selected again.

Brown had been installed manager of Sunderland within days of Murray's departure. His reputation suggested he seemed the ideal choice for a club seeking to restore their reputation. In 1968 'The Football Man' written by Arthur Hopcraft was published to universal acclaim and reprinted in 2006; it is regarded as a classic with the Guardian newspaper stating it a 'Masterpiece among sports books'. Hopcraft devoted a chapter analysing the 'Manager' and placed Brown alongside Stan Cullis, Stanley Mortensen, Sir Matt Busby and Sir Alf Ramsey as worthy of mention. The Hopcraft book qualifies as an exceptional reference for Brown, despite him being the only manager to relegate Sunderland twice. Brown, born in County Durham, was grammar school educated and led Sunderland on two occasions over 15 years, apart from a stint at Sheffield Wednesday. He played centre half in a losing FA Cup Final for Burnley where he cut his managerial teeth whilst developing a youth policy, which he would then refine at Roker with several of his protégées forming the backbone of the 1973 side. Brown, who was employed for a short while as a policeman after his playing career was over, was a straight talker who demanded and received respect from his players. He led by example, was teetotal and became a member of the Moral Rearmament movement. He was as fit as a fiddle. In 1970 he completed the Pennine Way.

Malcolm Allison, when not distracted by the good life, was a highly regarded innovative coach at the time England won the World Cup. In a Sunday Express article written in 1982 he was unstinting in his praise of Brown: 'In football terms I think of a man like Alan Brown who at Burnley, Sheffield Wednesday and Sunderland was one of the most brilliant teachers the game has ever known. Now he is doing nothing … the game thinks it can do without great men like him. Alan Brown is a giant compared with the likes of McMenemy but he's out of it and they're talking about McMenemy for England'. McMenemy is indebted to Brown for his first full-time job in football; in March '66 he asked him to leave Bishop Auckland and become an assistant coach at Wednesday. Brown encouraged all young players to take the FA preliminary coaching badge; one of his innovations was to install table tennis tables for players to use and improve their balance and reflexes. He could be unconventional if the occasion demanded; during one training session he accused the Sunderland defenders of lacking bottle and set about them by instructing them to head golf balls that he then proceeded to fling high above them.

The proof of Allison's accolade was everywhere in the game. Brown moulded the career path of many players into future managers with Jimmy Adamson and Brian Clough two examples. Adamson, under Brown's wing as a young player at Burnley, credited him with starting a youth policy from scratch that bore fruit when the unfashionable poorly supported Lancashire mill town took the League title in 1960. A mere two seasons later they were runners-up in both Cup and league. The discipline Clough learnt from Brown was inoculated in the teams he would later manage. He studied Brown at close quarters observing his tight control over players and his refusal to bow down to the men in grey suits.

In August '57 Len Shackleton, commencing his eleventh season at Sunderland, played in the first game, a 1-0 defeat against Arsenal. Those present in the 56,493 crowd were blissfully unaware that they were witnessing the last competitive game of his career. His 348 league and Cup games produced exactly 100 goals, including 97 in the league. That remained a post-war record for the club until the emergence of Kevin Phillips. Afterwards, despite great demand, he rarely consented to appear in exhibition or benefit games. As described by stalwart local sports journalist John Gibson in his informative book 'Wor Jackie. The Jackie Milburn Story', an exception was made for Jackie Milburn's testimonial in 1967, when determined not to tarnish the memories of his admirers, he underwent secret training sessions. Not a single person of the 45,000 who filled St. James' Park left disappointed, with the possible exception of goalkeeper Jack Fairbrother who failed to stop a banana shot from 'Shack' and damaged a finger in vain. At Roker, his team-mates were surprised when they discovered through a third party that a long-standing ankle injury had finally forced Shackleton to retire and that no effort had been made to prolong his career. His cavalier approach was never likely to find favour with Brown. The departure of Shackleton was a convenient collusion between player and club, the latter covered by an insurance policy and it is feasible that both parties gained financially. The arrival of Brown signalled the end of an era. A further casualty of the Brown purge was Billy Bingham, the established first choice right winger. Amby Fogarty, who cost only £3,000 from Glentoran, replaced Bingham who was transferred to fellow First Division rivals Luton in July '58. Bingham was vexed that Brown had not given him a fair crack of the whip and despite the growing relegation battles felt he was producing the best football of his career. He was vindicated five years later when he won a league championship medal with Everton.

Alan Brown was on a mission. He introduced the players to a new coach, George Curtis, who had managed the England youth side. Brown, with the assistance of the Middlesbrough manager Bob Dennison, formed the North Regional League to provide competitive football for the reserves. He overhauled the scouting set-up and commenced preparations for a training ground at Moor Lane, near Cleadon. Many years later, nearby land was purchased by the club and developed into a Premier League academy. When the first three matches were lost in August '57 it became obvious that the only objective remaining was to secure top-flight status. The puritanical Brown did not approve of unofficial inducements to sign players; he was acutely aware that the club had to be seen as whiter-than-white. Impervious to outside influence, he beavered away slowly changing the culture of the club. To many, the loss of the 'Clown Prince' rankled.

Of the 10 players that Brown introduced in his first season there was an even split between signings and those promoted within. An outlay of £52,000 on five players included Charlie Hurley, who at £20,000 became Brown's first signing. Hurley, distinguishing himself in the green of Eire, attracted attention at Millwall as a ball-playing centre half. George Aitken, although 33 years old, had successfully taken over the number 5 shirt from the departed centre back Ray Daniel. Sunderland, during their eleventh game, moved two points away from a relegation place with outstanding Aitken and two-goal Fleming instrumental in the 3-0 defeat of Luton at Roker. Brown, fixated on the future, dropped Aitken to grant Hurley a debut at Blackpool on 5 October '57. This game was devastating for the softly spoken Hurley, a day past the milestone of his twenty-first birthday, as Sunderland were thrashed 7-0. Malcolm Usher, writing in the Journal in the forensic critique of the times, described him as being weak in the tackle, lacking anticipation and being either unwilling or unable to embrace the role of a 'destructive stopper'. For the next game at Burnley, Usher, perhaps acknowledging his observations as unfair for a young man plunged into a struggling side, reported that Hurley showed a big improvement, notably in the air and in his quicker movement of the ball. Nevertheless, any change may have been superficial as Sunderland lost heavily 6-0 at Turf Moor. Despite the cry of 'post Hurley for Christmas' Brown kept faith. From unpromising beginnings, Hurley was voted 'Player of the Century' by supporters in the 1979 Centenary year. Whereas a trademark of the ungainly Leeds stopper Jack Charlton was to bully and impede a goalkeeper at a corner kick, Hurley pioneered a majestic run into the penalty box to produce a spectacular bullet header. He was however better acknowledged for his cultured defensive play and ability to dominate rival centre forwards. Johnny Giles recently named him in his all-time Republic of Ireland Eleven stating that, 'Hurley was ahead of his time … his control of the ball was exceptional … he could take the ball out of defence and would definitely fit the modern game'. Brown's side never recovered from the earlier defeats and in February '58 they slumped 7-1 at Luton followed by a 4-1 defeat from Blackpool before 28,127 at Roker, as relegation looked increasingly likely.

With Sunderland now bottom Don Kitchenbrand, a South African, arrived from Glasgow Rangers in March and his bustling forward play instilled belief that the club could extend their sequence of seasons in the top-flight since its inception beyond fifty-seven. When Nottingham Forest were overcome in the last home game it meant that a Sunderland win at Portsmouth, provided Leicester lost at Birmingham, would secure an improbable escape. After a double from Kitchenbrand secured two points Hurley, in his haste to discover the result at St. Andrews, sprinted off the field and collided with a policeman. On returning to the dressing room there was crushing disappointment when he learnt that Leicester had won. In a tight finish, Sunderland finished second bottom. Portsmouth and Newcastle were both level on points but possessed a better goal average.

Sunderland were league leaders in April '50, January '53, February '55 and November '55. The distractions of the FA Cup cannot be held responsible for those four seasons of disappointment and the other years of mediocrity. Neither can one man, although those who admired the unique Len Shackleton may often have wondered at the outcome if Sunderland had eschewed his genius for efficiency and had Murray opted for a less cavalier approach. A sprinkling of flamboyance in a land suffering the privations of rationing and enveloped by post-war drabness may have been a forgivable trade-off for an empty trophy cabinet. Joe Harvey, his former captain at Newcastle, stated that the Tynesiders would never have won anything if 'Shack' had remained part of it. Open to debate is the extent of the fallout from the FA disciplinary measures. During the second half of the fifties Sunderland were in decline.

Had Ted Ditchburn remained in charge it is problematic whether his spending spree would have continued but he would certainly have attempted to influence Alan Brown in his running of the team, in similar fashion to that of his relationship with Bill Murray. Ditchburn, now ostracised from the game, was heavily critical of his former directors: 'No one can have more sympathy than I for a great club. For I tried to make Sunderland the finest team in soccer. Now this … relegation. I'm not looking for scapegoats. But the present board surely have a case to answer. I feel they gave too much power to a manager appointed only last July. I say it's wrong for a manager to be the big boss. Team selections should be open to discussion and alteration'. There was widespread criticism in Brown's policy of throwing too many inexperienced players together whilst ignoring senior servants such as Bingham, Fleming and McDonald. The new manager would not have lasted five minutes under the old regime. Brian Clough stated that Alan Brown 'ran Sunderland like the dictator I was accused of becoming later in my career'. Brown, when it suited, could be a man of few words. After the defeat at Portsmouth he issued a terse comment of 'Sorry. I don't want to say anything. No. Nothing'. After a record unbroken membership of 57 years at football's top table, Sunderland were now in the Second Division. Words were inadequate.

Despite relegation, Sunderland were ninth best supported in the country, the only occasion since 1947-48 that they had been ranked outside the top seven crowd-pullers. Considering the absence of silverware their support was exceptional, especially given a widespread drop in attendances towards every season's end that affected all those clubs who were out of Championship contention and without the modern incentive of qualifying for European competition. Quite often, when the clocks moved forward and the heavy black pitches of winter dried to a dust bowl, it signposted a series of tedious contests resembling exhibition stuff, wrung out in front of quiet, scantily populated terraces. It was of little consolation that play was easier to follow, the ball and players framed in a monochrome backdrop as opposed to a sea of faces. Roker Park's fine, well-drained Irish turf may unlike other pitches have retained something of its summer lustre but long vanquished was the early season fanaticism of the dense queues that constricted and circled the ground, the latecomers untidily spilling into nearby streets. Nowadays, match to match attendance figures hardly differ. Season ticket holders are responsible for a vast portion of every ground's capacity and even if not present are counted as having passed through the turnstiles. Plainly, the Stadium of Light has hosted matches with thousands of season ticket holders absent. Evening occasions are a case in point; many followers are from a far-flung catchment area and therefore unable to attend through time constraints and an increasingly inconvenient number of kick-off times.

In the 2017-18 season Manchester City won the Premier League at a recently expanded Etihad. A freedom of information request disclosed a marked variance between the club's official attendance figures and those recorded by Manchester Police, an extreme example being a November midweek game against Stoke. An official gate of 53,407 was disclosed whilst the police, counting only those who actually attended, recorded a figure of 38,130. Before the gradual introduction of all-seater stadiums the vast majority of fans paid on the gate. All clubs, even the most successful, experienced a variation in crowd figures from one game to another. When Arsenal won the double in 1970-71 they had four attendances above 50,000 and nine in the range from 30,000 to 40,000. Their rivals Tottenham had three attendances above 50,000 with two below 20,000 including a crowd of 14,356 against Burnley.

The reasons for match-going have subtly altered since then. Previously, all clubs possessed a hard-core minority; the appearance of the floating fan was determined by a number of factors such as the attractiveness of the opposition, position in the table, recent form, the weather, importance of getting the two points or the opportunity to glimpse a new signing. The appeal of a sudden death Cup tie, in particular one heightened by the drama of a replay under the novelty of floodlighting, overrode the usual variables governing crowd figures. Today the popularity of football is at an all-time high. It is communal. Many are attracted to the game because of a basic human need to be part of something, to be with like-minded individuals who they would ordinarily have encountered in a bygone era through the everyday normalities of employment within a large workforce, residing in cheek-by-jowl terraced housing or the escapism of packed working men's social clubs.

A final look at attendances illustrates the underachievement at Roker. The relatively unfashionable provincial clubs in Lancashire of Blackpool and

Bolton Wanderers were FA Cup winners in '53 and '58 respectively on much smaller crowds than Sunderland. Bolton's average league placing was remarkably similar to that of Sunderland over the twelve seasons they shared First Division status. And yet, when the Wearsiders dropped out of the division, the average gate at Burnden Park of 22,029 was less than the 36,146 at Roker. Blackpool, losing Cup finalists twice in addition to their Matthews' inspired success in the year of the coronation, enjoyed no less than eight top seven finishes but never averaged more than 27,000. Preston's highest ever average gate was no greater than the 30,000 who witnessed their 1952-53 side agonisingly pipped for the title by Arsenal on goal average, only to lose the following year's FA Cup final. Although benefitting immeasurably from the loyal genius of Tom Finney, there was no wealthy benefactor at Deepdale and certainly no pampered footballers. This strident summary of Sunderland in the fifties, composed in 1962 by the internationally-renowned football writer Brian Glanville as part of his foreword to introduce a Billy Bingham autobiography, is worth relating: 'I have enjoyed his pleasant book, enjoyed especially reading about those half-mythic Sunderland days, when Len Shackleton, the tantalising virtuoso, Trevor Ford, Ray Daniel, Ken Chisholm and the rest composed a mountain of talent which, if it ultimately parturated a mouse in results, was rich in the ore of good anecdote'. In 1954 in Bologna, a younger Glanville encountered Alan Brown, who was assisting England manager Walter Winterbottom with coaching duties during an England under-23 international against Italy. Years later, the discerning Glanville remembered Brown as 'a Northumbrian of unpredictable moods (who) spoke about the possibility of Christ having set foot in his country'.

5

A BEHEMOTH AWAKENS

1958-59 to 1960-61

On 23 August '58, Sunderland were defeated 3-1 at Lincoln in their first taste of football outside the top-flight. The excellent crowd of 38,000 present for the home visit of Fulham were again disappointed by a defeat. Brown continued to ring the changes. In November Don Revie left for Leeds. Apart from Stan Anderson, every first-choice pick of Murray's last season had disappeared. The club were in a state of flux. After conceding no less than 27 goals in the opening eight games debuts were handed boldly to Cecil Irwin, Len Ashurst and Jimmy McNab, respectively 16, 19 and 18 years old. Ipswich spoiled their big day by winning at Roker but Brown, seeing potential in McNab, switched the vastly experienced half back Anderson to a forward position. The experiment did not last as McNab suffered a broken leg. Anderson, unsettled after Bill Murray's departure and the subsequent upheaval in playing staff, was returned to his best position. It was not until a draw at Huddersfield in the sixteenth fixture that Sunderland moved off rock bottom in the table. There was a gradual improvement to just below mid-table with Kitchenbrand a not-so-subtle centre forward, aptly named 'Rhino', finding a lower standard of football to his liking and scoring 21 goals. The Roker public did not turn their backs. The average gate was a respectable 27,772, only bettered in the division by Liverpool, who despite finishing well behind the promoted pair of Sheffield Wednesday and Fulham were the fifth best supported in England with 38,476.

With another finish in the wrong half of the table Sunderland's second season after demotion, although it did not excite, was notable for the introduction of Martin Harvey and Nick Sharkey, who in similar fashion to Irwin were then quickly rested and eased back gradually over a couple of years. Early in the campaign, Kitchenbrand's replacement Ian Lawther averaged at least a goal every two games. The signing of this Northern Irish 19-year-old was again evidence that Brown was looking at the future, but perhaps his best business until then was the short-term acquisition of Ernie Taylor who had commenced his league career at Newcastle back in January '46 and played with Shackleton. Taylor, a small and clever inside forward, is credited with providing the know-how for the Sunderland team to stabilise after relegation.

In 1960-61, Brown's third Second Division season, a corner was turned. The emerging baby-boomer demographic was captivated by a thrilling Cup run and older supporters regained their fervour, relishing the novelty of their team cast as the underdog. The Roker Roar came of age. Possibilities seemed infinite and yet, in the beginning, eleven winless games took Sunderland down to third bottom. Consecutive gates under 18,000 were not in themselves unusual but they were if occurring within the first half of a season. There was change in the air. Willie McPheat, a tall, raw, gangling centre forward claimed a place. John Dillon also debuted. Both were young. The darkness dissipated with only one defeat suffered in 20 league games. At Roker on Boxing Day 46,000 saw Hurley equalise against Sheffield United. The Blades were then beaten at Bramall Lane with a goal from McPheat and then on New Year's Eve Luton were hit for seven with Lawther scoring a hat-trick. In January '61, Arsenal were the visitors in an FA Cup third round tie. Euphoria abounded as two goals from Anderson overturned a half-time deficit on a quagmire of a surface. The crowd of 58,575 was the largest since a visit from Newcastle in 1954. Liverpool and Norwich, who were to finish third and fourth in the division, were beaten on their own turf as Sunderland stormed into the quarter-final. At Carrow Road, Hurley scored the only goal of the game in the closing stages with a powerful header; observers thought it his finest performance in a red and white shirt.

Sunderland were drawn at home against Tottenham Hotspur in the quarter-final. Spurs were closing in on the domestic double. Having lost once in their first twenty-five games, Spurs had the advantage of almost having the title sewn up when they embarked on their Cup campaign. The task was magnified when Cliff Jones put the visitors ahead. There were 61,326 in Roker Park and as Sunderland pressed in the second half a sustained roar grew louder, to the point when the Spurs captain Danny Blanchflower, noted for his level-headedness and intelligence, was unable to act or think straight. In his autobiography written shortly afterwards he stated, 'I have never seen such excitement, anywhere, as I did that day at Roker Park. The noise was unbearable; I could not feel my senses or clear my thoughts or concentrate properly because of the shrieking din'. Hooper took a right-wing corner in front of the Roker End. Hurley climbed, only for the keeper to parry his header to McPheat who bundled the ball over the line. Hundreds swarmed onto the pitch. The delay allowed Spurs to regroup and escape with their dream intact of a first ever Wembley appearance to go alongside the inevitable championship.

The record crowd at White Hart Lane is listed as 75,038 for a 1938 Cup quarter-final that Sunderland won with a Raich Carter goal. After McPheat's equaliser on Wearside, that number would have been surpassed had White Hart Lane's capacity allowed. Gates were locked half an hour before kick-off with almost 65,000 inside. Spurs in front of their own were not to be denied and won 5-0. The season tailed off but finishing sixth represented a big step forward and the last game saw George Herd, a highly rated Scottish international midfield player, make a first appearance after moving for £40,000 from Clyde. The headlines were reserved for the summer capture from Middlesbrough of Brian Clough for £50,000, a huge fee between clubs outside the top division. This gave followers a clear indication that Sunderland were back in business. Clough, as a Second Division player, had been capped twice by England. At that time the British transfer record stood at £85,000 when Gerry Hitchens switched from Inter Milan to Aston Villa. Clough, after returning from a holiday to Cannes, met Alan Brown at Southampton docks and was immediately impressed by the physique and manner of the Sunderland manager. He agreed to sign immediately. Clough was a goals machine. In the five seasons prior to meeting Brown he knocked in 194 league goals from 204 games. There were five goals against Brighton in a 9-0 win, four against Huddersfield, four against Doncaster, four against Ipswich and four against Swansea. Two penalties were converted in the Brighton game but not from Clough, as strangely enough, the man wearing blinkers within sight of goal did not take a single spot kick in his career.

Manchester City to this day, are the only club to score and concede 100 goals in a season. In their remarkable 1957-58 season they scored at least five goals on six occasions and suffered defeats of 9-2 and 8-4. Undeniably, the late fifties and early sixties saw a significant increase in goalscoring within the game. This trend was reversed as the domestic game adapted continental tactics with Alf Ramsey the new England manager dispensing with wingers in a 4-4-2 formation as the 1966 World Cup progressed. In an earlier era of plenty, George Camsell of Middlesbrough scored 59 Second Division goals during season 1926-27. It would be remiss not to mention an incredible purple patch of 26 goals that he accumulated within nine games. Yet Brian Clough's record withstands scrutiny in any era and the only blemish at first glance is the one solitary goal he struck in the First Division. And that last statement of his career will serve as a monument to his commitment and courage in overcoming an injury that few would have beaten. He was leading scorer in the Second Division three times and finished runner-up in the season that ended for him on Boxing Day.

6

PIPPED AT THE POST AGAIN

1961-62 to 1962-63

Sunderland now embarked upon a Sisyphean quest to restore what they considered their rightful place in the game. Twice about to summit, Sunderland stumbled and had to start again. In the summer of 1961, before the first of those seasons, Brown was asked what value he would place on his promising team. Without deliberation he gave the obvious figure of £90,000 for Clough and Herd and then said that the value of ‘my half back line of Anderson, Hurley and McNab would be millions’. This out of character statement from a normally guarded Brown sounded something that Bill Shankly might have said. Shankly’s Liverpool were on the threshold of great things and their ranking as promotion favourites was confirmed when they twice beat Sunderland by a three-goal margin on consecutive August Wednesday evenings, with both encounters attracting at least 47,000. Clough, off the mark on the first day of the season during a 4-3 defeat at Walsall, opened his Roker Park account in the second of those midweek games but a brace from Roger Hunt and Ian St. John eased Liverpool home. Had the Liverpool manager been so bold as to place such an irreverent value on his own back line, they surely would not have conceded 21 times in their first eight outings as Sunderland did. Sunderland however tightened up and at the other end of the field Clough resumed his customary command of the penalty box. He scored the first of his three league hat-tricks that season in a 3-0 win over Bury to finish with 29 goals from 34 appearances. The aforementioned Hunt, later a World Cup winner, led the chart with 41 goals. The Cup excitement from the Tottenham tie provided supporters with a strong belief that Sunderland possessed a fine young team capable of going all the way. A third round replay with Southampton attracted 58,527 spectators followed by a fourth round figure of 48,468 for Port Vale. In comparison, the average league attendance was less than 33,000. That was as far as Sunderland progressed, as Vale, mid-table Third Division, triumphed in the replay, watched by almost 30,000 at their spacious but somewhat underdeveloped ground. Jimmy Montgomery, after shadowing Peter Wakeham, had broken into the first team for a League Cup match with Walsall. With the exception of a couple of seasons when Hardwick and McColl managed the club, Montgomery would be more or less ever-present until 1976. After 41 games, with Liverpool out of sight, Sunderland were above Leyton Orient courtesy of a slightly better goal average. They charged to Swansea boasting seven straight wins. In the event, Orient defeated Bury 2-0 as Sunderland, unable to protect a lead given to them by Clough and denied the opportunity to extend it when the referee waved play on after Herd was blatantly upended in the penalty box, only managed to draw at the Vetch Field and therefore missed the second promotion position by one agonising point. Stan Anderson won his two England caps that season and was selected as one of the 22 players in England's Word Cup squad for Chile.

In the first away game of 1962-63 at Elland Road, Willie McPheat had his leg broken and career terminated after a nasty foul from the notorious Leeds enforcer Bobby Collins. The return encounter at Roker was the only time that season Collins was absent from the Leeds team sheet. In September the left winger George Mulhall was an important capture from Aberdeen. Jim Baxter, not overtly impressed by the team-mates he later inherited at Roker, made an exception for Mulhall recognising him as someone who could 'really play'. Six weeks later in November against Grimsby, another signing, Johnny Crossan, made his debut. In that game Brian Clough, even by his standards enjoying a purple patch, completed a hat-trick to score his thirteenth goal in eight matches as Sunderland emerged 6-2 winners before 43,000. Back in 1957, Sunderland agreed to give a contract to 17-year-old Crossan, then an amateur with Derry City. A fee of £6,000 was agreed and, as was the practice, Crossan would conveniently sign professional forms just before the transfer, therefore allowing him a legitimate split of the fee. Crossan however wanted all the proceeds bar £1,000 and as Derry disagreed the move was cancelled. Crossan was only on a short one-year contract and once this expired Derry were unable to prevent Crossan from signing for Coleraine. When Crossan's w club accepted a £7,000 offer from Bristol City, Derry annoyed at the previous breakdown in the deal with Sunderland, reported the saga to the Irish FA whilst also disclosing they had been paying the amateur a small wage. Crossan, controversially banned from playing in the United Kingdom, relocated abroad to Sparta Rotterdam and then Standard Liege. Syd Collings used his influence as an England selector to persuade the Irish FA to overturn the ban and for a fee of £27,500 Crossan's three-year exile was over. The slender Crossan emerged as an important maker and taker of goals, eventually to become the key figure in Brown's forward line.

On 26 December '62 Clough faced Bury in front of 42,000, with a tally of 24 goals in 23 games for a team in second position. On an ice-bound pitch, unplayable by current standards, he accidentally clashed with goalkeeper Chris Harker tearing a cruciate ligament. But for that he would surely have ended the campaign ahead of Chelsea's Bobby Tambling, who found the net on 35 occasions. At the age of 26 his career was effectively over. With Roker Park shrouded in misery, Bury took advantage to win 1-0. Their 3-0 win in Lancashire on another rock-hard surface completed an unlikely double. A lengthy deep freeze set in that created havoc for all activities and it was not until March when Roker first hosted league opposition in the New Year, as 62,420 hungry for live action watched a goalless duel with Newcastle. In the fourth round of the FA Cup, Sunderland narrowly avoided a major embarrassment from a Gravesend and Northfleet side lying third off bottom in the Southern Premier League. The part-timers, having advanced through no less than seven rounds in their stirring run, were expected to capitulate when George Mulhall gave the visitors an early lead on a muddy surface before a ground record of 12,032 that generated receipts of £2,345. When Brian Skingley equalised on 72 minutes, completely against the pattern of play, the tables were turned and Sunderland were relieved to survive a late onslaught. At Roker, on a frosty night of softly falling snow, there was no further drama as the home side scored three early goals and emerged 5-2 victors. Sunderland's fifth round away tie at Third Division Coventry was postponed. Manchester United awaited the winners. The Sky Blues, under the progressive management of Jimmy Hill, were impatient to match the economic success of their thriving motor-based manufacturing city. There were 40,449 in Highfield Road and thousands locked out. Crossan put Sunderland ahead but in the last ten minutes goals from Dieter Bruck and George Curtis, whose soft looping header Montgomery should have saved, left excited home fans in the closing stages having to be forcibly restrained from encroaching on the pitch. Coventry were to achieve promotion the following season with an average attendance of 26,017, ranked eleventh and only bettered by seven top-flight clubs.

Sunderland strove to overcome the loss of Clough. They were back on track after Crossan notched a hat-trick at Walsall before Norwich were blown away 7-1 on a memorable night under the lights, illuminated by the youngster Nick Sharkey, whose appearances over three years had not yet reached double figures. Contrary to myth, the aerial dominance of Hurley did not have a hand in any of the diminutive Sharkey's goals. He became the club's first player since Bobby Gurney to score five goals in a game. Len Hetherington disclosed in the Evening Chronicle that the Roker hierarchy rated him a future Hughie

Gallacher. This was no frivolous prophecy. Jimmy Greaves' nostalgic book 'The Heart of the Game', written decades later, considered the young Sharkey to be worthy of comparison with himself: 'In 1956-57 I scored 122 goals in a single season for the Chelsea youth team. In the sixties … Nicky Sharkey, as he was to become known, scored 140 goals in a single season for the Sunderland junior side in 1961'. Stoke City, the Good Friday visitors, attracted a huge crowd of 62,138. There was a double disappointment when the 48-year-old Stanley Matthews did not appear and the visitors, despite his absence, earned a goalless draw that maintained their position alongside the Roker side and Chelsea as one of the likeliest clubs to go up. Sunderland were on top of the table when they faced Chelsea in their final fixture. The London club, who had a further game to play, were four points adrift of Sunderland. Stoke, likewise with an extra game to fulfil, were tucked a point below the Wearsiders and strong favourites for pole position.

Despite constant rain 48,000 attended Roker Park. A draw was needed to avoid another near miss. Tyne Tees Television thought it a done deal; for a pre-recorded programme, which in the event would never be broadcast, they persuaded the players to give their thoughts before Saturday on achieving promotion as if the game was already won, a sure-fire way to cast a curse over proceedings. It was not as Harry Thompson in the Newcastle Journal saw it, 'They appeared on the field like neurotic ghosts; they played as though in a pressure chamber'. The reality was that Tommy Docherty, the effusive and abrasive Chelsea manager, had done his homework. He dropped Barry Bridges, Graham Moore and Bert Murray. In came a trio of experience. Frank 'the tank' Upton was deployed as an emergency centre forward, instructed to harry the normally unflappable Hurley with bustling Derek Kevan, another spoiler, ready to join arms. It was the third player introduced, Tommy Harmer, in his thirty-sixth year, the oldest and smallest on the field and making only his third appearance of the season, who scored the solitary goal of the game. Nicknamed Charmer by his colleagues, it was either his rump, backside or anybody's guess as to which part of his anatomy deflected a corner kick over the line. The narrative of the match would have been different had not the agile Peter Bonetti denied George Mulhall in the last minute. 'A wonderful team effort and some goalkeeping that was out of this world', said Docherty in the afterglow. Their left back Eddie McCreadie described his team's work as a 'mercenary job'. Chelsea duly overcame Portsmouth 7-0 in a rearranged midweek fixture in front of 54,558 to pass Sunderland on goal average.

7

THE MANCHESTER UNITED NIGHT

1963-64

Ask a Sunderland supporter, who remembers standing in an open Fulwell End or watching a winger retrieve the ball from a pile of straw before taking a corner, his favourite all-time eleven and you may be surprised at the answer. Stokoe's Cup winners are not the only choice. The team of Montgomery, Irwin, Ashurst, Harvey, Hurley, McNab, Usher, Herd, Sharkey, Crossan, Mulhall will roll off the tongue quicker than Montgomery, Malone, Guthrie, Horswill, Watson, Pitt, Kerr, Hughes, Halom, Porterfield and Tueart. The 1963-64 season, nearly one of the greatest in the club's history, will then be recalled in bitter-sweet fashion.

Without a hint of the drama to unfold Sunderland made a solid start; they sat second in the table behind Leeds after their tenth game, a 3-3 draw with Cardiff in front of 37,287 at Roker. The Welshman Ivor Allchurch's hat-trick was cancelled out with a pair from Sharkey and a final equalising goal from Hurley. There was controversy when Brown, keen to encourage youth, abruptly dropped club captain Stan Anderson, replacing him with 22-year-old Martin Harvey for the midweek match at Plymouth. That was Anderson's last appearance for Sunderland. Anderson, who had surpassed Charles Buchan's record of the most outfield appearances on Wearside, found Brown unapproachable and endured the long journey knowing that as a travelling reserve he would not play. His sensational move to Newcastle came as much a shock to him as supporters; only after Sunderland agreed to his transfer did Anderson discover his destination. He eventually gained the unique distinction of playing for and captaining Sunderland, Newcastle and Middlesbrough.

The rivalry with Leeds, apparent since the McPheat incident, intensified when the two clubs were locked in a Christmas double-header. Sprake,

Reaney, Bremner, Charlton, Hunter and Giles formed the nucleus of a team that would dominate English football. Don Revie impregnated them with a professional, intimidatory and ruthless approach. The first encounter with Leeds, on a shocking pitch at Elland Road ended all square with the home side, a game in hand, preserving their three-point lead at the top. The ill-feeling between the clubs surfaced on the Saturday return at Roker Park. It was a brawling, spiteful game with punches randomly thrown, no less than 39 stoppages for fouls and a Leeds player stretchered off with a damaged knee to a chorus of booing from a sizeable minority in the 55,000 crowd. No players were dismissed. The Daily Express commented that the game 'should have been given an X certificate as it was not suitable viewing for the children'. Sunderland triumphed however, with goals from Herd and Sharkey ending the visitors' 20-game unbeaten run.

Jimmy McNab and Len Ashurst were the acknowledged hard men of Sunderland. Every team possessed at least one player who could look after not only themselves but also their team-mates if the occasion arose. Vigilante behaviour was necessary to compensate for incompetent or lenient officialdom. It was a rare event for a player to be given marching orders. Rather than feign injury after a heavy tackle the wounded party would scramble up to avoid revealing a weakness to the opposition. Tommy Smith was a Liverpool defender with a deserved reputation for tearing into a player but who nonetheless, like the Leeds defender Norman Hunter, was considered hard but fair. Rather than intend to hurt an opponent, Smith preferred verbal threats to unsettle him. In his autobiography 'Anfield Iron', he recalls a match when Steve Kindon, a pacy young Burnley winger went flying past him. Smith said to him, 'If you go on the outside of me again, I will break your leg son'. Kindon complained to the referee only to be told, 'It's a man's game, son. If you can't look after yourself, go and do something else in life'.

Sunderland now embarked on an unbeaten sequence of their own that lasted 14 games and took the Roker team above Leeds and into an exciting FA Cup run with hopes high of winning the trophy. A week after Sunderland beat Bristol City 6-1 in a fourth round tie in January '64 they climbed to the top of the Second Division and then enjoyed another six-goal romp over Swindon, on this occasion featuring a Sharkey hat-trick. Johnny Crossan, in a rich vein of form, scored two goals in each of four consecutive games, divided equally between Cup and league. Sunderland were drawn against reigning league champions Everton in the fifth round. Such was the demand to watch this game that there was no room in the Clock Stand paddock to accommodate the brass band and their instruments; the pre-match entertainment comprised canned music. A vast majority of the all-ticket 63,000 were in heaven when Sunderland with McNab, Hurley and then an own goal all inside twenty minutes swept away the visitors en route to a 3-1 win; Everton had not lost for eight games and were not to lose for another eight. A matter-of-fact Brown said, 'We had no special plan to beat Everton. We simply set about the job of beating them just like any other team'.

Sunderland's time had surely come. On the Wednesday evening after the Everton game 45,000 thronged Roker for the visit of Norwich; three days later 44,000 for a 3-0 win over Derby County when, after naming an unchanged team for thirteen matches, Brown replaced the injured McNab with Dave Elliott. These were remarkable numbers, considering interest in the national game was waning after the post-war boom. Sunderland averaged 41,262 in the league that season only bettered by the two Merseyside clubs, Manchester United and Tottenham. The previous season that was marred by the Harmer goal, the average of above 40,000 was in excess of the Old Trafford support.

A particularly virulent strain of Cup fever took hold. 16,000 made the trip to Old Trafford for the sixth round match. Manchester United were the holders. George Best at 17 was all the rage. Matt Busby was quietly rebuilding from the 1958 Munich disaster and had Denis Law and Bobby Charlton. Johnny Crossan edged Sunderland ahead at the interval before Hurley put through his own net. Crossan was then clumsily upended by Shay Brennan, converting the penalty himself. A third goal from George Mulhall should have given Sunderland an unassailable position. But Montgomery, concussed after a goalmouth melee and perhaps not fully recovered, was beaten with only three minutes remaining by a rare Charlton header. Agonizingly, there was enough time for Best to squeeze an equaliser. The five teams in Monday's draw included three outside the top-flight. West Ham were no more than mid-table First Division. Excitement was unrestrained. The pairing of Swansea and Preston guaranteed a Second Division team at Wembley. Sunderland were drawn against the Londoners at Hillsborough, if as expected, they finished off United. There was no time to make the Wednesday night replay all-ticket. The hotbed of soccer held its collective breath and waited. And waited.

On the evening of 4 March '64, a sequence of events unfolded in and around the ground to which nothing in the history of Roker Park before or after compares. County Durham constabulary anticipated a crowd of around 70,000 and placed 100 officers on duty to cope with the inevitable few thousand or so latecomers that would ordinarily be locked out on such an occasion. Unexpectedly long queues formed from midday and as supporters arrived early straight from work, the narrow terraced streets became dangerously congested. Chief Constable William Tait rushed a hundred reinforcements to Roker in vain. He said that the 'crowd exceeded all our calculations - I have known nothing like it'. The battle was lost. At 6.45 pm the police allowed no more in the ground. This was a signal for the seething masses to break ranks, climb perimeter walls and cut through barbed wire in order to gain entry. Others, panicking to escape a growing crush, scrambled over parked cars to find refuge in nearby gardens. During the rush hour from work, the shock effects had been felt far away; a one and a half mile traffic jam blocked the A1 between Newcastle and Gosforth. Mrs Emma Johnson, of Sandringham Terrace, a row of houses running beside the Fulwell End, told a local journalist, 'Thousands were jammed between my front door and the football ground'.

A huge gate at the Roker End then collapsed under the pressure of those crammed outside. A raging torrent of humanity burst through, storming steps towards the crowded, vast, open terrace. Although eighteen people suffered broken limbs no lives were lost. Sadly however, there were two fatalities on this evening; one was a 16-year-old girl from Pelaw, near Gateshead. The Journal headline on the Thursday morning screamed 'Riot At Roker Park' with a sub-heading of 'Two die, 80 hurt, 50,000 shut out'. It was plainly no exaggeration. Sunderland hospitals were overwhelmed and were forced to call in off-duty nurses. Police motorcycles patrolled streets to enable access for ambulances.

A special train carrying hundreds of away fans terminated at Seaburn station only for it to be ordered back to Manchester without anyone alighting. When the turnstiles were closed there were as many outside the ground as inside. The official attendance of 46,727 was probably twenty thousand less than the actual number in the stadium; although an overflow thronged the ash perimeter track, popular estimates that 80,000 were present are fanciful. However, it is certainly not beyond reasonable doubt that up to 120,000 set out to watch the Manchester match and almost half returned home either caught in heavy traffic or unable to force their way to within touching distance of an entrance. Bobby Charlton, in his autobiography, stated that it took the team bus an hour to inch round from one side of the ground to the other. Len Hetherington writing for the Evening Chronicle in his usual theatrical prose, summed it up succinctly, 'a night of tragedy and terror outside the stadium and tension and near triumph for Sunderland inside'.

Yet again, victory was snatched away with a late goal. Sharkey put the home side ahead before Denis Law took the tie into extra time but when Maurice Setters put through his own net on the slippery pitch, the last four beckoned. With two minutes of the extra thirty remaining, Bobby Charlton did what he and the crowd least expected. He produced another header, this one however without venom, but enough to evade Montgomery's flailing grasp.

The derby with Middlesbrough the following Saturday proved anticlimactic and not because it was a goalless draw. Fans stayed away, traumatised by their midweek ordeal. A large hoarding covered a gap where a Roker End exit gate once stood. Thoughts switched to Huddersfield, venue of the second replay. No chances were taken with crowd arrangements, the decision to make the game all-ticket vindicated with a 55,000 sell out. And again, Sunderland scored first with Sharkey obliging shortly after the interval. As a heavy, rain-sodden pitch exacted its toll, Manchester United were roused into decisive action. Denis Law, suddenly his gladiatorial self, shirt sleeves stretched over arms, equalised within seconds and United were on their way to a 5-1 victory with the former Huddersfield striker, revelling on familiar territory, ending with a hat-trick.

There was an immediate reaction to the defeat when Newcastle won the Tyne-Wear game by the only goal. The record books show an attendance of 27,341. For practically everyone who turned up at St. James' Park there was a matching number that stayed at home, convinced the game had been rained off. Stan Anderson's testimonial at Roker a couple of months later actually attracted a slightly larger crowd. Dropped points either side of the second replay were the deciding factor in conceding a tight title race to Leeds. The loss at St. James' Park was in fact the only defeat since an anomalous 5-1 December reverse on a frosty, unplayable Northampton pitch. The Yorkshiremen in turn had only suffered one defeat since the festive falling out. Come the penultimate game against Charlton, Sunderland enjoyed a four-point cushion over third placed Preston whilst boasting a much better goal average. The visitors took an early lead before George Herd equalised and then in the last minute Johnny Crossan notched his 22nd league goal of the season. 50,000 fans saluted Charlie Hurley and his team-mates on a lap of honour. A final day draw at Grimsby featured a seventeenth goal from 33 league games for Sharkey. There was a settled team in which nine players made at least 37 league appearances; indeed Montgomery, Ashurst, Crossan and Mulhall were ever-present. Sunderland finished two points behind Leeds United with 61 points from 42 games.

With an eye on the forthcoming 1966 World Cup, Roker Park underwent a refurbishment with some of the cost met by an FA grant. New, taller floodlights had already been installed for the 1962-63 season; they were visible from the Newcastle to Tynemouth coast road and Leam Lane in Gateshead. The original pylons were donated to the home of South Shields at Simonside Hall. The Fulwell End was roofed over in 1964. As previously mentioned, the upper part of the Clock Stand was converted to seating. For the tournament itself, temporary benches were fixed to the Fulwell End and both paddocks. In addition to group games that were shared with Middlesbrough, Wearside hosted a quarter-final tie between the Soviet Union and Hungary, which attracted a disappointing crowd of 26,884. There was more than a grain of truth in Stan Anderson's view, all of a decade earlier, that the World Cup was not as important as the FA Cup. It wasn't until the conclusion of the 1966 tournament, when the nation had been force-fed international games and West Germany were beaten 4-2 in the final, that the competition was no longer an acquired taste. Wembley was almost 13,000 short of capacity when England commenced their Group stage with a sterile draw against Uruguay. The quarter-final attendance of 90,584 against Argentina on a sunny Saturday afternoon, again fell short of a full house.

Sunderland made an eye-watering profit of £114,000 in their promotion year. That figure had only ever been exceeded by Tottenham, who had made £123,000 during their double season of 1960-61. Looking back over proceedings, Syd Collings interpreted a 5-3 victory over a 'world-class' Benfica side midway through the season, a game he regretted missing because of business commitments, as 'a warning to Europe that we mean to be in there, at the earliest possible moment, challenging for top European honours, either as First Division champions or FA Cup winners'. Of his manager he wrote, 'Mr. Alan Brown cannot be praised too highly. It is particularly pleasing that he should be enjoying success as the reward for all the work which he has put into building and developing our playing resources'. The Sunderland chairman looked forward to a well-earned vacation.

8

BAXTER AND LITTLE ELSE

1964-65 to 1967-68

Despite huge takings of £122,523 from season tickets, the summer progressed without transfer activity. Six weeks before Sunderland kicked off the 1964-65 season, Syd Collings was at St. Andrews in Scotland watching The Open golf tournament. He was rocked with the news that Alan Brown, whose root and branch reform of the club was bearing fruit, had sensationally resigned to become manager at Sheffield Wednesday, having emerged first choice from 50 applicants. No reason was advanced for his abrupt departure. Brown may have been dismayed at the lack of funds for team strengthening, he may have thought himself worthy of an improved contract or may have been disappointed at the lack of a bonus. Sunderland gave each player a generous £1,000 reward and on discovering that Brown received nothing they arranged an impromptu collection. Len Ashurst, in his autobiography 'Left Back In Time', claims Brown had asked the directors to sell him his club house, at the prevailing value when he moved in, and that this request was refused.

The Sunderland players were well-paid in this era. Competing for the top honours, Manchester United and Liverpool were not as generous. Matt Busby and Bill Shankly had a tacit agreement to suppress the burgeoning wage demands that accrued from the abolition of the maximum wage in January '61. They were initially reluctant to pay more than £30 per week with £10 a point bonus. When United won the FA Cup at Wembley in 1963 Busby did not relent on a previously agreed bonus of £200. It is well documented that the standout Fulham player Johnny Haynes became the first £100 per week player. Haynes, a multi-capped England midfield maestro surrounded by willing artisans at best, almost single-handedly preserved unfashionable Fulham's top-flight status throughout the sixties but only received those wages after his chairman, the comedian Tommy Trinder, made a rash promise he never suspected he would have to honour. Some Second Division players were offered a pittance of an increase on their old contract; not so at Roker. Ron Reynolds, recalling his time under Ted Bates at Southampton in a book titled 'The Life of a 1950's Footballer', stated that his team mates, with the exception of future England international Terry Paine, whose wages more than doubled to £45, were only offered between one and two pounds. On the threat of strike action, Bates consented to a £5 increase. Hurley, who was initially offered £60 per week, found himself much better off than his Irish Republic international colleagues who were fully established within the First Division. In the previous near-miss promotion season, the players were handsomely looked after with an unusual lavish bonus system. If Sunderland were in a top-two position after 10 matches each player received £300, after 20 matches £600 and 30 matches £900. Regardless of how promotion was achieved, a guaranteed maximum total bonus of £1,200 became payable, dependent on the number of appearances made. The ever-present Roker players were paid £900, as in the twenty-ninth game they defeated Norwich to guarantee second position after 30 games. Ironically Sharkey, who scored five against the Canaries, received nothing; the bonus was not part of his contract as he had started the season as Brian Clough's understudy. When England won the World Cup three years later, their FA bonus was divided equally amongst the 22 leaving each squad member £1,000. Sunderland players under Alan Brown had received a similar amount for failing to win promotion.

Rudderless Sunderland did not hit the ground running when First Division soccer returned. Six goals were shared with Leicester before 45,465. The occasion is memorable because it featured debutant goalkeeper Derek Forster, who at 15 years and 185 days became the youngest ever player to appear in the top-flight. A training injury to Jimmy Montgomery had coincided with reserve goalkeeper Derek Kirby being ruled out of a pre-season game. Gordon Banks was Forster's opposite number and remembers the schoolboy acquitting himself well. For a modest fee, Sunderland bought Sandy McLaughlan from Kilmarnock as cover. Forster's distinction was overtaken in 2022, and that by only four days, when Arsenal's midfield scholarship prospect Ethan Nwaneri was introduced on the Emirates pitch with only three minutes remaining of an Arsenal Premier League match against Brentford. He did not touch the ball.

Despite consecutive away defeats the early September midweek match with West Bromwich Albion was a big attraction for 52,000 as it announced the return of Brian Clough to competitive action following his twenty-month absence. However, in Clough's words the comeback, which lasted all of three matches, was 'a desperate but futile attempt to hang on and prolong a career'. In the next match Clough netted his one and only First Division goal as a crowd of nearly 50,000 witnessed the resumption of rivalry with Leeds. Clough's goal and then two from Crossan, all in a ten-minute second half spell, saw Sunderland roar back from two down before Leeds spoilt the afternoon with an equaliser. This was no leisurely rehabilitation for Clough. He played a third time within seven days. A fixture list quirk had given Sunderland three consecutive home fixtures. Hurley's late equaliser against Aston Villa papered over defensive problems as the club drifted. Clough could perhaps have continued in a lower class of football, with razor-sharp reactions partially compensating for a lack of mobility. However, his knee would always be less than perfect and Sunderland were anxious not to lose insurance compensation reputed to be worth around £40,000. Nick Sharkey regained the number nine shirt and his goal against Blackburn finally secured two points for Sunderland at the ninth attempt.

Sunderland sifted through eighty unsuitable applicants, continuing their managerial search. They dithered then widened their net, only to suffer rejections from prime targets. Towards the end of September, Tommy Docherty refused an approach to discuss terms. In October Don Revie was offered the Roker vacancy and came very close to accepting. He was disillusioned with a lack of support from the Leeds public; a lucrative five-year contract tested his loyalty. Billy Bremner feared the worst. The Yorkshire Post lamented his expected departure. Revie changed his mind when Leeds offered vastly improved terms. This is hardly surprising with hindsight, for Revie would later be called 'Don Readies' and stereotyped as knowing the price of everything and the value of nothing, after he had walked out on his position as England manager in favour of the United Arab Emirates. However, the Leeds manager with a reputation as a deep thinker from his playing days was nothing if not complex and it is possible that, given his family values, he was unwilling to abandon a tight-knit group of players that he had nurtured from apprentices. Inevitably, some would have followed him to Roker. The Revie regime at Leeds spanned a further ten seasons, over which time they never finished outside the top four.

On 28 November '64 George Hardwick was appointed as caretaker manager after an approach by a worried chairman Syd Collings, as Sunderland languished near a relegation place. Hardwick, a former Middlesbrough full back capped many times for England, had player-managed Oldham followed by coaching stints abroad before returning home to look after the Ayresome Park youngsters. His invitation to manage came as a surprise. An intelligent, honest man with confidence in his ability, he was not concerned for the security of a contract as Collings had intimated the position would be permanent, on the proviso of relegation being avoided.

'Gorgeous George' Hardwick, of dashing good looks that in a later era would almost certainly have allowed him to utilise his football fame to guarantee a lucrative income outside the game, did not court popularity. He continued to select the in form McLaughlan when Montgomery returned to fitness. The deposed, former first choice goalkeeper only appeared once in the first team after New Year and concluded a frustrating period by submitting a formal transfer request. Supporters were also dismayed when Crossan departed to Manchester City. In addition, Brian Usher was replaced by Mike Hellawell, a pacy, direct winger as the first eleven was overhauled. Sunderland agreed a huge fee of around £70,000 with Dundee for their coveted forward Alan Gilzean. They were able to offer much better terms than Tottenham but lost out when Gilzean accepted less money in exchange for his longing to play alongside Jimmy Greaves. Charlie Hurley, now aged 28, was plagued by fitness problems and was dropped over the Easter period when he struggled against Wolverhampton Wanderers' Hugh McIlmoyle. Hurley, the undisputed king of Roker Park, had been voted runner-up to West Ham's Bobby Moore in the prestigious Football Writers' Player of the Year award. For a Northeast player outside the top division to achieve this was testament to his standing throughout the country, with the possible exception of London. However, over the following five years he missed almost as many First Division games as he played.

Since Hardwick's arrival, a run of 18 points from 15 games had banished relegation fears. His habit of criticising players in public did not impact team spirit. No home match was lost until Boxing Day and over the season, 12 of the 14 league victories were at Roker Park. There was confidence that the moderate return of 37 points from 42 games could be improved. Noting the potential of Brian Clough, he enrolled him on an FA coaching course and gave him responsibility for the youth team.

Hardwick was shocked and hurt when Sunderland went back on their word and did not offer him a contract. He felt that the board was annoyed when he failed to consult them on promoting Clough and were not keen on his aim of grooming the outspoken young man as a prospective number two. Regardless, Hardwick may have been too forthright for their liking. Clough, who would shortly commence his managerial career at Hartlepools United, always claimed he had good relations with the Roker hierarchy and blamed the new Sunderland manager for ending his career on Wearside. That was Ian McColl, fresh from his resignation after a four-year stint as Scotland national team manager. McColl signed a five-year contract on 21 May '65. An emollient and sometimes withdrawn character, he represented a cultural change from the authority and firmness of Hardwick, let alone the innovative coaching and moral code of Brown. McColl was a civil engineer, owner of a garage and without any experience of the hands-on, full-time responsibility of club management. He did not have the final say in picking the Scottish eleven, as in similar fashion to his England counterpart Walter Winterbottom his proposals were subject to scrutiny by a selection committee. Therefore, the tasks of formulating line-ups, resolving daily tensions within a squad of players, contract negotiations and developing relationships with a board of directors were foreign to him.

Less than a week into McColl's regime Sunderland stunned the soccer world when they signed Jim Baxter from Glasgow Rangers for £72,500. For sheer impact, nothing at Roker or the Stadium of Light since, apart from events of 1973, invite comparison. Baxter, a genius with the ball but blighted by his drinking and gambling habits that made him a real-life Damon Runyon character, was a living legend in Scotland. Questions why Sunderland could attract such a player, without competition from bigger clubs in England and the Continent, begged asking. The answers centred on Baxter's excessive nocturnal activities and problematical recovery from a broken leg that scared away potential suitors. Matt Busby refused the opportunity of signing him for Manchester United, presumably worried that Baxter's party animal instincts would destabilise team spirit. Instead, he took Pat Crerand from Celtic; less gifted but more reliable. Crerand later described Baxter as 'George Best before George Best'. Baxter was devastated when the Tottenham manager Bill Nicholson, looking to replace Danny Blanchflower, met him in a Glasgow hotel and agreed terms only to unexpectedly call off the deal later. Again, the reputation of a man who had acquired the sobriquet 'Bacardi Baxter' counted against him. Baxter, his Rangers career reaching an impasse, was desperate to go anywhere provided the money was right. The great Hungarian Ferenc Puskás was honoured to drink with Jim Baxter. The brilliant cricketing all-rounder Gary Sobers was another who counted Baxter as a dependable partner to while away the small hours. Pelé is reliably credited with saying that Baxter should have been born a Brazilian. At Rangers, Baxter was selected for a Rest of the World eleven to play England in an international at Wembley to mark the centenary of the FA. He may have been the first name on the team sheet such was the esteem his left foot, or claw as he named it, was held. Glasgow Rangers fans regard him as their all-time favourite. With Baxter on his game dictating the play, Rangers were almost immune from defeat in the Old Firm games, losing twice in eighteen matches. Alex Ferguson, who played alongside him said, 'Baxter was a magician on the park, a player who in the words of one admiring victim, could have put a size five football in an egg cup'. Denis Law rated him man of the match at Wembley in April '67, when Scotland inflicted on England their first defeat as World Cup holders. Never to be forgotten was the chutzpah of Baxter as he arrogantly played 'keepy-up' with the ball as a demoralised England surrendered. In mitigation Jack Charlton had broken his big toe after only 15 minutes and Ray Wilson limped around the pitch unable to retire because no substitutes were allowed. However, there were no caveats when Baxter, playing arguably his finest international game, scored twice as Scotland defeated the 'Auld Enemy' 2-1 at Wembley four years previously. Norman Giller, a respected southern-based Daily Express journalist, wrote that 'Rangers were well worth watching for the performances of the one and only Jim Baxter, a perfectionist of a player and a prince of playboys.'

In December '64 Baxter's world imploded. Seconds remained of a game he had dictated to ensure Ranger's passage to the quarter-finals of the European Cup with a 2-0 win over Rapid Vienna in Austria. Baxter tormented the Rapid full back one final time. He received an ill-tempered kick that broke his leg and he hardly played for Rangers again. Disenchantment had set in long before that defining incident. Baxter considered a basic £45 a week wage at Ibrox an insult; he wanted away.

Sunderland readily bowed to his demands. They agreed £80 a week and a generous £20 per point bonus plus extras, a package exceeding the offers of either Nicholson at Spurs or anyone else. In line with regulations, Baxter received 5% of the transfer fee but there was a feeling that he had received more, albeit on an unofficial basis. Len Ashurst confirmed years later in his autobiography 'Left Back in Time' that Baxter had pocketed no less than £17,000 from Sunderland, after an initial demand of £20,000. Ashurst realised from the off that Baxter would be a disruptive influence within the dressing room. His abrupt arrival in the wake of McColl raises the possibility that the new manager made the acquisition of his former international player a condition of his job acceptance. When news of the signing broke, Syd Collings said that Sunderland had been keen on Baxter for two years but was puzzled when pressed why no approach to Rangers had been made over that period. He then added 'I understand his broken leg has healed well and we are assured by Rangers it will not affect his play'. It only took Alf Greenly, writing for the Newcastle Journal, a single sentence to sum him up rather well, 'Baxter who runs a Jaguar and who is shortly to be married, likes the good things in life and it was the bigger cash which could be earned in England which prompted him to first ask for a transfer in December 1962'. Perhaps the reporter knew him better than Collings.

During his honeymoon period Baxter provided an expectant Roker crowd with every reason to hope that the fee paid was worth every penny and that it represented a major step for Sunderland in their return to challenge for honours. At first however there was the little matter of an eminently forgettable friendly with Celtic, as the visitors gained a measure of revenge for the torment they had received in Old Firm clashes from the Baxter of old, when they hammered Sunderland 5-1 at Roker. There was encouragement however when the opening day of the 1965-66 season brought a narrow defeat at Leeds even though most of the second half was played with ten men. George Mulhall was dismissed for abusive language after complaining to a linesman about a high and late challenge from Billy Bremner. The rivalry with Leeds persisted. A draw at Upton Park followed. Wearside eagerly awaited the midweek home league debut of Baxter. They were not disappointed. Baxter scored two and made two in a 4-2 victory over Sheffield United. The visiting goalkeeper Alan Hodgkinson was spellbound by the brilliance of Baxter, 'There was gold leaf sunshine in an aqua blue sky over Roker Park and one might have been forgiven for thinking that when Jim Baxter was born, above him a star danced … In the second half, however, Baxter upped the ante, playing thirty-yard passes of such exquisite weight and direction to John O'Hare and George Herd they landed like snowflakes on the toes of their boots. Throughout the final forty-five minutes, Baxter slid, stroked, swerved, chipped and drove passes like a watchmaker's feel for weight and precision.' Baxter attracted 42,147 for this game then 48,626 the following Saturday to watch a 2-1 win over West Ham.

In October, with Sunderland comfortable in mid-table, McColl spent £50,000 to tempt the free-scoring Neil Martin from Hibernian. Martin eventually achieved something that eluded Sunderland's all-time record scorer Dave Halliday, namely that of scoring 100 goals in both Scotland and England. McColl was gradually reshaping the team. A wind of change was blowing through Roker that did not bode well for long-standing terrace favourites. Sharkey, of five-goal fame, and whose impressive haul of 21 goals from 35 matches during the campaign that included Hardwick's temporary tenure, was no longer first choice. Hurley, a colossus when fit, would be replaced the following season by a £30,000 capture from Stoke, the rugged and unvarnished George Kinnell, a second cousin of Baxter. There were stories of lax discipline and Baxter taking advantage of McColl's perceived favouritism. Often lost for words McColl was no great orator. In the latter days of his management when he gathered everyone together, some players would take bets on the length of time it took him to commence talking.

The fashionable rumour at the time was of friction between the non-English players with Protestant and Catholic forming different cliques. This was simply not true. Billy McNeill who captained Celtic to a 1967 European Cup final win regarded Baxter as a close friend and in his opinion was the greatest ever midfield player Scotland produced. Baxter was noted for crossing sectarian divides in his socialising. With drinks on the table, no divide anywhere was too great. When Sunderland travelled to the capital for a weekend or midweek fixture, Baxter engaged a network of famous and infamous friends. The football came second. It was the arrogance of Baxter and disrespect he showed to lesser mortals by burning the candle at both ends that rankled team-mates. The expected improvement with Baxter and Martin in tandem did not materialise and the season petered out but not before a belated relegation scare that was only put to bed in the very last game, a 2-0 win over Everton. The propensity of the public to vote with their feet had reduced attendances for a couple of matches to just over 20,000 in the New Year. A pattern emerged of a team dominant on their own turf and anything but on their travels. No club in the First Division had such a marked difference between home and away results. Of the 14 wins collected in McColl's first season only one was outside the Northeast.

During most of the sixties, Alan Brown's initiative in forming the North Regional League meant that Sunderland Reserves were restricted to playing the second string of clubs such as Rotherham, Hull City and Middlesbrough and non-league clubs such as South Shields and Ashington. The Central League, including the reserve outfits of Newcastle, Sheffield Wednesday, Leeds and the Manchesters, was reluctant to permit new entrants, therefore young prospects coming through at Roker and established players seeking match practice faced unsuitable opposition. In November '67, Sunderland Reserves defeated a Darlington side 12-1. The scorers were listed as Gauden (3), Moore G (3), Hughes (2), Kerr (2) and Suggett (2). There was an ongoing debate if this was detrimental to their development. Brown however, and to a lesser extent McColl, tended to promote promising youth team players quickly into first team action without recourse to a long spell in a transitional reserve set-up.

The fruits of the Brown youth policy, underpinned by the discoveries of astute chief scout Charlie Ferguson, delivered the prestigious FA Youth Cup to Sunderland in 1967 and 1969. There was a losing final appearance in 1966 and a run to the last four in 1965. The names of Horswill, Todd, Pitt, Kerr, Hughes, McGiven, Chambers, Suggett and Tueart feature in those Roker finals. The depth of talent was such that less well-known youngsters Colin Beesley and John Lathan were, alongside Ritchie Pitt, selected by the FA to attend a one-week coaching course at Lilleshall. Ferguson, previously a scout at Burnley, linked up with Alan Brown when Brown arrived there as manager in 1954. He had a reputation for unearthing talent in and around his home town area in Dunbartonshire; for Sunderland his first notable find there was Nick Sharkey, with Bobby Kerr the most valuable.

During the 1966-67 season Colin Todd became a regular in the side. He was a cultured half back, mature before his time, who could tackle, pass cleanly and read the play; with the possible exception of Stan Anderson there has never been a better defender brought through the ranks at Roker. Clough, his youth team manager for a short time, was fully aware of his capabilities and eventually took him to Derby for a British record fee for a defender of £170,000.

All clubs nowadays possess Academies. Their vigilant, possibly overprotective development of young players is light years away from the time when a player short of his 18th birthday was deemed ready for a debut to seize a permanent place. Indeed during the following three seasons in a struggling team, Todd only missed three league games out of a possible 126. Bobby Kerr like Todd made a bow in the first team. They added vitality. For a few brief months promise flickered with an unbeaten league run which coincided with Cup progress and Kerr's introduction.

There was a poor start in August and September '66 but gradually, with Neil Martin proving his worth, goals flowed, although the usual difficulties away from home persisted. The aforementioned Todd, from Chester-le-Street, quickly established himself. Martin, who left penalties to Baxter, managed 20 top-flight goals that season. Thirty-three years elapsed before Kevin Phillips bettered that. Martin was a player who remains underrated and until very recently was almost forgotten, performing in an overlooked period within the club's history. There were three consecutive wins in autumn, including a 3-0 defeat of Newcastle that marred the debut on Tyneside of their record signing Wyn Davies. The third of those games was a 4-1 victory over Sheffield United on a mild Guy Fawkes afternoon. A fightback from 3-1 down to overcome Burnley 4-3 was followed by a 5-0 drubbing at champions-elect Manchester United who fielded Best, Law and Charlton. With little shortage of entertainment at Roker, no immediate danger of relegation and Baxter sometimes capable of something more than the odd cameo, a corner was being turned. Over a festive double-header with Aston Villa the points were shared with both games ending 2-1 in favour of the hosts. A cold Boxing Day of freezing mist reduced the home attendance to 30,000.

Newly promoted Manchester City wrapped up the old year. Debutant Bobby Kerr, 18 years old and barely 5'4", scored the only goal. Johnny Watters, the valued Roker physiotherapist, described him as a Rolls-Royce engine in a Mini. Those leaving early would have had to wait until Sunday afternoon for the 'Shoot' highlights to see his golden shot. The Kerr goal commenced a sequence of 12 games without defeat, including three Cup games with Leeds. He was labelled a lucky charm. His introduction coincided with resounding early round home FA Cup victories of 5-2 and 7-1, against Fourth and Third division opponents Brentford and Peterborough respectively. Brentford had been ahead after the interval before Martin's second goal levelled matters and Baxter took over. There was also a change from traditional red and white stripes to red jersey, red shorts and white socks, something that persisted until the Cup run ended, although the stripes momentarily returned for the fourth round game.

Peterborough, a relatively new club that had entered the League in 1960, brought a huge following, swelling the attendance to 44,000. Neil Martin scored a hat-trick establishing a six-goal lead after 50 minutes. Before automatic movement within a tiered pyramid system, admittance to the Football League depended on a vote at the Annual General Meeting. Before the system was scrapped, Hartlepool United were re-elected on eleven occasions. Non-league football was regionalised. The Northeast clubs of South Shields, North Shields, Blyth, Stockton, Ashington, Spennymoor and Horden CW voluntarily competed in the Midland League. This was where Peterborough resided when they gained enough votes at the AGM to displace Accrington Stanley from the Fourth Division. Each year the bottom four were compelled to apply for re-election alongside any ambitious non-league clubs. However, as only league members were eligible to vote, they exercised an 'old pals act' whereby there was a tacit agreement to maintain the status quo by voting for each other and invariably the four league clubs would receive the most votes.

Peterborough had enjoyed remarkable attendances at their impressive London Road ground but it was their FA Cup exploits that compelled clubs to vote for them. Months before their successful vote Peterborough had taken 15,000 fans to Sheffield Wednesday for a fourth round tie which attracted over 51,000 to Hillsborough. En route they defeated Shrewsbury, Walsall and Ipswich and remarkably attracted a crowd of 9,922 for a qualifying game against Bury Town of the Eastern Counties League. Against Northeast clubs in the Midland League, an aggregate of 25,000 saw home matches against Ashington, North Shields and Stockton. Although football was losing its mass appeal, the Cup continued to attract huge interest and for a club hoping to gain admittance to the league, it provided an opportunity to showcase their ambition. Hereford United underlined this. After being thwarted several times, they were elected in 1972 on the strength of defeating Newcastle and holding West Ham to a draw.

Leeds United at home in the fifth round was the main feature on a special Match of the Day programme, enlarged to cover three venues. The all-ticket crowd of 55,763 who crammed Roker Park on a windy day saw Baxter deliver an inch-perfect pass to Martin, who stroked a bobbling ball past Sprake. It did not take Leeds long to level. There was little between the sides; O'Hare came closest when he struck the woodwork for Sunderland whilst Baxter, relishing his moment on the big stage, chose to raise his game. He was lucky to only receive a booking when, without provocation, he deliberately hurt Giles although for the Leeds player it was certainly an example of he who lives by the sword, dies by the sword. Little football was on display. Leeds, as expected, started by kicking anything that moved. Bremner laid down the gauntlet with a nasty piece of work on George Herd. Sunderland were not slow to retaliate but both sides escaped serious censure from a lax and lenient Ray Tinkler. Overshadowing every incident, and ironically unrelated to the general tone of the game, was the sad conclusion to a clash between Bobby Kerr and Noman 'bites yer legs' Hunter. Despite his nickname, the Eighton Banks-born Hunter was generally regarded as hard but fair. His tackle on Kerr was not malicious; observers thought the broken leg Kerr suffered was accidental. Initially, he returned to his feet, and hopped a short distance to the Main Stand touchline before falling over in shock. Over 18 months passed before he made a return to first team action. Whoever succeeded in the replay would host the modest opposition of Manchester City in the quarter-final.

The decision not to make the replay all-ticket, an echo of the Manchester United night at Roker three years previously, almost had fatal consequences. Elland Road was besieged. Officials were slow in reacting and when the turnstiles were finally closed 25 minutes before kick-off the ground was dangerously overcrowded. Some of the 20,000 travelling Sunderland contingent were locked out; the official crowd of 57,897 smashed the ground record to smithereens. After only ten minutes action there was a calamitous collapse of crush barriers near a corner of the pitch. Fortunately there were no fatalities although a fleet of ambulances were summoned to take nineteen casualties to hospital, two of whom were detained overnight. Tinkler, again officiating, suspended play for quarter of an hour; Edelweiss from the Sound of Music film was relayed over the tannoy to bring calm. Proceedings restarted with some fans perched on a stand roof and others populating touchlines. As at Roker, Sunderland took the lead. O'Hare converted a Herd pass but Leeds equalised within a minute. This was a terrific contest, refreshingly without spite. Both teams, Leeds unusually, showed a sportsmanlike spirit. McColl said, 'I thought it was fantastic the way the crowd applauded both teams at half-time, full-time and extra time. I have never seen anything like that before'. Before hostilities were renewed there was a mundane trip to Stoke where Kinnell, Baxter, Herd, Mulhall and O'Hare were rested, which allowed a debut for Colin Suggett, who like Todd was from Chester-le-Street. Sunderland unsurprisingly lost 3-0, to remain on 29 points from 31 games.

The second replay at Hull the following Monday night before an all-ticket 40,000, ended unceremoniously. Leeds led for most of the game but against the run of play Allan Gauden, deputising for Kerr, equalised with 11 minutes remaining. To those with red and white eyes, Sunderland were in the ascendancy. That was until, with extra time looming, Jimmy Greenhoff theatrically threw himself over the 18-yard line in response to a legitimate tackle from Cecil Irwin. Referee Ken Stokes awarded a penalty without hesitation. There is a belief that Revie, the master of gamesmanship, a sporting euphemism for cheating, had instructed his players to go down under any tackle if made anywhere near the white chalk which defined the penalty box border. Cue mayhem. As Johnny Giles waited patiently for no less than five minutes before converting the winning kick, rival players brawled in a mass melee. George Kinnell broke ranks from the main body to chase the Leeds winger Johanneson as Stokes struggled to calm inflamed feelings. There were no dismissals until the last moments of the match when two Sunderland players, Herd and Mulhall, were ironically sent off for the relatively mild offence of surrounding the referee, after disagreeing with a free kick awarded to Leeds. The final whistle was a signal for mayhem; Baxter threw punches at Bremner whilst Charlton and Martin were pulled apart after a slanging match threatened to turn nasty. It was scant consolation that Leeds themselves were eventually to fall foul of officialdom. Trailing 1-0 late in their semi-final at Villa Park, Terry Cooper had a goal disallowed against Chelsea for offside that the Leeds team were adamant should have stood. Worse came in the last minute when the referee ruled a defensive wall had not retreated the full 10 yards from a free kick and therefore invalidated Lorimer's strike. Sunderland's season predictably petered out and even though at 31,731 the average gate was the ninth best in England, it represented a drop of 3,000 on the previous average.

Nick Sharkey, no longer an automatic selection after Neil Martin's arrival, had been quietly released to fellow First Division outfit Leicester City halfway through the season. As if to question McColl's judgement, Sharkey scored twice on his home debut for City against Newcastle in the month of May and days later repeated the feat against Chelsea to secure victories for his new club. However, the former boy wonder was unduly sold to Third Division Mansfield, where despite scoring one of the goals that dispatched West Ham's trio of World Cup winners from the FA Cup, he conveniently returned to the Northeast with Fourth Division Hartlepool. Having just turned 27, only a short stint at non-league South Shields was left of a once promising career. Sharkey, a popular figure in Fulwell's Mill View Social Club, settled on Wearside whilst working as a sales representative, latterly establishing himself as a leading figure in Sunderland's former players' association, before his passing at the untimely age of 71. In the summer, Ralph Brand was signed from Manchester City for £5,000. Brand, a forward similar in height to Sharkey, was near the end of his usefulness and had played alongside McColl at Ibrox and selected by him for Scotland. Supporters were perplexed again when another small ration was assigned to secure Brian Heslop, a young defender from Carlisle United.

With Brand and Heslop in place Sunderland started the 1967-68 season surprisingly well with a draw at Leeds; the misdemeanours of a Canadian tour, in which Baxter's party instincts were aided and abetted by Kinnell, reduced to an embarrassing footnote. With memories fresh of Baxter running the World Cup winners ragged, the midweek visit of Fulham on a warm August evening was heading for a comfortable conclusion until the architect of that famous Wembley occasion became embroiled in fisticuffs with John Parmenter and both were sent off. A 21-day suspension hung over Baxter. Sunderland prospered a short while and after defeating the Londoners and Everton in successive home games, they achieved a rare away win at

Leicester. Against West Ham at Roker, Sunderland, gifted a lead from Bobby Moore, were heading for a tenth point from seven opening games until Moore, Hurst (2), Peters and Redknapp scored within fifteen devastating minutes. Baxter, his 21-day suspension imminent, contributed little. The reporter on the teatime BBC Radio Sports Report stated that the Sunderland bubble had burst. Charlie Hurley remained out of favour and the following week as his teammates suffered a 3-0 loss at Burnley, he languished alongside Martin Harvey at a rain-lashed North Regional League encounter against South Shields at Simonside Hall. Towards Christmas Sunderland took two points from six games. McColl was on borrowed time. The average gate after four games had stood at 39,747; except for the Newcastle derby it wasn't until the second coming of Alan Brown in February, that Roker again witnessed a 30,000 league crowd.

Sunderland were desperate to offload Baxter after his sending off and were resigned to a heavy loss on the fee paid to Rangers. According to Ken Gallacher in his excellent book 'Slim Jim Baxter. The Definitive Biography', Ian McColl spoke to the Manchester City manager Joe Mercer, who he presumed was interested. Mercer said in no uncertain terms, 'No way I want him near this club'. There was a final hurrah from Baxter a month before the curtain came down on his Sunderland stay, a performance acknowledged as the last worthy of his name and one that moved McColl to gush, 'one of the greatest players who ever walked'. This was his return to the game after serving the suspension resulting from the Fulham fracas. He was champing at the bit. Such was his mastery of Nottingham Forest during a 1-0 victory, such was his vision and touch evocative of halcyon days, Johnny Carey the visiting manager was seduced into persuading the committee at the City Ground to buy him. McColl was astonished when Forest, without recourse to haggling, offered £100,000. The Forest chairman, Tony Wood, commented when the business was concluded, 'I regard him as one of the best footballers in the world'. He was obviously blissfully unaware of Baxter's off-the-field interests. The transfer was confirmed on 2nd December within 48 hours of a home defeat by Chelsea. Carey, delighted with his 'early Christmas present', could not have envisaged Forest offloading Baxter within 18 months as damaged goods, on a free transfer to his spiritual Ibrox home.

McColl's future may have been subject to scrutiny but his transfer market activity was not curtailed. Raith Rovers were satisfied with a sizeable fee of £40,000 for their relatively unknown midfielder Ian Porterfield. The left-footer, although eliciting comparison with Baxter who likewise had played at Kirkcaldy, made a promising beginning on Wearside before being judged unready for senior football. Following a Boxing Day defeat at St. James' Park, Porterfield made his debut at Roker in the return festive fixture. Sunderland surrendered a 3-1 lead; the abiding memory is that of John

McNamee the visiting man-mountain of a centre half celebrating his equaliser three minutes from time by swinging on a crossbar. Ollie Burton his defensive partner had converted two penalties whilst Colin Suggett, now cementing a regular berth in the team, scored his eighth and ninth goals of the season. It was apparent that the input from Martin and Suggett was not enough to override defensive shortcomings, therefore with money to spare from Baxter's sale, McColl signed a full back Geoff Butler from Chelsea for £60,000. Butler had been at Stamford Bridge only a short time after his previous move from Middlesbrough and only made a couple of appearances for Sunderland before moving on to Norwich.

Despite 10 league games without a win, steadily falling rain on a January evening and the modest Second Division opposition of Norwich, a third round FA Cup replay lured 33,000 to Roker. An unexpected 1-0 defeat evidently sealed the fate of McColl, as despite winning at Sheffield Wednesday in the next game through a Ralph Brand goal, he was dismissed and replaced by Alan Brown, who was therefore returning for a second spell in charge following his shock departure in 1964.

After the Cup exit there were two surprises. Neil Martin had kicked his last ball for Sunderland and departed to Coventry City for £90,000. After starting the season in characteristic fashion with 10 goals in 16 appearances Martin, suffering from Baxter's departure, was amidst a barren patch and demoted as an unused substitute at Hillsborough. Debuting in the number nine shirt was McColl's final signing Gordon Harris, a seasoned midfield enforcer, who came from Burnley for a fee of £68,000. Harris, his thinning hair combed in such a way as to disguise a growing baldness, had seen better days and ran with a slight limp. His first game at Roker Park coincided with the commencement of the reign of Brown, who had left Wednesday after three and a half years having taken them to the 1966 FA Cup final, where after a 2-0 interval lead they surrendered the trophy to Everton. The movements of Martin and Harris suggest that the changes afoot were an open secret.

Alan Brown was appointed 9 February '68 and a larger than usual crowd of 31,735 welcomed him back to familiar territory for the visit of Tottenham, who spoilt the homecoming by triumphing 1-0. Experienced utility player Calvin Palmer became his first signing, taking the expenditure at Roker over and above the Baxter and Martin largesse. Worryingly, the Spurs game was the start of four defeats; with one solitary win in fifteen games the club were second bottom. Brown however instilled spirit within the dressing room and a run of 16 points from 12 games carried Sunderland to safety. The return to the fold of Hurley was welcomed. On the last day of the season, Suggett and Mulhall secured a surprise win at Old Trafford in front of 62,963. In order to gain a second consecutive title, Manchester United needed to win and pray that Manchester City did anything other at St. James' Park. A 4-3 City win rendered United's defeat irrelevant.

9

FENDING FOR THEMSELVES

1968-69 to 1969-70

In 1968-69, the first full season of his second coming, Alan Brown gave Charlie Hurley a huge vote of confidence when he jettisoned George Kinnell. Brown's team was a curate's egg of senior players raging against the dying of the light and a collection of newcomers bursting forth from a highly successful youth team. Results were therefore predictably unpredictable. Leicester's defeat on 7th September, through goals by Porterfield and Mulhall, placed Sunderland in eighth position with nine points from eight games. There was controversy in the next match at Molineux. After leading through a Billy Hughes goal, a late Wolves equaliser that many thought offside denied them another victory. In a heated dressing room exchange Calvin Palmer incurred the wrath of Brown, who promptly excluded him from the next two games. Wolverhampton and the volatile Palmer did not mix. In the previous season, shortly after signing him, Brown had taken his team to a cinema during an away trip there. Palmer walked out unannounced before the end of the film and was handed a one-match ban. Ironically, for all Brown had made him a first signing, Palmer continually crossed the manager's strict disciplinary line.

At the age of twenty, Colin Todd wore the careworn appearance of a seasoned professional and had already accumulated England caps at under-23 level. It was sink or swim for those youngsters around him. Todd missed his first game for eighteen months in October when Sunderland suffered an 8-0 humiliation at West Ham. Geoff Hurst illegally punched his first goal into the net but there was no doubt surrounding his other five. The Sunday People newspaper awarded merit marks out of 10. Hurst received a perfect 10 as opposed to the usual mark of eight or nine that a 'star man' might achieve; everyone else including the unemployed goalkeeper was marked as a nine.

Alan Brown's concise analysis afterwards of 'It was an even game. We conceded four in each half' would certainly not be acceptable in today's environment of 'on message' soundbites. He was neither an empty vessel nor a talking head.

Dwindling gate receipts and the rapid emptying of club coffers just before and after Brown's return left no option but to promote internally. Although Billy Hughes, displaying genuine promise, had broken into the first team others such as Moore, Lowery and Beesley found the transition difficult. A week after the carnage of a November 5-1 mauling at Tottenham, a promise of tomorrow flickered. Sunderland tackled Jimmy Adamson's resurgent Burnley, who within a run of six consecutive wins and a draw had defeated champions-elect Leeds 5-1. The Newcastle Journal reporters Ken McKenzie and Bob Cass enthused, 'The day was truly notable for 19-year-old forward Billy Hughes, who showed up better than the much boosted and talented, Burnley babes'. They were assured that he looked a future top-line prospect. Evergreens Herd and Harris scored in the 2-0 win but both picked up injuries. Any apprehension at the return match with West Ham, on the last Saturday before Christmas, quickly dissipated when Sunderland helped by two early strikes from Palmer and Harris gained a measure of revenge for their Upton Park nightmare. Hurley, on this occasion magnificent, reduced Geoff Hurst to that of a mere mortal and one solitary goal.

The Roker Boxing Day goalless draw against Sheffield Wednesday watched by 26,333 featured a debut by Dennis Tueart who replaced George Mulhall. Sunderland sat twelfth in the table. Chairman Syd Collings was encouraged to comment in a New Year message, 'The progress of our younger players augurs well for the future … Our position at the moment, around the middle of the league table, means that it will be extremely unlikely that we will be among the leaders at the end of the season … There is also every chance of a good run in the Cup; we have the ability to go far'. His rose-tinted spectacles were only in situ until the very next game. Sunderland suffered a comprehensive 4-1 defeat at home in the third round of the FA Cup by a Fulham side who finished bottom of the Second Division. The immediate reaction was a 3-1 defeat at Everton that commenced a fourteen-game sequence that yielded only six points. For George Herd, a vital cog in midfield with an eye for goal, the final curtain beckoned. He returned after a short layoff but only played four more games in his Roker career. Herd's last appearance featured yet more capital punishment, a 5-1 setback at Chelsea. Through bad weather this was the club's first game for three weeks, during which period a ring rusty side were unable to use a snowbound Moor Lane training ground and were left with little option but to utilise Roker beach. Ritchie Pitt, at 17 years old a boy in a man's game, was introduced somewhat prematurely later in the season and had the daunting task of filling in for an injured Hurley. Pitt's five-match winless stretch included a 1-0 defeat by West Bromwich Albion on 10 March '69 that produced an attendance of 15,769, the lowest in eight years for a league match at Roker.

Three games from the end of the season Sunderland, two places off relegation, were looking over their shoulder. The uncertainty was banished with a blast from the past and peek into the future. A patched up Hurley, whose long-standing mobility problems had worsened, faced Wolves in his last ever competitive appearance on Wearside and shackled the dangerous Derek Dougan whilst, at the other end of the park, the 19-year-old Tueart wowed a 21,000 crowd. He headed Sunderland into a lead then rounded off a scintillating performance by beating two defenders then intelligently playing a pass to the overlapping Palmer, who whipped in a low centre that Bobby Kerr lashed home. The 2-0 victory which just about guaranteed safety was followed by a 2-1 success at Burnley in the penultimate away game, the only occasion Sunderland tasted victory on their travels. Their record of ten home wins compared with one away was unusual but hardly remarkable in an era before teams benefitted from luxury travel and first-class hotel arrangements. In addition, with clubs fielding a significant proportion of local products and a blanket absence of foreigners in the game, the motivation for players to succeed on their own turf was high. Manchester United won thirteen at home but only two away whilst Stoke, amongst other clubs, displayed a noticeable home bias with all of their nine victories coming at the Victoria Ground.

Over the five seasons since promotion, the Wearsiders had never finished above fifteenth. Leeds, in securing their first major trophy, cantered to the title with a record 67 points, no less than 34 ahead of Sunderland. Their relatively modest goal tally of 66, which numbered 23 more than Sunderland, was as much a reflection of the defensive dogma now prevalent in the English game as the cautious nature of Don Revie.

Considering a goalscorer was more than ever a prized possession, it was disappointing when Colin Suggett was sold to West Bromwich Albion. Selling a valuable asset with an assured future had never been the Sunderland way. He had been leading scorer in the two previous campaigns with 14 and 9 league goals and netted each time in four derbies against Newcastle. The £100,000 fee stood comparison with a new British record of £165,000 that Leeds had paid for Allan Clarke. Joe Baker, a recognised striker at Arsenal where he won England caps, now past his zenith, was signed from Nottingham Forest for £30,000 as Suggett's replacement. The £10,000 outlay on Gateshead-born Colin Symm from Sheffield Wednesday reserves, a player Brown knew from his management spell there, completed the grand summer outlay.

Coventry, newly promoted Crystal Palace twice, Burnley and Sheffield Wednesday were the opposition in a modest-looking start to the 1969-70 season. Charlie Hurley, released on a free transfer to Second Division Bolton Wanderers, was not part of it. Alarmingly, Palace took three points from Sunderland and from five matches the club only mustered one goal and two draws. Brown blooded teenager Mick McGiven on the opening day and the even younger 17-year-old Bobby Park, in the next match. McGiven, a tenacious player, acquitted himself well and was ever-present whilst the slender, versatile Park made a substitute appearance in the second game, before an unbroken run in the second half of the season underlined his undoubted potential.

The case for the defence unravelled when the first of the big guns entered the fray at the end of August. Without breaking sweat, the City slickers of Manchester eviscerated Sunderland 4-0 at Roker, easing into a two-goal lead after eight minutes. Their neighbours United rounded off a miserable month for the Wearsiders with a 3-1 victory at Old Trafford. A second round League Cup dismissal at Roker by Third Division Bradford City followed. The players, never short of effort, were outraged at criticism by shareholders at the Annual General Meeting who questioned their commitment. Brown sent out a defiant message, 'We have certainly been hit in the solar plexus. We will not tolerate slackers.' Even his detractors could not deny that he himself, was a fitness fanatic and that if nothing else he would lead by example. From Syd Collings there was talk that the club was ready to make a splash in the market once new finance was attracted. It remained talk. When a win finally materialised against Nottingham Forest, a completely unexpected two points were earned at Tottenham in the next outing. The home side, lacking conviction, were coming off a 5-0 loss at Derby and were beaten by something of a fluke when Mike England, challenging Baker for a high ball, collided with one of his defenders to accidentally put through his own net. Pitt, ruled out with injury, had been replaced at centre half by Brian Heslop, who held down a regular place for the remainder of the season. Usually never more than a stand-in during his time at Sunderland, he was transferred to Fourth Division strugglers Northampton for a modest fee within a year. Perhaps Brown should have kept Hurley and wrapped him in cotton wool. The comic Peter Cook, a Spurs supporter, unwittingly placed Sunderland's shock win in perspective when he classed the entertainment value of the game as being less than that of watching a fish finger defrost.

There was no follow through at Roker Park after the back-to-back wins. Only a difficult winter ahead remained when two consecutive home games produced one point. Chelsea were held to a goalless draw before a 1-0 midweek defeat by Burnley, watched by 20,000. Joe Baker had managed four goals in 31 starts during his previous campaign at Forest; at Roker he fared worse. Not for lack of effort. Despite encouragement from a dwindling hard core who endorsed his wholehearted approach by repetitively chanting 'Joe

Joe Joe Baker', nothing went right. After nineteen goalless games he was withdrawn from a lightweight forward line. The promising Park scored the decisive goal in a December match against Ipswich that guaranteed only a third victory of the season. The gate of 12,739 for a First Division match, considering everything was still to play for, was an extraordinary indication of apathy. There were no demonstrations or protests. They simply voted with their feet. The Roker End resembled a stark, brutalist mausoleum. On the same day the next lowest attendance was 17,000 at Stoke. At this stage Sunderland were by no means adrift but the public were losing patience, criticising the directors for a lack of ambition, and the manager for a perceived series of strange decisions. Ian Porterfield, having fallen out with Brown in the summer, had not kicked a ball in anger. The transfer-listed Palmer, who surely would have improved the midfield or back four, had not been selected since the early weeks. On a local radio programme he bizarrely commented, 'The reputation Northeast people have for friendliness and hospitality was a fallacy. I would like to get back to the Midlands where they don't have to know you before they will come up and make you feel at home'. Of greater concern, a few months later under the influence of alcohol, he was the subject of an early hours high-speed police chase in South Shields before he smashed his car into a garden wall. He was banned for one year, charged with dangerous driving. A free transfer beckoned.

An improvement of five points from five games was taken into the final Saturday when Sunderland travelled to Maine Road and emerged 1-0 winners through a Dennis Tueart goal. Sheffield Wednesday and Crystal Palace, both in trouble at the foot of the table, had lost and Sunderland, handed a lifeline, finished their season with consecutive Wednesday evening home games against the Merseyside pair. When Palace completed their business with a home victory over Manchester City, who were distracted by a second leg Cup Winners' Cup semi-final against Schalke 04, Alan Brown's side required three points from two tough games to stay up.

It was improbable that Sunderland would vacate a relegation position occupied since August. Everton, at full strength, featuring their fabled midfield trio of Kendall, Harvey and Ball, were newly crowned league champions and wanted a victory to match the recent record points haul of Leeds. Everton, on top, hit a post in the early exchanges but a spirited home side urged on by 28,774 competed well, only a lack of composure and undue haste preventing them from breaking the deadlock. Liverpool, becalmed in fifth position, had nothing riding on the outcome. Bill Shankly's assistant Bob Paisley was from Hetton-le-Hole. His dream as a kid to play for Sunderland was dashed when manager Johnny Cochrane deemed him too small. Tommy Smith, the Liverpool captain, later admitted that the normally animated Shankly was very subdued on the night and did not give his usual, inspirational team talk. Sunderland, one final push from salvation, suffered stage fright. The eagerness against Everton was replaced by a nervous caution. Liverpool, guilty of missing easy chances, held off for as long as possible before Chris Lawler, without celebration, struck an 86th minute winner. There was a silent acceptance from 33,000 with a sizeable chunk of the Fulwell End staying behind for twenty minutes after the final whistle to proclaim their unrequited love for the club.

Gordon Harris finished leading scorer with only seven goals. A tally of 30 goals was a new historical low. Baker and Harris were well into the veteran stage of their careers. The full back pairing of Cecil Irwin and Len Ashurst was at an end. At Highfield Road in March Ashurst had played his last game of a long Roker career. In accumulating a record 452 outfield league appearances plus six as substitute, he had overtaken Stan Anderson and was marginally second behind goalkeeper Ted Doig, whose career spanned the Victorian and Edwardian eras, in the all-time list of league appearances. Ashurst became player-manager at Hartlepool. Jim Montgomery would eventually overtake all with 537 league appearances. The average gate of 21,790 was eclipsed by 22 clubs. Alan Brown had another rebuilding job on his hands. This was not 1957; Sunderland did not possess the funds, attendances or standing to attract players. A saddened Hurley, following his former team's demotion from afar commented, 'I always said that Sunderland made a mistake when they let me go and I have never changed my feelings. You must remember that this was not the opinion of a young professional relatively new to the game but of a player who knew the situation there and who knew exactly the way the club was heading. The club made mistake after mistake after they got promotion. We were raring to go. Then came the Alan Brown shock. He went and we had no manager. There was the chance to make the club great again, but it was allowed to slip away. The only ones I feel sorry for are the players and supporters. Nobody else'.

10

VOTING WITH THEIR FEET

1970-71 to 1971-72

No great confidence existed in an instant return to the First Division as Sunderland bobbed around mid-table in 1970-71. Despite another majestic Colin Todd display, a midweek home defeat in October from Hull resembled boys against men, as seasoned campaigners Terry Neill, Houghton, Chilton and Wagstaff dictated proceedings. Brown's paymasters would not sanction £30,000 for a Scunthorpe unknown called Kevin Keegan. A first signing for more than a year materialised when full back Dick Malone arrived from Ayr United. The novelty put a couple of thousand on the gate as Sunderland defeated Bristol City 1-0 through a Mick McGiven goal, in front of 17,335. Unexpectedly, just before Christmas, as if produced from a conjurer's hat, Sunderland smashed their transfer record when a bid of £100,000 was accepted by Rotherham for the centre half turned striker, Dave Watson. It was the joint highest amount paid for a Third Division player and an astonishing fee for a relative unknown, regardless of Sunderland's financial situation. Watson had only recently made the switch to centre forward. He scored on his debut in a 1-1 draw at Watford adding to his season's tally of nine in eighteen games for Rotherham. Watson's first appearance at Roker was a Boxing Day match with Middlesbrough. Despite snow flurries, 42,000 turned up to see Kerr and Hughes earn a draw.

Inevitably, Colin Todd departed in February '71. His sad finale, a 4-0 defeat at Roker by Cardiff, was witnessed by 11,566 with only a few stragglers remaining at the end. At Derby County Brian Clough was searching for a successor to Dave Mackay. Cocksure of Todd's capabilities, having closely witnessed his development in the Roker youth side, he unhesitatingly broke the British transfer record for a defender. Clough's single-mindedness was measured by more than the £170,000 fee. He did not seek permission from his chairman Sam Longson, who on receiving a telegram from Clough, took a sharp intake of breath when he realised Derby would have to contend with a huge overdraft. Clough's characteristic boldness was vindicated as Todd went on to amass 27 full England caps. Of far less concern to supporters was the news that Keith Collings had assumed the mantle of chairman following a short period when his father Syd had vacated the position in favour of Jack Parker.

Clearing the first obstacle in any Cup competition was a depressing jump too high. Fourth Division Lincoln ended League Cup interest in the second round. An evening third round FA Cup game at home to Orient brought confusion to sparsely populated terraces and a threadbare experimental defence. Sunderland emerged in all white with Gordon Harris wearing a number five shirt; the visitors had only packed their all red home strip. Orient, as the 3-0 scoreline suggested, were more than comfortable on a bewildering night. This was the last appearance for Joe Baker, despite ten goals in sixteen league appearances suggesting he had finally found form. Towards the end of the season, a series of eight games that produced only one goal enticed merely 8,596 for the visit of Swindon. Attacking the Fulwell End Sunderland netted five times in the first half, with Kerr and Hughes contributing two each, before coasting in 5-2. The jury remained out on the effectiveness of the number nine Watson.

Not for more than half a century, at a time when football was markedly less popular, had the average gate of less than 16,000 been so low. As the 1971-72 season dawned there was no transfer activity. Against promotion favourites Birmingham City, a creditable 1-1 draw was gained but heavy rain restricted the attendance to 9,749, the lowest opening day figure at Roker Park since 1904. The weather was a dampener, as was the absence of 17-year-old boy wonder Trevor Francis, ruled out with injury. He had burst to attention in the previous campaign scoring eight goals in three matches, including four against Bolton. The afternoon was completely overshadowed by a terrible accident on the slippery surface. The high hopes of Alan Brown for his teenaged prodigy Bobby Park were cruelly dashed when the highly rated and versatile youngster, replacing Cecil Irwin in the back four, sustained a career-ending double fracture of his right leg from a tackle by Ray Martin. The sickening crack was audible within the main stand paddock. Losing Park was a major blow. Irwin returned for three matches before moving to non-league Yeovil as player-manager. He had made over 300 appearances after commencing his regular full back role on the opposite side of the pitch to Len Ashurst. Before a ball was kicked against Birmingham the Sunderland manager, not noted for hyperbole, took everyone aback with a bold prediction of promotion. Monsoon conditions or not, the thin line of die-hards sheltering under umbrellas at the back of an otherwise empty Roker End suggested the public were not convinced. It may have been a ploy by Brown to instil much-needed conviction into his young team.

Increasing hooliganism was a problem but there was still an appetite to watch a winning team. Throughout the season Birmingham, with Francis playing at St. Andrew's, attracted five Second Division crowds in excess of 40,000 and a quarter-final FA Cup gate of 52,500 against Huddersfield. Midlands rivals Aston Villa, Third Division champions-elect, also boasted remarkable numbers with three crowds above 45,000, including 48,110 for a match against Bournemouth that Match of the Day made their main feature. At Roker, youth was given further licence when 16-year-old substitute Jimmy 'Chico' Hamilton headed the winner in a 4-3 victory over Preston. This inspired a run of three consecutive victories, the first such sequence for five years. On a warm autumn afternoon 24,000 were tempted for the visit of Second Division leaders Norwich. Tueart, now a first team regular, put Sunderland one up before Norwich came back for an undeserved point.

A spate of home draws followed. Against Luton, Watson opened the scoring with a low, raking shot but Sunderland were unable to extend their lead when Chris Nicholl dived full length to handle a goal-bound shot, only for Billy Hughes' penalty to strike the inside of a post and roll teasingly along the goal line. The visitors then scored twice before Mick McGiven rescued a point. Northern Premier League South Shields entertained Notts County in the second round of the FA Cup at Simonside Hall. Shields succumbed 3-1 against opponents who fielded Willie Carlin, Tony Hateley, Don Masson and Les Bradd. The attendance of 8,144 was a mere 3,689 less than the number at Roker who saw Sunderland defeat Fulham on the same afternoon. A season later at Meadow Lane, Sunderland would oppose eight of that County side in a third round tie. The last fixture before Christmas should have produced a vital win over Millwall, who were second in the table, five points ahead of Brown's team. The Roker crowd, witnessing a rare appearance from Derek Forster between the sticks, were deflated when the visitors stole a draw with two late goals that arose from corners at the Fulwell End. Sunderland were becoming difficult to beat but seven draws from nine matches confined them to the fringe of the promotion race.

After nine attempts there was finally progress beyond the initial round of a domestic competition when Sheffield Wednesday were beaten at Roker Park. The FA Cup fourth round tie with fellow Second Division side Cardiff City was washed out, therefore both clubs were in the velvet bag for a place in the last sixteen. Whoever progressed would contest with Leeds United at home. There was sudden interest on Wearside. Sunderland drew at Ninian Park and the replay was scheduled for a Monday afternoon to avoid government-imposed restrictions on electricity usage in response to a coal strike by the National Union of Mineworkers. Leeds, potential fifth round opponents and a huge attraction, were positioned a close second to Manchester City in the First Division and drawing unaccustomed praise for a recent conversion to entertaining, attractive football. For long-suffering Sunderland followers there was the added spice of a chance to gain revenge for the penalty injustice at Hull that soured the three-match saga with the Yorkshiremen in '67. Getting past Cardiff was judged a formality. Aside from their fellow Second Division opponents sitting second bottom of the table, they were forced to rush centre half Don Murray back into action after his deputy Richie Morgan had limped off in the previous game. What the Welshmen did have in abundance, however, was the wherewithal to handle the big occasion. In front of 40,000 on a blindingly bright day, Cardiff settled quickly taking a deserved lead through Brian Clark and should have put proceedings well beyond the reach of a nervous home side in a dominant first half. Only three minutes remained when Bobby Kerr, six yards out and facing the Roker End, unexpectedly poked home a low left-wing cross. Alan Brown appeared on the pitch before extra time to rally his young team. For thirty minutes, the roar that had been dormant for years was roused. As a rattled defence in front of him buckled, Billy Irwin in the Cardiff goalmouth stood firm. 48 hours later Cardiff won the second replay at an almost deserted Maine Road. The touchpaper remained unlit.

Shortly afterwards, in another midweek afternoon kick-off, Sunderland achieved a fourth consecutive league victory by defeating Portsmouth 3-2. John Lathan, unable to secure a regular place, managed a hat-trick as the club climbed to third but the attendance of 8,273 was markedly different to that of the first Cardiff replay. Momentum stalled through an unfortunate postponement of a match with Watford. Roker Park was blanketed in a sea fret as thousands waited in vain outside the ground.

Third position however proved transient as Sunderland fell away to fifth, six points adrift of second-placed Birmingham with an inferior goal average. Norwich were champions; all four clashes with the two promoted clubs ended all square. The encounter at Carrow Road featured the sad loss of half back Martin Harvey who sustained a career-ending injury. Harvey, the last outfield survivor of 1964, made over 300 league appearances and represented Northern Ireland on 34 occasions. In an early seventies' Roker Review, there was mention of a comment from a wag in the crowd, impressed with Harvey's stylish wing half movement, likening his legs to those of Brigitte Bardot. The Saturday evening Sunderland Football Echo that included match reports, general gossip and readers' letters is no longer published. For 29 years from 1950 Billy Butterfield, using the pseudonym 'Argus', was the main correspondent. Harvey found amusement in explaining to opposition players that the name Argus was derived from Greek mythology and referred to a giant with a thousand eyes who never missed anything. Harvey concluded by saying that every one of the eyes was red and white.

The final fifth place comprising only nine defeats from 42 games, with Dennis Tueart and Dave Watson sharing 26 goals, should have augured well for the future. Despite an encouraging season, the average gate of 15,906 was far from an improvement and only served to underline a growing apathy. Again, no signings were made during the close season. All was not well with Billy Hughes and Tueart who were restless to develop their burgeoning talents in pastures new.

11

THE MESSIAH AND THE MIRACLE

1972-73

Competitive football returned on 12 August '72. Leeds were defeated 4-0 at Chelsea. They were reduced to ten men in the first half when the departure of goalkeeper David Harvey with concussion coincided with Mick Jones hobbling off. Their travails at Stamford Bridge would pale against their end-of-season fate. Sunderland lost narrowly at Middlesbrough. After ten games seventh position was attained with a 4-1 win over newly relegated Nottingham Forest. John Lathan scored twice; Forest had not won a league game at Roker since 1906. It was the last victory Brown oversaw. Time was running out on his long-term vision to nurture a young group of players to maturity. McGiven, Kerr, Hamilton, Lathan, Tueart, Hughes and Watson occupied shirt numbers seven to eleven in Brown's final months in charge; with the exception of Watson all were brought through from the youth team. In defence, Pitt and Jackie Ashurst were vying for the centre half spot, Mick Horswill a teenager from Annfield Plain was established at half back and Keith Coleman, another youngster, featured at left back. The loss of Martin Harvey was keenly felt.

It all started to go to pieces in the second half at Oxford United's Manor Ground. After taking the lead through Bobby Kerr, Sunderland were routed 5-1 with a 29-year-old Scottish forward, Hugh Curran, helping himself to a hat-trick. The storm clouds were gathering. A subdued crowd of only 11,618 witnessed a tepid goalless encounter with Fulham. The club were marooned in fourteenth without immediate cause for panic but falling gates were a concern. Shortly afterwards, there was a civilised meeting between chairman Keith Collings, vice chairman Jack Ditchburn and Alan Brown to agree a parting of the ways. Brown, six months remaining on a five-year contract, took his departure philosophically and was confident he was leaving his successor a legacy of good youngsters. Perhaps he realised his methods, so relevant in his first reign at Roker, were now outdated. With the privations of the post-war years a distant memory, Brown's values increasingly jarred against a more open, less deferential society and his second period at Roker had unwound with him out of touch and unable to adapt. Dogmatic to the end, he became reluctant to sign the very experienced players that his young side needed lest they contaminated the high moral code that he preached. Trainer Billy Elliott took charge on a caretaker basis. The telephone was ringing again at Roker Park. The press speculated on a replacement, putting forward anyone with a Northeast connection as a candidate. The name of Brian Clough figured heavily but Sunderland made no approach. The first game without Brown attracted the largest league gate for nearly a year, albeit a modest 18,717, to see a 2-2 draw with Aston Villa. For the visit to Carlisle, Elliott switched Dave Watson to centre half and despite a 4-3 defeat stuck to his guns when he announced an unchanged side for Bristol City. At Ashton Gate this proved to be another defeat.

Sunderland, without fanfare, unexpectedly appointed 42-year-old Bob Stokoe as manager. Stokoe, from Mickley in Northumberland, was centre half in Newcastle's 1955 FA Cup winning team. This, coupled with his arrival from modest Second Division Blackpool and a reputation of working within a shoestring budget did not, at the beginning, endorse him to supporters. Stokoe commenced his low-key management career at Bury before doing the rounds at Charlton, Rochdale and Carlisle. He allowed a group of players that Brown had ruled with a rod of iron to express themselves and perform without apprehension. He defused tension by bringing humour into a situation, even allowing his charges the odd drink without looking over their shoulders. He was however a sore loser and when the occasion demanded capable of maintaining a grudge. Keith Peacock, a career-long player at Charlton, relates a tale in his excellent autobiography 'No Substitute', that gives a revealing insight into Stokoe's personality. At Charlton, Stokoe felt he was unfairly sacked. All of five years later, he relished revenge when Peacock and his old club were at Bloomfield Road in a vital end of season game which, in contrast, meant little to Blackpool but everything to their manager. He fired his players up to the extent they crushed the South London club 5-0 to relegate them. A gloating Stokoe popped his head round their dressing door exclaiming, 'I know some of you weren't even at the club when I was there, but I want you to know that I'm bloody glad that Charlton have gone down'.

For players accustomed to Brown, his less formal approach was refreshing. When Sunderland ran out at Roker Park, his initial game in charge, the team wore black shorts, a throwback to tradition before Brown's change to white. A 1-0 defeat to Burnley, who were running away with promotion, was no disgrace but with only one win in thirteen, the situation was growing serious. However, two late goals from Hughes and Kerr overturned a 2-1 deficit at Portsmouth to prevent a drop into the bottom two. The gate for the Fratton Park game was only 5,783. The following week Portsmouth hosted Middlesbrough and only 4,688 were present. Decades past, December saw a traditional pre-Christmas drop in crowds across all clubs. Following a goalless draw against Preston on 16th December a flu epidemic, which did not noticeably affect other clubs, wiped out Sunderland's festive schedule with three postponements. This gave Stokoe breathing space to assess the job at hand and he realised Sunderland needed experience to bring the best from his inheritance.

Stokoe was in the right job for a manager who did not possess an open chequebook. He contacted his former team-mate Joe Harvey and persuaded the Newcastle manager to part with fringe players Ron Guthrie, David Young and Ray Ellison. Harvey would have recalled a favour from Sunderland when Dave Elliott was allowed a move in the opposite direction and helped United avoid relegation. This occurred in autumn 1966 shortly after the Geordies had lost 6-0 at bottom club Blackpool. During his time at Sunderland Stokoe signed four other players who were either at United or had played there previously: Robson, Moncur, Gibb and Foggon.

Guthrie was typical of so many footballers who patiently bided time in the reserves, relying on injury or a suspension to displace a recognised first-teamer and who were also unwilling to uproot when the relocation package from an interested club was less than generous. Having been a career-long understudy to left back Frank Clark, he was aged 28 when joining Sunderland and had only accumulated 52 full league appearances. Young was labelled a utility defensive player; although a regular in the Newcastle Reserves Central League side he had nevertheless made nine consecutive First Division appearances at the beginning of the season. The acquisition of an unknown 34-year-old coach Arthur Cox to work with Billy Elliott would prove a masterstroke. His playing career ended with injury at the age of 19 so Cox, having served under Tommy Docherty, had amassed a wealth of knowledge within the game. Stokoe's protracted and ultimately futile attempt to prise back John O'Hare from Derby County kept Sunderland in the news. Only no publicity is bad publicity.

As the seventies unfolded, some of the managers in the game were becoming larger than life characters, instantly recognisable on television, their personas in stark contrast to the old school stereotypes of Harry Catterick, Bill Nicholson, Bertie Mee, Don Revie, Ted Bates or Tony Waddington. Malcolm Allison at Manchester City was one such outgoing individual. Freed from a partnership with the sombre, senior Joe Mercer, the exhibitionist within Allison flourished unchecked, with photographs adorning the tabloids of him posing in a bath with actress Fiona Richmond. Stokoe found contentment on a deserted Seaburn beach, walking his black Labrador Jed. Allison, without 'Uncle' Joe to rein him in, extravagantly purchased the talented but maverick show pony Rodney Marsh at the end of the 1971-72 season and his introduction to a team leading the First Division only succeeded in proving the adage 'if it ain't broke, don't fix it'. Marsh was, perhaps unfairly, held responsible for City conceding a tight title race. Not long after Stokoe arrived at Sunderland, Allison emerged from the Roker Park tunnel on a wild, windswept night. There was a swagger and boldness as he walked towards a foaming Fulwell End with a raised hand leaving no one in doubt what he expected from his players.

With the flu epidemic over, Stokoe said somewhat uncharacteristically, 'We will go like bombs in the New Year'. Although returning to action with a convincing 4-0 score line against Brighton, the validity of Stokoe's prediction was mitigated by the visitors having suffered their tenth consecutive defeat. An attendance of 12,573 reduced the season's average to 13,748. The pigeons in the quiet corners of the Clock Stand remained undisturbed.

There was a stuttering start to the FA Cup campaign. An 81st minute goal at Meadow Lane from Dave Watson saved face against Third Division Notts County, after Montgomery had kept the tie alive with a splendid save that denied Les Bradd a second. The return was arranged for the following Tuesday evening following a decision to bring forward midweek matches by 24 hours. Stokoe, staring into the dark, wintry, Nottingham sky as if to provoke the fates, was hopeful of a 20,000 crowd at Roker. He had targeted the Cup as a quick fix to stir interest in a moribund club. Although the draw paired the victors with Reading of the Fourth Division, it was not the expectation of a clear run to the last sixteen that sparked demand for the replay, rather the potential return of their manager Charlie Hurley, who was praying for a Sunderland win so his players could experience the magic of a Cup tie on Wearside. A surprising 30,000 turned up at Roker for the County game. Sunderland obliged their extra support through an early Watson goal that calmed nerves. The relaxed attitude Stokoe had introduced was evident after Dennis Tueart added a second in the closing minutes. The young forward, as if to exorcise the memory of Alan Brown, ran towards the dugout in celebratory fashion before checking his stride to allow a reverential low bow of his head in the direction of Stokoe. It was a rare moment of happiness that many presumed would not last.

The quest for reinforcements continued. With Watson proving a success at centre half, Stokoe persuaded John Hughes to leave Celtic and team up with his brother Billy. His home debut against Millwall was cut short with a career-ending injury but only after his chaotic, forceful running had caused consternation for team-mates and opponents alike, in addition to long overdue entertainment for a home crowd. The attendance of 22,781 was a big jump on the previous league turnouts of 11,529 and 12,573 and in the background was the anticipated return of Charlie Hurley. Kerr and Tueart scored in a 2-0 win as the improvement continued. The upturn could perhaps be attributed to the not uncommon short-term impact of a new manager. The coming hurricane was not foreseen. The distinctive criss-cross iron latticework on the main stand balcony that had always been coated in black paint was now a freshly painted bright red. Astonishingly, the club's fortunes were about to see a transformation that nothing in post-war history, before or after, would equal.

Losing Hughes to injury forced Stokoe to act. Vic Halom was signed from Luton for £30,000, good business for someone who had 10 goals from 25 games. Halom had not missed a match for the Hatters until omitted for a third round FA Cup tie. Therefore, he was not Cup tied. Pound for pound, that was Stokoe's best example of being able to squeeze a tight budget. There was also an element of luck, as without the loss of John Hughes and his failure to persuade Derby to release O'Hare the course of history may have been markedly different.

Fortune again intervened. Ritchie Pitt, a local lad Brown blooded in a losing First Division side, had struggled after the retirement of Martin Harvey having been unsuccessfully paired with Mick Horswill at the commencement of the 1972-73 season. Days after Stokoe was appointed, Graham Taylor, the future England manager, was settling into his first managerial job at Fourth Division Lincoln City. A £15,000 fee was agreed between the clubs but Pitt was reluctant to drop two divisions. Unexpectedly, Arsenal came in with a loan deal and the decision of the 21-year-old to reject Lincoln was vindicated. An injury to Young forced Stokoe to reluctantly recall Pitt, with little choice but to select him. He quickly formed a formidable partnership with Watson in the centre of the defence.

Reading were lively opposition at Roker, taking the lead before Tueart equalised in an eventful first half. After that, the heroics of goalkeeper Stephen Death ensured a replay and both clubs learnt on Monday lunchtime of a fifth round tie at Manchester City or Liverpool. City, enjoying a rich seam of form, had held the runaway First Division leaders Liverpool to a draw. The Reading programme proudly noted that for the second year running, 'we are the last Fourth Division side in the FA Cup' and then, 'That trip to Roker Park was really something. I'm sure the result alone made the journey well worthwhile for the thousand or so fans who made the trek to the Northeast by cars and two special trains. But there was so much more to the occasion. That fanatical Roker crowd, for instance. They greeted Charlie Hurley with a roar of appreciation – but that was all they gave away … The Roker Roar shook the stadium and must surely have helped Sunderland keep us under pressure'.

A season's best of 33,193 were present at Roker. Reading averaged barely 5,000 in the league but had pulled in 10,361 for their third round win over Doncaster. 19,793 packed Elm Park for the floodlit replay with Sunderland. The magic of the Cup was with the visitors; Watson was switched to his old position of centre forward and together with Tueart and Kerr scored first half goals in a 3-1 canter. Ritchie Pitt, recalled from Arsenal, played under Stokoe for the first time. When Watson returned as centre back in the next match, a narrow defeat at Sheffield Wednesday, Pitt gave way to Watson with Halom making a debut. The home match against Middlesbrough, a week before the fifth round City tie, was the first time Stokoe fielded the exact future Cup-winning starting eleven. The Roker crowd, revelling at the sheer ferocity of a performance that swept Boro away saw Sunderland finally live up to Stokoe's bold prediction that they would 'go like bombs'. There was a quiet start with Horswill giving Sunderland a half-time lead but then, in the space of 23 minutes, the visitors were blown away with further goals from Halom, Hughes and Tueart.

After Manchester City had overcome Liverpool at Maine Road in front of 49,572, they were installed as competition favourites by virtue of an expected easy passage into the last eight. They had Bell, Summerbee, Lee and the luxury of Marsh. Yet another enormous crowd, this time 54,478 but including thousands of visiting fans who were positioned in the vast Kippax shed running sideways along the pitch, saw Tony Towers give City an expected lead. Horswill retaliated when he seized upon a short, misplaced Joe Corrigan goal kick and then in the second half Billy Hughes finished off a brilliant jinking run to put Sunderland 2-1 up. Hughes' goal was a breathtaking example of his genius; on his day he was the standout, albeit unpredictable match-winner of Stokoe's finest eleven. In the 78th minute Mike Summerbee swung over a corner that Montgomery mistakenly palmed into his own net.

Those present for the replay at Roker on a charged Tuesday night experienced their singularly best, most remembered match of a lifetime at the famous ground. They arrived in droves from Saturday evening to purchase a ticket. By late Sunday morning all were sold with thousands turned away empty handed. A home draw with fellow Second Division team Luton Town who had dismissed Newcastle in the fourth round offered the barely believable prospect of a place in the last four.

The Roker roar is an elusive beast. It can go missing for years, only allowing a pale imitation to appear intermittently. When in the mood it can shake the foundations of not just an emporium but an empire. Manchester City kicked off, their light blue shirts a blur of movement under the dimpled brightness of the floodlights, and as they advanced towards the colossal sway of 20,000 flickering Roker End faces, a tumultuous howl rocked them. The sheer mass of the crowd drew the pitch in. There was no hiding place. The noise did not abate. No flag waving, no singing; mere bedlam. Following a bout of smart passing across the City defensive line, Bobby Kerr fed Vic Halom with a short ball on the right edge of the penalty box that Halom smashed into the Fulwell End net. There seemed no time for the euphoria to subside before Hughes evaded his marker in a packed goalmouth, to put Sunderland two up. City were unnerved. Now it was the cue for most of the 51,782 to boom out 'When the reds go marching in'. Only at half-time did the noise subside, replaced by the raw sound of the chart hit 'Mouldy Old Dough' before that in turn was swamped by an animated hubbub. When play resumed City asserted themselves for a few anxious moments. Francis Lee reduced the arrears from six yards and was then denied an equaliser when Montgomery's legs instinctively blocked a goal-bound shot. There was no stopping Sunderland. With the game stretched, Hughes concluded a break down the right at the far post to complete a famous 3-1 victory. In the space of ninety minutes the Cup odds for Sunderland were slashed from 100-1 to 25-1. They were 250-1 in January. A humbled Malcolm Allison meekly offered his congratulations to the Sunderland players and said the better team had won.

Joe Cummings, who covered the Northeast for the Sunday Mirror, remembered the morning after. He encountered a London-based journalist wandering around the ground convinced that the noise generated by the Roker Roar was a 'wonderful gimmick'. The journalist assured Cummings he had been to most of the world's great stadiums but never experienced anything like the previous night. He had returned to find the hidden amplifiers.

Vouchers were issued for the home match with Oxford that guaranteed a ticket for the quarter-final with Luton. The kick-off was delayed twenty minutes as 40,000 turned up. This was third highest in Britain bettered only by 54,369 at the Goodison Mersey derby and 46,735 at Manchester United. The nearest Second Division gate was 24,007 at Aston Villa. The club were box-office again. A late goal from Watson broke the deadlock. In addition to the Cup run there was a strong expectation of a surge up the table resulting from a glut of rearranged fixtures. At the beginning of March, Sunderland had played at least four games fewer than any team in the division and as many as seven fewer than some clubs.

Luton were managed by 'happy' Harry Haslam, who professed to have nothing to fear as his side had already done the double over their opponents: they possessed a director by the name of Eric Morecambe. With everything to lose, the quarter-final encounter at a sunny Roker, which attracted an all-ticket 53,151, was a taut affair, resolved with second half goals by Watson and Guthrie. Only then the crowd roared, only then the bunting came out and as the Fulwell End was transformed into a mass of red and white scarves, everyone realised the club were semi-final bound. It was almost impossible to take it all in. The best was to come.

The last four featured two of the three heavyweights within the English game. When Sunderland arrived at Hillsborough, their title-chasing opponents Arsenal were a single point behind leaders Liverpool. Leeds in third position, due to play Wolverhampton Wanderers at Maine Road, were five points behind Liverpool with two games in hand. Arsenal were a form team; a 1-0 defeat by Derby on the previous Saturday was only their second setback in 23 matches. The majority of the country anticipated a repeat of the Arsenal-Leeds '72 final. An unprecedented second domestic FA Cup and league double within three seasons was a realistic possibility for the north London club. Unfortunately, the Derby game proved more costly than the surrender of two points. Veteran club captain and defensive lynchpin Frank McLintock was carried off with a torn muscle, never to play for the Gunners again. Arsenal were hurriedly forced to press centre half Jeff Blockley, recovering from an injury and missing for five matches, back into action for the Cup.

There were other concerns over Blockley. Bertie Mee signed him from Coventry the previous October with every expectation of him replacing McLintock. He won his one and only cap for England shortly after his arrival. Joe Mercer, who sold him, rated the fee he negotiated as one of the best bits of business in his managerial career. Peter Storey, the Arsenal half back wrote in his autobiography 'True Storey', 'Bertie had paid Coventry £200,000 … and he was supposed to be a good player, although I never saw any startling evidence'. McLintock revealed later that it only took a couple of training sessions alongside him before he realised his place at Highbury was not under threat.

Vic Halom ran Blockley ragged. Halom, of low centre of gravity and broad shoulders, was a bundle of railroading menace. He seized on a terrible back pass from Blockley to put Sunderland ahead. He forced McNab to clear a shot off the line and then left three defenders flailing as he created a clear opening, only to be denied by Wilson. It could and should have been three-nil at half-time. Arsenal did not lie down; Montgomery, alert to a nasty deflection, switched direction at the last second to prevent an equaliser from Hebburn-born George Armstrong. With Blockley substituted and Arsenal throwing on John Radford, another forward, Hughes stretched the lead to 2-0 on the hour with a calculated back header. There was tension in the closing stages when Montgomery removed the sting from a Charlie George shot only for it to squirm over the line, reducing the deficit to a single goal. As Arsenal frantically prepared to take a last-gasp corner in front of the massed Sunderland support, the referee sounded the final whistle. The crowd imperiously called for their messiah and waited. Stokoe emerged pitch side, unable to mask his emotion as he acknowledged the adulation. Logic dictated that this was the high point of the Cup run. Arsenal, the team of George, Radford, Alan Ball and Ray Kennedy should have had enough firepower to overcome a Second Division side, regardless of their problems. With only one win in their remaining five fixtures, they conceded the title to Liverpool. A full-strength Leeds, having beaten Wolverhampton Wanderers in the other semi, lay in wait.

Sunderland had never managed to get the better of Revie's Leeds but never willingly surrendered to them. Leeds of course, had pipped them for the Second Division title and three years later ended their Cup dreams after a bitterly contested set of matches. Leeds were now a different and more formidable adversary. Although retaining a characteristic professionalism that strayed into illegality, Revie had modified their cautious, safety-first approach for a system that allowed the players greater expression.

Days after the Hillsborough game Hughes scored a hat-trick against Huddersfield at Roker, then on the following Saturday Portsmouth were beaten. Burnley and QPR were both out of sight at the top of the table but the Wearsiders, in eleventh position with games in hand, were hungry to finish as high as possible. There was no inclination to ease up; they were in form. Before the final an article from John Kay in The Journal correlated a rise in industrial productivity with the Cup run. The Coal Board at Wearmouth Colliery, shipyards of the Austin and Pickersgill Group and the Thorn factory making television tubes all witnessed increased activity. The Sunderland town clerk James Gardner was quoted, 'For once Sunderland is being projected as a success story rather than the usual cloth cap and heavy unemployment image.'

In the week before the final the Sunderland players, on £1,000-a-man win bonus, were camped at Selsdon Park Hotel in Croydon. They had gathered thirty points from twenty-one games including thirteen wins to sit seventh in the table. By changing the first eleven only sparingly, Stokoe cannily maintained momentum. The Cup Final back then was a huge media event comprising live BBC and ITV coverage and a seemingly endless build-up that included a Friday evening trailer. Sunderland, and in particular Billy Hughes, reduced the BBC man Barry Davies to laughter during the long-standing pre-final ritual of interviewing the players. Hughes kept setting off a laughing box. The players, lounging about casually dressed, were in stark contrast to the nervy-looking, formal, suited and booted Leeds team. Stokoe was outwitting Revie in other ways. He made public his feelings on the 'professionalism' of Leeds and implied that he wanted Ken Burns, the referee, to make the decisions and not the Leeds captain. Davies had a unique window on the Sunderland camp and felt their confidence of causing an upset so strongly that he was emboldened to bet Bobby Charlton a fiver that the underdogs would win. Another clever move from Stokoe was in agreeing to a surprise request from ITV to have a live camera on the Wembley-day team coach, despite Bertie Mee trying to persuade him otherwise. Brian Moore, the final's ITV commentator, was convinced that this helped the players to take their minds off the pre-match pressures. Revie, riven with paranoia and superstition, would have dismissed out of hand such an innovation. Gary Sprake, a goalkeeper under Revie, later commented, 'he was an utterly brilliant manager but knotted with fear'.

Revie's Leeds, after losing at Wembley against Liverpool in '65 and Chelsea in '70, had won the trophy for the first time when they defeated Arsenal in the 1972 final. The players were not allowed to celebrate. A painstakingly, meticulous Revie imprisoned them in a hotel, stone cold sober and in limbo, counting down the hours before a Monday evening game at Molineux, where a solitary point was required to achieve the domestic double. Despite centre forward Mick Jones being ruled out with a dislocated shoulder sustained in the Wembley final and despite his strike partner Allan Clarke and winger Eddie Gray forced to play with strapping, this should not have been an occasion to enhance the reputation of a battle-weary Leeds for choking in sight of the winning line. Wolverhampton Wanderers were halfway through a two-legged UEFA Cup final with Tottenham. However, before a crowd of 53,000 they tore into Leeds, establishing a two-goal advantage before Bremner retaliated to set up a frenzied last half hour. After a limping Clarke was substituted, a desperate Leeds failed to convert one of their many chances. The League had gone; the memory of Wembley was now bitter-sweet. With only Second Division opposition standing in the way of FA Cup glory, those same Leeds players were determined to have the celebration that they were denied only twelve months previously. That in turn ratcheted up the pressure on them.

Bobby Kerr and Billy Bremner, at 5'4" and 5'5" respectively, were the two smallest captains ever in Cup Final opposition. Sunderland did not allow Leeds to settle. With the country behind them, the first team in a final not to field an international player were unperturbed by the occasion. Within seconds, Allan Clarke was left unmistakably hurt on the ground by Pitt, who was lucky not to receive a booking. Watson effectively shackled Clarke's combative strike partner Jones whilst the puppy of the pitch, Horswill, snapped terrier-like at the heels of Giles and Bremner, disrupting the fulcrum of the Leeds midfield. Leeds, intimidatory as a matter of course, were unaccustomed to opponents intent on getting their retaliation in first. The treacherous Wembley turf, saturated with rain, gave referee Ken Burns every reason to exercise tolerance. On 32 minutes the unexpected happened. A left-wing corner from Hughes was chested by Halom into the path of Ian Porterfield, who cushioned the ball with his left thigh and then volleyed right-footed into the goal. As the afternoon progressed it was clear that Eddie Gray, touted as a potential match-winner, was unable to get past the supposed weak link of Malone who was generally excellent throughout, and on the rare occasions he did, Kerr covered admirably and lived up to his nickname of 'The

Little General'. An enduring moment of the club's history was an incident halfway through the second period. Jimmy Montgomery made his all-time famous double save, miraculously preventing an equaliser and effectively winning the Cup. He palmed away Trevor Cherry's header into the path of Peter Lorimer, who blasted the ball towards an empty net. The Sunderland goalkeeper somehow threw himself off the ground to deflect the goal-bound shot on to the bar, where it ricocheted to safety. Ironically, if Lorimer had not struck the ball so hard it may well have passed through the outstretched fingers of Montgomery. The innocuous Gray was substituted. Two signal vignettes from the latter stages, rather than any particular passage of play, emphasised that Leeds, no longer the strutting playground bullies, were done for. Porterfield, upended by Bremner, condescendingly ruffled the ginger hair of his assailant. Then Halom, a law unto himself when the need arose, rashly charged the stationary goalkeeper David Harvey and his ball into the goal. Before the end, a disconsolate Norman Hunter said to Tueart, 'It looks like it's going to be your day, Dennis'. Instead of cautiously sitting back, a tired Sunderland team, mining deep reserves of willpower, continuously counterattacked a ragged Leeds and finished the stronger.

At the final whistle, Stokoe sporting a red tracksuit, fawn mackintosh and a trilby, sprinted onto the turf and embraced his goalkeeper. Montgomery's double save will rank for posterity with that of Banks's denial of Pelé in Mexico. There was an extra spring in Stokoe's step, as he had disliked Revie ever since an incident when he had been manager of Bury, when the Leeds manager asked him to instruct his players to take it easy. Indeed, in 1977 the Sunday People did an exposé of the Leeds title-decider at Molineux, which was resolved in the High Court when Bremner sued the newspaper and a Wolves player Danny Hegan for alleged libel. Hegan stated in the People that some of the Leeds players offered bribes to their opposite numbers before the game. Bremner won his libel action thanks to vital evidence given by the Wolves forward Derek Dougan, who claimed that he was completely unaware of any attempt to tamper with the result.

Revie ranked the Wembley loss as his worst moment in a long career of playing and managing. There is a photograph of him taken minutes after the end of the final wearing his 'lucky' coat. He is on the Wembley turf, shoulders hunched, hands in pockets, a look reminiscent of the cartoon character Dick Dastardly. His captain Billy Bremner, almost in tears, is in pensive hands-on-hips mode. In the cartoon there is always the sniggering, smiling dog called Muttley who, despite appearing to be Dastardly's partner in crime, always took great delight in his inevitable downfall. On this May afternoon there was more than enough schadenfreude from the millions of TV viewers to compensate for the missing Muttley. Afterwards, Revie broke down in tears at the Savoy banqueting hall and was unable to finish a speech to his players.

The game 'felt like a bad dream' to John Giles, an outstanding midfield player with enormous ability that he complemented with a hard edge, earning him the accolade from fellow professionals of 'the silent assassin'. Giles admitted years later that the whole experience 'still has a horrific quality, the biggest disappointment of my career'. Hunter, in his autobiography 'Biting Talk', states, 'that defeat rankles with me more than any other'. Bobby Kerr, in a completely off-the-cuff moment, took the champagne filled FA Cup into a dressing room of shattered losing players. Past caring, they obliged him by sportingly taking a sip. Bob Cass, a well-liked local journalist, was drying out after having been thrown, fully suited and booted, into the communal bath.

On Wearside they partied like there was no tomorrow. The town centre, eerily empty in the afternoon, was now awash with a flood of people, old and young alike who linked arms, danced and shouted themselves hoarse. There were crowds in the train station at midnight waiting to greet the first of the returning supporters, ready to lift them shoulder high. It was New Year's Eve, Coronation Day and VE Day all rolled into one. Everyone was fleetingly caught in the moment; for some the events would be stamped indelibly on their memories.

Sunderland were the darlings of not just the nation but even Fleet Street, then the home of national newspapers. The esteemed Geoffrey Green of The Times cast aside any notion of impartiality when he sported red and white colours in the Wembley press box. Amidst the celebrations they had to fit in remaining fixtures on the following Monday and Wednesday. Over 26,000 were at Ninian Park to see the Cup winners, easily dwarfing their previous largest crowd of 16,364 on the opening day. Although Cardiff required a point to avoid relegation they had the safety net of another game after that, at home to Hull. The 1-1 draw left a bleary-eyed Sunderland to face a homecoming on the Tuesday night and a final match 24 hours later against promoted Queens Park Rangers. The team travelled north, before transferring near Durham to an open-topped Northern service bus that was conveniently awaiting repair, after its roof was sliced off after colliding with a low railway bridge in Jarrow.

With 43,000 in Roker, what should have been an entertaining, celebratory evening soured quickly when tackles from both teams flew in, causing the referee to ask for calm from captains Terry Venables and Kerr. Sunderland had paraded the trophy around the ground and it was left on a small table near the halfway line. During a goalless first half Tony Hazell, either intentionally or accidentally, sent the cup spinning to the ground. This did not endear him to the crowd but was not the catalyst for what was dubbed by the national press a night of shame for Sunderland. Stan Bowles was known as a maverick and an entertainer who employed his superior skills to rattle opponents. He was the archetypal seventies playboy, an obsessive gambler, the type of footballer that would have been regularly overlooked by an England manager. Shortly after Rangers had taken the lead on the hour, Bowles, not for the first time, tackled a Sunderland player from behind. On this occasion Mick Horswill retaliated by throwing a punch, leaving referee Peter Reeves with no option but to dismiss him. The bookings of Guthrie and Pitt for reckless challenges on Venables and Bowles respectively, sufficiently enraged a supporter to charge towards the referee, only to be restrained by Sunderland players. The referee, having completely lost control, called everyone off the pitch with an abandonment not out of the question. A loudspeaker address to the crowd by Bob Stokoe defused the situation and when the teams came back after a short delay, Bowles scored twice in a couple of minutes as Rangers won 3-0. Years later, Bowles spiced up his autobiography by claiming that he had knocked the cup over to win a wager with his team-mates. That, however, was one bet that Bowles did not place. The margin of Sunderland's defeat meant that they dropped to a final sixth placing by virtue of Bristol City then having a better goal difference.

12

A BEGINNING OR AN END?

1973-74 to 1975-76

A peasant nurturing his tiny smallholding, eking out a day-to-day existence, has a gift that is denied the emperor of the land despite his wealth and vast possessions. The peasant can endlessly imagine and dream about everything he knows will be always out of reach, a state of mind the emperor is robbed of, because by virtue of having everything he has nothing to crave for and therefore nothing to occupy his imagination or dreams. This parable is as relevant today as it was yesterday. When George Best sat with his team-mates and Matt Busby after overcoming Benfica at Wembley to achieve their all-consuming ambition of the European Cup, it dawned on him that for them it represented an end rather than a beginning. He realised that he, himself, was standing at the very pinnacle of his career and suspected that in the years ahead nothing would come close. What possibly could Sunderland, the club, supporters, manager and players experience in the future that could rival that unforgettable ride of the preceding months?

Len Hetherington in the Evening Chronicle dubbed Stokoe 'Klondike Bob'. Since the Manchester City night Roker Park averaged 34,228 over eight league matches. Gate receipts were unprecedented. An original record of £15,481 dating back to Leeds in 1967 was surpassed as early as the fourth round. The quarter-final Luton game realised £26,106. At Wembley, as the FA and opposition teams received approximately equal shares of the £233,800 receipts, Sunderland were guaranteed almost £80,000. Would the hunger for success remain after the gold rush? Would living the dream prove a different proposition from striving for the dream? Would the FA Cup success be the start or finish of something? The answers came only too quickly. Before the trophy was safely on Wearside, Stokoe was quoted in the Daily Mirror in the Monday morning aftermath, 'I'm set to go through hell after the heavenly experience of Wembley. The chase is already on for my Cup-winning stars … as for the future we should not take anything for granted. Promotion is the aim and what we mean to get'.

The expected Charity Shield with Liverpool did not occur as the champions opted for a pre-season continental tour; therefore Sunderland arranged a friendly with Tottenham that was lost 1-0. The new season kicked off with a visit from Orient. The first year of 'three up, three down' heightened expectations but there was an early reality check when Gerry Queen put the visitors ahead before Hughes quickly equalised. The match day programme opened by stating that 'today's the day that over 40,000 fans on Wearside have been waiting for since Cup Final day last May 5th'. The attendance was a slightly disappointing 28,211. Despite the club being awash with money, no additions to the playing squad were made, which was surprising allowing for the extra demands of a Cup Winners' Cup campaign. Nevertheless, a superb volley-cum-overhead kick at Oxford from Dennis Tueart that commentator Brian Moore called 'the goal of the season', earned a win in Sunderland's fifth game to maintain an unbeaten start. Sunderland then became entangled in Europe and the League Cup to the detriment of promotion hopes. Their continental debut against Vasas Budapest, marked by goals from Hughes and Tueart, involved a tiring midweek trip to Hungary and on returning to league action there was a 1-0 home defeat by Luton. In the closing stages Ritchie Pitt fell awkwardly near the touchline to sustain the injury that brutally ended a promising career. The FA Cup winning team was no more.

For the Vasas return supporters were annoyed by a doubling of admission prices to £1 standing and £2 seated. A Tueart penalty guaranteed progress in front of the 22,762 who were prepared to stump up the extra. The brighter floodlights, upgraded for colour TV and European competition, only served to highlight the constant rain and a string of missed chances. Jackie Milburn, in the press box, summed up the foreign opposition as 'overcoached thoroughbreds'. At the Baseball Ground, just before the close of Clough's Derby County reign, a late brace from John Lathan earned Sunderland a reprieve in the League Cup second round. Before the Derby replay, a first leg tie with Sporting Lisbon offered a route to the quarter-finals. Despite outplaying the Portuguese, conceding a late goal meant that only a 2-1 advantage was established for the away return.

The following midweek was dominated by two matches against Derby, both attended by over 38,000, which excepting a derby with Middlesbrough, provided Roker Park with the largest crowds of the season. A Tueart penalty miss on the Monday night had meant another tiring replay within 48 hours. A neutral ground was ruled out; Sunderland guessed the coin toss correctly to gain home advantage. For the extra game on Hallowe'en night, Vic Halom gave the best display of his career with a brilliant hat-trick. Len Hetherington in the Evening Chronicle reported, 'Derby County were last night caught and engulfed by a Sunderland tidal wave which left them lying like so many pathetic pieces of First Division flotsam on the Roker beach ... a superb Dave Watson decisively settled the argument about his entitlement before Roy McFarland to the England No. 5 shirt'.

Sunderland were now due to face Liverpool in the third round but England, with an international friendly against Italy at the same time, wanted one player from each team in their squad. With Sunderland unwilling to release Watson, the FA placated Sir Alf Ramsey by delaying the League Cup game a week. This was the classic, festering club-versus-country row that had always compromised the selection of players for national duty and would only be resolved years later when it was agreed that no domestic fixtures would overlap international games. As it happened, Watson would not be selected to make his England bow until the following April in Portugal, when he partnered Colin Todd in a goalless game.

Sandwiched between the Derby marathon and the Lisbon adventure was an unglamorous, vital league match at Hull. Stokoe wanted to emulate the 1969 Inter-City Fairs Cup-winning feat of Newcastle. He controversially rested the full forward line of Kerr, Hughes, Halom, Porterfield and Tueart; the game was lost 2-0. In the cauldron of the José Alvalade stadium, 50,000 fanatical Portuguese outnumbered 300 from the Northeast. Uncharacteristic mistakes from Watson and Montgomery handed the classier home side a deserved 2-0 victory, 3-2 on aggregate. It was Stokoe's first defeat in sixteen Cup ties.

A coal mine overtime ban on 12th November forced the government into a series of economy measures. As floodlighting was barred from sporting events, afternoon kick-off times were brought forward to 2.15 pm. For the third round League Cup tie, an unlit Roker Park was enveloped in gloom when Liverpool and the BBC Sportsnight crew arrived. The overcast weather wasn't entirely to blame. Dennis Tueart had just forwarded a written transfer request. Toshack and Keegan ended interest in the competition with the consolation that this would allow space to rekindle promotion hopes.

League form however did not improve and problems mounted when Billy Hughes joined Tueart in asking for a move after a defeat at Bolton in early December. A third round FA Cup replay exit to Carlisle United followed and when a season's low of 16,509 witnessed a drab goalless draw with Oxford, the magic of Wembley was far off. Despite seven defeats from the previous 12 matches, time remained for a belated promotion push especially as Middlesbrough, benefitting from Jack Charlton's first year in management, were a mile clear of the field leaving a cluster of mediocrity in their wake. Into February, Halom and Hughes obliged with four goals between them to beat Millwall 4-0. Despite losing the home Boro derby on a day when Tueart and

Kerr were dismissed, Sunderland maintained a steady improvement and when they defeated Carlisle before 34,179 on Good Friday, the third promotion spot was in dispute; Halom and Hughes scored again. Hope was quashed when the next games against Bristol City and Carlisle were lost, the latter determined by a disputed Chris Balderstone penalty. The rural Cumbrians, encased in a former northern frontier of the Roman Empire and never considered genuine contenders, unexpectedly climbed two places to third position on the last Saturday of the season by virtue of defeating Aston Villa and a couple of favourable results elsewhere. Two late Sunderland goals at Roker Park stopped Blackpool in their tracks after Micky Burns had provided a 50th minute lead and there was another Orient stumble, a team that although shot with nerves having won only 2 of 14 previous games, remained favourites to claim the final promotion place in their fixture on FA Cup Final eve. They required a victory over Villa to overtake Carlisle. A drawn contest that disappointed 29,766 at Brisbane Road, allowed Carlisle, with 49 points from 42 games and averaging 8,270, to grasp their place in history.

Unlike the joy along Hadrian's Wall, the feeling on Wearside was one of cautious optimism, now that the seemingly never-ending hangover from Wembley had finally abated. Uncertainty clouding the future of Dennis Tueart had been resolved on 11th March with a transfer to Manchester City, where he was joined by Mick Horswill. Tueart was valued at £250,000 with Horswill a makeweight at £100,000. Included in the transaction was the gift of a highly promising midfield player Tony Towers, whose valuation was assessed at £125,000. In the same month Towers had played in a League Cup final and as an established first choice in the City side, the fee seemed generous compared to the figure disclosed for Horswill. City doubled Tueart's weekly basic wage from £60 to £120. A potential for extras based on win bonuses, crowd figures and first team appearances inflated the complete package well above the prevailing £40 average wage in the UK. A government pay freeze to combat spiralling inflation was forwarded as a lame excuse for the inability of Sunderland to keep Tueart.

Towers' introduction had contributed to the late upturn in results. The signing of Rod Belfitt for £70,000 was not however judged a success. Unlike the previous summer, Stokoe realised the need for improvement and two important additions helped Sunderland off to a flyer in the new season. Bryan 'Pop' Robson, aged 28, was considered the best uncapped striker in the game when he signed from West Ham for £140,000. In the 1972-73 season he was leading scorer in the First Division with 28 goals. He started his career at Newcastle, winning a Fairs Cup winner's medal, but had left Tyneside for Upton Park in a swirl of controversy, after criticising United for a lack of professionalism. Bob Moncur, captain of Newcastle and formerly Scotland, was the other signing, a vastly experienced, commanding centre half who was the right side of thirty. This pair, with the addition of Towers, who received three England caps whilst at Roker, galvanised Sunderland into scoring 12 goals from an opening four fixtures.

With the Second Division featuring newly relegated Manchester United, managed by Tommy Docherty who was striving to reclaim their place at the top table, there was no shortage of interest. This was reflected in the phenomenal coverage Sunderland received on Match of the Day. The programme transmitted highlights from two matches each Saturday evening. Sunderland appeared on the programme on no less than six occasions, including four features as the main match. In total, Match of the Day broadcast sixty-four matches during 1974-75. The series commenced in August '64. Sunderland's visit to Stamford Bridge that month was only the second ever programme transmitted. They were then shunned until March '67 when BBC cameras first visited Roker Park; there was little excuse to ignore a fifth round FA Cup tie with Leeds. In an era of showing the highlights of one match per episode, there had been over 80 visits to First Division grounds before that broadcast.

For visitors to Wearside a point was the sole objective. In October '74 the BBC cameras relayed Aston Villa's dour suppression of Halom, Hughes and Robson; Roker Park suffered five such goalless stalemates. Craven Cottage provided better entertainment for the nation. In the first twelve minutes Fulham were blown away by a Robson double and a Bobby Moore own goal as Sunderland occupied second in the table, behind a resurgent Manchester United, who had recovered from an interval deficit to beat Villa before 55,000. Robson then scored twice to ensure two points against Notts County on the same afternoon that United surprisingly lost at Hull, therefore setting the stage for a late November collision between the two heavyweights of the division. Sunderland were only three points adrift with a game in hand. The gates were shut on 60,585 in Old Trafford. The spectacle was voted match of the season by BBC viewers. Stuart Pearson's early goal was met with swift retribution from the swashbuckling, impudent Billy Hughes, who revived the pomp of his Cup-winning season by scoring twice. It should have been game over by half-time. Robson, put clean through by Hughes, allowed Alex Stepney a merest fraction of time to narrow the angle and smother his shot. Manchester United were not inclined to look a gift horse in the mouth. They emerged emboldened in the second half and flipped the contest 3-2 in their favour. Frank McGhee of the Daily Mirror wrote, 'Manchester United's win over Sunderland leaves only one real issue to be settled in the Second Division this season. Who will go up with the pair of them next spring? I can't believe that teams with as much as both proved they have to offer to the First Division could be denied the chance to provide it once again'. Hours after Sunderland's next match, a marauding 4-1 victory over Portsmouth, Ian Porterfield who had orchestrated the strings in midfield during a one-sided game, tragically nearly lost his life in a car crash and suffered a fractured skull. The return game with Manchester United was in January; a chasing Sunderland needed a win. An all-ticket 45,796 witnessed an inspired shut-out from Stepney. Afterwards, Docherty commented, 'I am delighted we got a point, but I cannot honestly say we deserved it. I thought Stepney and Buchan were tremendous.'

The absence of Porterfield contributed to a New Year slide of only 10 points from 12 games that allowed Villa to overtake. For a neutral it was a fascinating implosion. For Stokoe it increased the pressure, as he wrestled with a commitment to quit if promotion was unachievable within two seasons. At Blackpool, Sunderland fought back from two down only for Billy Hughes to miss a penalty, before being undone by a stunning solo strike from Mickey Walsh two minutes from time that was voted goal of the season by the BBC viewers. Hughes' spot kick was tipped on to the woodwork by John Burridge against a backdrop of two animated, white-coated Bloomfield Road figures who stood directly behind the netting. The Match of the Day cameras were at Roker to capture another penalty miss when Tony Towers hit the bar facing an emergency West Bromwich Albion goalkeeper Gordon Nisbet. Only for the penalty did Nisbet, an outfield player, take charge of the green jersey from a stricken John Osborne, who spent most of the match hobbling around the goalmouth after an earlier incident. The disadvantaged Osborne eventually succumbed to a 65th minute Halom header before two goals from Robson settled matters. On the final Saturday, the Rokermen travelled to Villa Park, in hope rather than expectation, where faint promotion ambitions were killed with a 2-0 defeat in front of 57,266, enabling Norwich to bag the third spot by defeating Portsmouth. Even a Sunderland victory would have left the Canaries in the driving seat as they were still to play Aston Villa in a rearranged fixture. There was no doubting the pedigree of the three clubs above Sunderland. The League Cup final featured Villa and Norwich, the only instance of two clubs outside the top division contesting a major domestic final; Manchester United on their return to the First Division would finish four points behind champions Liverpool a year later.

The entertainment Sunderland provided made another season outside the top-flight difficult to stomach. Robson and Hughes, with 19 and 15 goals respectively, were the principal goalscorers. A settled eleven, more so than the '63-64 team and any other in the club's history, included Malone, Moncur, Kerr, Hughes and Robson as ever-presents with Montgomery, Watson and Towers only missing five games between them. Notably, Dave Watson was first choice England centre half having been capped 14 times whilst playing outside the top division. A downside of missing promotion was the granting of Watson's wish to leave Roker. Manchester City paid £175,000, permitting Sunderland to take the promising centre half Jeff Clarke in part-exchange, who had broken into their first team with 13 appearances at the start of the previous season.

From August '75, Clarke and Moncur formed a good partnership. Stokoe sacrificed flair for functionality. A forward, Mel Holden, came from Third Division Preston whilst Tommy Gibb and Dennis Longhorn were signed for small fees. Later in the season, Roy Greenwood and Ray Train arrived from Hull and Carlisle respectively, deals typical of Stokoe's bargain basement mentality. Sunderland were not promotion favourites as Chelsea were expected to bounce straight back after relegation. At Roker, the two teams met on the opening day of the campaign when 28,689 witnessed Robson score first in a 2-1 defeat of the Londoners. From September Sunderland were never out of the top three and at crucial moments in the season were able to grind out results. The absence of Hughes, who missed most of the campaign with a broken leg, was overcome. After taking only one draw from five away games, Sunderland faced a defining run of five consecutive away games that stretched until the end of March. The unspectacular but markedly improved return of four points was enough to maintain momentum. Penalties were converted at one end and saved by Montgomery at the other. Relegation bound York City came to Roker on the evening of 30th March and in front of 33,000 were denied a point when Montgomery dived full-length to save an Ian Holmes penalty. Three days later at Notts County, Montgomery saved another penalty, as the Wearsiders eked out a goalless draw. For the first time in a 42-match season there were no home losses, with only the two Bristol clubs taking a draw. This compensated for mediocre away form and allowed Sunderland to clinch promotion on a sunny Easter Monday watched by 51,893, at the same time ending Bolton's challenge through a 2-1 victory, with goals from Towers (penalty) and Robson. Stokoe commented, 'I'm more relieved than elated that promotion has been won. I have done what I was brought here to do and the important thing is that Sunderland are in the First Division'. Of greater importance was the question of whether they were equipped for the challenge. 40,000 saw Sunderland wrap up the title by defeating Portsmouth; the average gate of 31,250 was bettered in the country by only six clubs. Sunderland's total of 56 points was three more than Bristol City and West Bromwich Albion.

On FA Cup fifth round day, Bolton Wanderers were leading the division, two points ahead of Sunderland, both having played the same number of games. The Lancashire club were involved in a three-match marathon with Newcastle, watched by an aggregate of 139,245, before being knocked out of the competition at a neutral Elland Road. Following the first encounter at Burnden Park, Bolton suffered 6 defeats in their remaining 13 games, leaving them one point short of third position. For Sunderland, the excitement as always was with the Cup. Stoke City at the Victoria Ground, fielding the disparate talents of Shilton, Greenhoff and Hudson, represented a formidable barrier to a quarter-final place. Stokoe outfoxed his opposite number Tony Waddington by fielding Jack Ashurst in a number eight shirt as an extra centre half. A dogged display made it worthwhile for 8,000 visiting fans in a huge 41,176 Potteries crowd.

The Stoke replay was another memorable occasion under the lights. The scene was set with uplifting theme music from the film '633 Squadron'. After Mel Holden put Sunderland ahead with a quarter of an hour remaining, Denis Smith promptly equalised but with extra time likely, Pop Robson sparked celebrations with a goal that had the majority of 47,583 dreaming of another Wembley appearance. No one left early. The spider's web of concrete steps in the bowel of the vast Roker End squeezed a noisy torrent of euphoric humanity into the narrow streets below. A visit from Third Division giant-killers Crystal Palace in the sixth round represented a marvellous opportunity. They were managed by Malcolm Allison, basking in the limelight again, living with a former Playboy club model 20 years his junior. The defeat on Wearside with Manchester City, which had forced him out of Maine Road within weeks, seemed ancient history. Palace triumphed at Chelsea in the fifth round and had already disposed of Leeds. At Elland Road, Allison stoked the pre-match atmosphere, predicting the score with three fingers raised as he strutted the touchline. At Chelsea, before hostilities commenced, he had paraded in front of the Shed. Allison was at it again on Wearside, walking defiantly up to the Fulwell End. He was serving a lifetime FA touchline ban, therefore forced to spend the ninety minutes cloaked almost anonymously in the directors' box, his trademark lucky fedora the only visible evidence of his presence. For all the hype and a capacity 50,000 crowd, the Palace tie was a let-down. Without the night air to inspire, without the strands of sea mist dancing in the rays of the floodlights and deprived the adrenaline rush of an underdog, nothing went right. Dennis Longhorn and Tom Finney hit the woodwork but Sunderland failed to capitalise on heavy first half pressure. In the second half neither the team nor supporters stirred. Towards the end, the highly rated Peter Taylor left Joe Bolton and Bobby Moncur in his wake to set up Alan Whittle for the only goal. It was a case of what might have been when Sunderland discovered Palace were drawn against Second Division Southampton in the last four. For Allison the game was up; the Saints under Lawrie McMenemy went on to win the FA Cup.

13

A TRAVESTY

1976-77

There was certainly a case for strengthening the first team squad. The starting eleven for the Crystal Palace Cup tie included Longhorn and Finney, honest journeymen who within a short time would find their level in the lower divisions. Vic Halom, having lost his place to Holden, departed for Oldham. The money spent in haste on Train and Greenwood should perhaps have been withheld until promotion was achieved and used to buy someone of proven ability. There was a parallel with the club's only other promotion in 1964 when, for different reasons, no signings materialised.

Stokoe was unduly cautious as he prepared for his first game at Stoke. In a repeat of the previous visit to the Victoria Ground, he drafted Jack Ashurst as an extra defender and the home side were restricted to a goalless draw. Sunderland received a taste of their own medicine when a 36,668 Roker crowd, welcoming the return of First Division football and visitors Leicester, witnessed another stalemate. During proceedings, the championship pennant that was billowing above the Roker End suddenly disappeared, never sighted again. On the second Saturday of the 1976-77 season, four goals were shared with Arsenal in an entertaining first half at Roker with 41,000 in attendance; three drawn games hinted at consolidation. Under Stokoe Sunderland had a terrible record on the south coast and in the West Country. At Bristol City they embraced tradition to lose 4-1. This setback, which could so easily have been worse, threw the club into a tailspin. Worrying reports emerged of a stressed Stokoe suffering debilitating bouts of migraine. The avant-garde brilliance of his 1973 team was nothing more than a memory.

Within weeks there was frantic transfer market activity as the search intensified for an elusive victory. Jimmy Montgomery, holder of a record number of 537 league appearances, saw his long service at Roker terminated abruptly when he was summarily despatched to Birmingham. Barry Siddall the Bolton Wanderers goalkeeper replaced him. Moncur was dropped and replaced by an on-loan Jim Holton. Forward Bob Lee cost a hefty £200,000 from Leicester and a cheap punt was taken on Alan Foggon from Manchester United, who had only made three substitute appearances at Old Trafford, following a lengthy spell with Middlesbrough. On Teesside, Jack Charlton cannily evolved a style of play to utilise Foggon's speed but on Wearside no such contingency was made. Holton, a raw, giant centre half had twice recovered from a broken leg and not featured in Tommy Docherty's United team for eighteen months. Docherty, aware Sunderland were vulnerable in defence, telephoned Stokoe with a sales pitch extolling the virtues of Holton stating that he was 'superb in the air, a magnificent tackler, good distributor of the ball, reads a game well and never gives less than 100% in games and in training'. Docherty said a hundred thousand would not buy him and the streetwise Stokoe countered 'I know. I am one of them'. With the seed planted, Stokoe eventually reconsidered. He took Holton on loan within the seven-day period when Lee, Foggon and Siddall arrived.

Following a home defeat by Aston Villa, which stretched the winless league run to nine games, Stokoe succumbed to the mounting pressure and offered his resignation. Chairman Keith Collings was reluctant to accept but Stokoe stood firm to end his four-year reign. Stokoe's race was long run; in reality the winning of promotion had been his finishing line. Only a matter of days before his resignation, Robson was allowed a return to West Ham. This unforgiveable piece of business would haunt Sunderland. Ian McFarlane, who had surprisingly replaced Arthur Cox in the summer, stepped in as caretaker to oversee a flimsy revival that took Sunderland off rock bottom. Bob Lee's first goal at Coventry, which helped secure a first win of the season on 30th October, commenced a run of five points from four games during which time the Holton move was made permanent.

In July '06 a bronze statue of Bob Stokoe, sculpted by Sean Hedges and authorised by Niall Quinn, was unveiled outside the south-east corner of the Stadium of Light. It is unmistakably him, a fitting memorial to a legend. It captures his unique combination on 5 May '73 of trilby, mackintosh and tracksuit. The Football Association's famous competition had never before experienced anything like the drama that day produced and never will again. Stokoe's achievement in winning the FA Cup is unsurpassable. Promotion, albeit at the third attempt, was praiseworthy but merits no more than a footnote. Yet Stokoe like all flesh and blood was fallible. With the notable exceptions of players past and present signed from Newcastle, the part-exchange trades with Manchester City and the masterstroke of attracting Vic Halom from Luton, his record in the transfer market was poor. However, any criticism of Stokoe will always fall on barren ground. His Wembley triumph trumps everything that anyone could have possibly achieved at a club in Sunderland's state that grey autumn day when he quietly arrived without a welcoming committee.

Sunderland appointed Jimmy Adamson as their new manager. He was synonymous with Burnley. He captained the Lancashire club to a league title in 1960, a remarkable achievement for a town populated by 80,000. He gained recognition as a first-class coach at Turf Moor before succeeding Harry Potts as manager and nurturing a fine young team that won the Second Division in the year of Sunderland's Cup success. Uphill battles against low crowds and Bob Lord, the autocratic owner of Burnley, took their toll and Adamson was unemployed when Sunderland approached him. For anyone except Brian Clough, following in Stokoe's footsteps was a tall order. Adamson's policy of importing his backroom staff and players with Turf Moor connections was not likely to go down well unless results on the pitch, that arbiter of everything in football, were exemplary.

Seven consecutive defeats without so much as a goal scored was Adamson's calling card and when Sunderland stopped the rot with consecutive goalless draws, they had suffered a run of two points from eleven games including a sequence of ten games without a goal. Rooted at the bottom, an out-of-form Sunderland were disadvantaged by playing games during a spell of bad weather at a time when their confidence was low and other clubs at the wrong end of the table were able to build a cushion of games in hand. The Pools Panel sat three times in January concocting their imaginary results; on each occasion Sunderland took the field three times and lost. With necessity the mother of invention, Adamson gave youth a fling. Three local lads, Gary Rowell from Seaham, Kevin Arnott from Gateshead and Shaun Elliott from Haydon Bridge, played together for the first time at the back end of the losing run. The latter pair made league debuts in a defeat at Leicester, days after playing in a third round FA Cup dismissal at Wrexham. At Filbert Street Adamson placed the tall Lee and Holden together, tacitly signalling that Billy Hughes was surplus to requirements. He took the experienced centre half Colin Waldron from Old Trafford and replaced full back Dick Malone with Mick Docherty from Maine Road. Both newcomers had served him well at Burnley. On a rainy, mild, Friday evening in January, with a season low 21,407 present, a Mel Holden goal against Bristol City ended the longest scoring drought in the club's history to earn only a third victory in 26 games. The unusual scheduling avoided a clash with the Tyne-Tees derby.

The transformation was startling. The next three games, all at home, were emphatically won. Middlesbrough, West Bromwich Albion and West Ham were beaten 4-0, 6-1 and 6-0. Lee, Holden and Rowell scored at least once in each of those games with Lee putting three past Albion. Sunderland's task of staying up remained Herculean. 11 points from 25 games had become

19 points from 29 games but the sudden climb to eighteenth position offered little comfort because the four clubs beneath them, on either 18 or 19 points, had played significantly fewer games. All had at least two games in hand, with Bristol City and Derby no fewer than four.

Don Revie, the England manager, was impressed with the emerging youngsters saying, 'Sunderland are really capturing my attention at the moment. The improvement stems to a great extent from the form of Gary Rowell, Kevin Arnott and Shaun Elliot'. Revie thought Rowell a 'particularly exciting prospect'.

The circumstances of a Sunderland defeat at Maine Road, in their first away trip after the Roker scoring spree, angered a remarkable travelling midweek contingent of 10,000. A highly debatable penalty, awarded by Bert Newsome and converted by Dennis Tueart, surprised even the Manchester City players. Before that incident Holden, despite not being offside and no one interfering with play, had a perfectly good goal disallowed. The following away match at Villa Park was lost but those two defeats were the only setbacks over an 18-match spell that yielded 25 points. On Good Friday, a two-goal lead against Newcastle was squandered with United equalising in the final minutes but then a draw at Leeds and a 2-1 victory over Manchester United on Easter Monday restored momentum. Towers converted a vital penalty in the Manchester game and two more in the remaining fixtures. Sunderland fought like tigers. Jim Montgomery, now keeping goal for Birmingham, made an emotional return to Roker for the last home game of the season and was beaten by a powerful Holden header nine minutes from time. Sunderland were no longer relegation certainties; with two away fixtures remaining they looked down from the heady heights of sixteenth. The impetus continued when Rowell and Kerr cancelled a two-goal Norwich lead at Carrow Road. Apart from rearranged matches in the days prior to the FA Cup final, the First Division was nearly done. Those encounters however were of paramount importance for Bristol City, Coventry, Stoke, Sunderland and West Ham, all striving to avoid joining doomed Tottenham.

There was every chance that the Sunderland fans, before even arriving at Everton for the final match on Thursday night, would be celebrating. This hinged on the outcome of three matches on the Monday. As it happened, the defeat of Stoke that confirmed them as the second relegated team, left Sunderland rueing the results elsewhere. Provided West Ham lost or Bristol City failed to win, safety was assured. Neither happened. Unfortunately, although their respective opponents of Manchester United and Liverpool represented the two heavyweights of the English game, the involvement in a forthcoming FA Cup final ensured they brought severely weakened sides to Upton Park and Ashton Gate. Ironically, it was Bryan Robson, transferred by Stokoe in his last days at Roker, who had almost single-handedly kept West

Ham's season alive. Against Tommy Docherty's lightweight United, he scored twice as his side, despite conceding after 25 seconds, won 4-2 to guarantee survival. West Ham therefore finished with a sequence of 23 points from 19 games and Robson, who appeared in 16 of those games, scored on 12 occasions. Bristol City, their players incentivised by a £1,500 bonus and watched by a record league crowd of 38,688, defeated the league champions Liverpool to take their fight into a final game. City's haul of 16 points from a possible 30 meant that Sunderland and the Hammers were not the only club upsetting the formbook. The 'great escape' however seemed merely delayed, not derailed.

Alfred Hitchcock could not have scripted a better finale. Sunderland needed a draw at Goodison Park to make certain but would still avoid relegation provided the Coventry versus Bristol City game did not end all square. The latter scenario seemed unlikely. All three clubs were level on points, Coventry possessing the worst goal average. Perhaps it would have been better if Sunderland needed to go all out for victory at Everton, without a potential safety net. Despite the backing from a travelling support of 16,000 in a crowd of 36,075, the Wearsiders, a pale imitation of the team that had risen Lazarus-like, were defeated 2-0.

The referee delayed the Highfield Road kick-off because of congestion outside the ground caused by nearly 37,000 turning up. Reports suggest a delay of fifteen minutes but Jimmy Hill, then Managing Director of Coventry, claimed it was five minutes. The home side established a two-goal lead before the visitors equalised with 21 minutes remaining. With Bristol City pressing, news filtered through to supporters listening to transistor radios that Sunderland had lost. Hill then instructed the Radio Sky Blues presenter to announce the score within the stadium. With minutes remaining, Norman Hunter, playing for Bristol City, implored the referee to blow for time as the ball was being pointlessly passed back and forward between a line of opposition players, unwilling to advance from their own half. Hunter said in his autobiography 'Biting Talk' that it was the most bizarre situation he had experienced in football. The Guardian newspaper the following morning commented, 'What had been an intensely physical contest dissolved farcically'. Hill's justification for his announcement was for the 'theatre, drama and entertainment' it would produce. The Daily Mirror claimed he raced to the announcer's box with the result, screaming 'get it on the board'. A dark night for Sunderland; for those present on that wretched Merseyside evening the events are ingrained in their DNA. The league secretary Alan Hardaker went through the motions of reprimanding Coventry, before quietly dropping the matter without tangible reparation. The fury directed at Jimmy Hill, a person the game considered royalty for abolishing the maximum wage and revolutionising television coverage, quickly abated. Yet, as the years have passed resentment towards the now deceased Hill has resurfaced almost with a vengeance, fuelled by the modern scourge of social media that has manufactured a synthetic rivalry between a growing number of Coventry and Sunderland supporters.

14

NO ONE WANTS US

1977-78 to 1978-79

Jimmy Adamson was buoyant at the commencement of the 1977-78 Second Division season. Although the shock of relegation lingered over the summer he believed that promotion prospects were excellent. But Sunderland started with a 3-0 defeat at Hull and the 3-0 midweek victory over Burnley, in front of an excellent 31,405 crowd, proved the only success in 12 games that included a two-legged League Cup exit. A purple patch of 15 goals in 5 games returning 9 points proved an aberration as the club drifted in mid-table. Bristol Rovers ended FA Cup hopes early. Supporters were not enamoured with Adamson's signings, in particular Wayne Entwistle and Roly Gregoire from lower division clubs. The insubstantial £30,000 paid for Entwistle was the exact amount received from Derby County for Billy Hughes. Only a couple of years after his swashbuckling performance against Manchester United at Old Trafford, the career of a footballer many fans fondly remember as their favourite was in decline. A younger Hughes emulated World Cup winner Alan Ball and incurred the wrath of Alan Brown by wearing white boots. His main achievement for Sunderland, 73 league goals in the top two divisions, is only surpassed since 1945 by Shackleton, Rowell and Kevin Phillips. He passed away at the age of 70 and in 2020 was posthumously inducted into the club's Hall of Fame.

The influential Tony Towers, capped for England on Wearside, had proved a huge miss in the wake of relegation after his transfer to Birmingham City, and with Lee and Holden not meeting expectations there was uncertainty. As an interminable season dragged on, supporters lost faith in a manager not renowned as a good communicator. Despite a fine footballing brain, his scholarly manner and stilted appearance counted against him. Consecutive home crowds dropped to under 12,000. A burst of wins realised a flattering sixth-place finish. Gary Rowell could look back on 18 goals, including the first five of 26 penalties he would take for Sunderland, only one of which he failed to convert. A cursory glance at the final table reveals a fraught time for many clubs as remarkably, seven were locked on 38 points a mere single point ahead of relegated third bottom Blackpool. Four points separated 13 clubs.

Sunderland made a laboured start to their second year in the second tier. Adamson, aware of a substantial minority wanting him out, was receptive to a vacancy at Elland Road where Leeds were finding it difficult to replace Jock Stein, who had left to manage the Scotland national team. Stein's 44-day tenure at Leeds was coincidentally the same length as Clough's back in '74. On 25th October, eleven league games into the '78-79 campaign, Adamson, absent for two weeks from Roker Park with gastroenteritis, sensationally resigned and immediately signed a three-year contract at Leeds. He was never under contract on Wearside.

Before Adamson walked out he had the immense satisfaction of putting one over his former club Burnley or specifically, his nemesis Bob Lord, in a torrid game at Turf Moor. The first half was a kicking match littered with bookings. Just before half-time Michael Henderson, already cautioned, received a second yellow. Joe Bolton became the second full back to receive his marching orders for a second bookable offence. Bolton, from nearby Birtley, was the undisputed hard man of Sunderland, a latter-day Billy Elliott or Jimmy McNab. Sunderland commenced second half proceedings handicapped with only eight outfield players. Burnley did not expect them to go for the jugular. Rowell scored on the hour; minutes later he converted a penalty. The home side reduced the arrears but that was all. What credit Adamson could take for the victory is debatable; his assistant Dave Merrington invigorated the dressing room in the interval as the Sunderland manager made himself scarce after lashing his players with a short-lived volcanic outburst. The Turf Moor match emboldened the team to beat West Ham in front of an improved crowd of 23,676. Rowell again scored twice, again including a penalty.

Brian Clough, at the height of his powers having steered Nottingham Forest to the league title only a year after promotion, was the unanimous choice to replace Adamson. Within 24 hours of the Sunderland job becoming available, the Forest chairman Stuart Dryden refused a request from Keith Collings to approach Clough stating that, 'every humanly-possible effort will be made to prevent Clough leaving the club'. Clough, befitting his unpredictable nature, adopted an ambiguous stance. In the meantime Merrington, a former Burnley player, assumed temporary managerial duties whilst stressing he was holding the fort until a replacement was found. Welded to Adamson, he was earmarked as his assistant at Elland Road. Speculation continued. On the eve of a vital Forest match with Everton, the Nottingham Evening Post ran a report headed 'Dryden's plea - end Clough rumours'. It stated that Clough had not made his own position clear and Dryden made reference to a series of 'conflicting reports'. The following day, 4th November, Sunderland were at home to top-of-the-table Stoke City. Merrington, who claimed that Clough was the 'only logical choice to build on all the hard work that Jimmy Adamson and I have put into this club over the last two years', wanted a big crowd to make Clough aware of the clamour for him and the potential on Wearside. The ante was raised further by an Evening Chronicle front-page headline of 'I want to talk to Sunderland' that appeared on newsagents' placards a mere couple of hours before kick-off. The reporter Mike Currie had received the quote after intercepting Clough, just as he was leaving home en route to the Everton game at the City Ground.

The 25,170 Roker Park turnout was gripped with Clough mania but Stoke, managed by Alan Durban and including the experience of Howard Kendall, Mike Doyle and Denis Smith, survived an early onslaught before taking the points with a goal on 88 minutes from Brendan O'Callaghan. By a sobering Monday, the frenzy abated. Forest announced that Clough was to accept a seven-year contract and the man himself made all the right noises to exonerate his indecision over the previous ten days. Although he said he had been 'so close to taking the job he always wanted', he probably used Sunderland's interest as a bartering tool for enhanced remuneration and security at Forest. Clough is on record as stating that when he and his assistant Peter Taylor controversially left Derby in 1973, he would have taken the Sunderland job without hesitation. This conveniently overlooks the fact that with Stokoe in charge during that period, it simply could not have happened. No doubt, over the course of time there had been several talks between Clough and the Sunderland hierarchy. A younger Clough would have crawled on all fours for the chance to manage at Roker. Opportunities were denied; aside from his dismissal in 1965 from youth team duties he was overlooked after the departures of McColl and Brown. When Sunderland eventually called, Clough deemed it too late and a suspicion exists that his enigmatic behaviour was a deliberate ploy in order to avenge past rejections.

Collings did not waste time. He made an official approach to the Southampton chairman Alan Woodford, for permission to contact Lawrie McMenemy. This was within 48 hours of someone from the Northeast, possibly a journalist, receiving positive vibes from McMenemy. Unlike Clough, the new Roker target gave little away although privately, he found the interest unsettling and deserving of serious consideration. He was unconvinced that the south coast club appreciated his achievements of winning the FA Cup in 1976, promotion and First Division consolidation. Woodford convened a board meeting. McMenemy expressed his desire for the

Sunderland job and Southampton, compelled to act, surprised him with the offer of an eight-year contract. Collings, unable to take no for an answer, offered to helicopter him to Roker for talks but McMenemy was not swayed. The uncertainty did not affect the players. Merrington had instigated a revival. A Methodist lay preacher with a fiery outlook, he had taken no prisoners when part of a rugged Burnley defence in the sixties. Following a late winner against Brighton, an appreciative crowd chanted his name. Wayne Entwistle boosted Merrington's stock even higher when he skated to an orange-ball hat-trick against Bristol Rovers on a snow-covered surface. With Sunderland lying fourth he was offered the managerial role on a permanent basis. Merrington, unable to break free of Adamson, decided it was the correct time to finally become his right-hand man at Elland Road. As options narrowed, Sunderland settled on the low-key caretaker appointment of former player Billy Elliott who had also served as Alan Brown's number two. Ken Knighton was promoted from reserve to first team coach.

The players, respectful of his long association with the club, immediately responded to the earthy Elliott. Despite a home loss to lowly Cambridge in his first game on 16th December, Sunderland were soon stringing results together. A remarkable unbeaten away record stretched from November '78 to September '79. Steve Whitworth, an experienced right back capped seven times by England, arrived from Leicester. A rearranged third round FA Cup tie against an Everton team placed second in the First Division, was memorable. As a blizzard swept in, a successful penalty from Rowell followed by a Bob Lee goal ensured a fourth round visit to Burnley. When Sunderland travelled to St. James' Park on 24 February '79 they faced a Newcastle side defeated in four previous outings. In a game still talked about, Rowell bagged a hat-trick with Wayne Entwistle making the final score 4-1. The 37,507 present the following mild and calm Monday evening, the largest crowd of the season, were fully expected to witness a resurgent Sunderland storm past Burnley and book a fifth round match on the Saturday at Anfield. On Wearside only weeks previously, Sunderland had comfortably defeated the struggling Lancashire club in a league match, on a pitch disfigured by large circles of burnt grass, a consequence of using braziers to prevent frost forming.

A special Cup night of theatre, enhanced under the lights, was expected. Within the ageing Clock Stand, a thousand and one intermittent flickering sparks betrayed the presence of those hidden under its dark recess, as a constant fug of tobacco smoke wafted across a glossy sheen of green grass. The paddocks, half bathed in artificial light, resembled a shooting gallery as silhouettes weaved in and out of the remaining spaces at the ends. In a corner of the ground where viewing was impaired, a small part of the whitewashed rampart at the rear of the Roker End and a few stark concrete steps were visible. Latecomers, emerging from crowded gangways, created a series of shock waves before everyone in the vast open-aired terrace coalesced to a pink, fleshy blob. The contrast with an inky black sky provided a canvas that few West End productions could aspire to equal. A wall of sound and popping flashbulbs greeted the emerging teams. Even before battle commenced a wave of triumphalism rattled the rafters. Lighting was extinguished within the main double-decker stand as the clock on the red Leitch lattice balcony ticked towards half past seven. It triggered a domino effect as everyone standing sat down quickly. Another noise welled up as the players hastily changed ends and as the match started, an urgent, louder roar drifted over the rooftops of the tightly woven terraced streets out to the North Sea. At twenty-five minutes to eight there was silence. The identity of the young Sunderland goalkeeper between the Fulwell End posts was a mystery to some in the stunned crowd. Ian Watson's first touch was to pick the ball out of the net. Within a quarter of an hour, Watson fumbled the ball a second time when, to the uninitiated, it was easier to save; after the self-assured Barry Siddall unexpectedly failed a late fitness test the 19-year-old had been pitched in at the deep end. The encore to Rowell's derby hat-trick did justice to a Hammer House of Horror film. Sunderland's 3-0 defeat by Burnley was a gift for the headline writers: 'Roker Choker'. The following Saturday, in his solitary league appearance for his hometown club, Watson creditably kept a clean sheet as a goal from Wayne Entwistle earned two points.

The memorable win at St. James' Park commenced a run of seven league wins out of eight. The aberration was a defeat by Crystal Palace, a talented side that included Vince Hilaire and Kenny Sansom, who in benefitting from the wisdom of their young manager Terry Venables, were futuristically dubbed 'The Team of the Eighties'. Palace, every inch justifying their status as promotion favourites, coasted to a more comfortable victory than the 2-1 scoreline suggested, delivering a reality check to a large crowd. After this chastening night, 14,000 fewer turned up against Orient to witness Gary Rowell score the only goal. Sadly, this game echoed Clough's bad luck from Boxing Day 1962. Rowell, on 21 goals in 32 games, sustained serious knee damage that ruled him out for the remainder of the season, restricting him to a handful of appearances the following term. Promotion hopes were dashed. A further blow was suffered when an injured Jeff Clarke missed the run-in. Billy Elliott plugged the gaps. Jack Ashurst replaced Clarke; Alan Brown replaced Rowell. Undaunted, Sunderland won the first two of their three Easter fixtures and climbing to second in the table, relished a Monday afternoon encounter with rock bottom Blackburn Rovers. At a squally Roker, a Derek Fazackerley penalty again quietened a large turnout. Young Roly Gregoire, surprisingly given his first start of the season and as it transpired his last in a Sunderland shirt, missed an absolute sitter in front of the Roker End.

The defeat, only a second in eighteen outings, was excused by Elliott's decision to rest Lee and Buckley.

Palace, Stoke and Brighton maintained their challenge. Undeterred, another away success set up a perfectly poised Wednesday evening. With three games remaining Sunderland, if they achieved a four-goal margin over Sheffield United, would go top for the first time. The fun started in the second half when Bob Lee, who had never rediscovered his scoring burst of the relegation season and often been used effectively in midfield, put Sunderland 4-1 ahead. The next scorer was United's impressive Argentinian Alex Sabella, whose prompt response seemingly ended any chance of a summit ascent. In the 87th minute Wilf Rostron converted his second penalty of the game. Moments later he completed a hat-trick putting Sunderland 6-2 up. It was far from over. With a delirious Roker End behind him, Siddall celebrated the save of a last-minute penalty that preserved the four-goal lead. The penultimate match was a throwback to all our yesterdays. The season's second largest crowd of 36,526 witnessed a numbing 2-1 defeat from lowly Cardiff City that rendered the forthcoming final Saturday as unsuitable viewing for faint hearts.

Sunderland needed to win their final game at Wrexham in May '79 and hope that either Stoke or Brighton failed to win. In the event that both were victorious, Palace would have had to lose one of their two remaining games. Brighton opposed a Newcastle team becalmed in mid-table and duly built a three-goal half-time advantage. The attendance of 28,425 was rather different to the games immediately before and after; the visits of Bristol Rovers and Wrexham attracted 9,925 and 7,133 to Tyneside. Crystal Palace scored a vital match-winning goal at Orient on the hour but, as the afternoon progressed, the failure of Stoke to break the deadlock at Notts County seemed of little consequence, given that Sunderland were trailing at Wrexham to a 58th minute Joey Jones goal. In an instant it changed. Rostron scored on 80 minutes and Brown on 83. Between those goals Barry Siddall produced an improbable, instinctive save at close quarters from Dixie McNeil. At the final whistle thousands of jubilant Sunderland fans within a 12,000 contingent swarmed onto the Welsh turf, momentarily blissfully unaware of a development at Meadow Lane. On 88 minutes Stoke City's desperate quest for a winning goal against Notts County was answered. As at Goodison Park two years previously, the disappointment was immeasurable. The following Friday evening Crystal Palace, before their record crowd of 51,801, defeated Burnley and in the process leapt from fourth to first, thereby pushing the Wearsiders outside a promotion place. Sunderland's fifty-five points was a mere one less than their league-winning season under Stokoe. Billy Elliott's efforts were awarded with a substantial golden handshake.

During the closing weeks of the season Tom Cowie, an outspoken board director, said that Sunderland 'must have a top manager'. The nakedly ambitious Cowie also mentioned his desire for ‘new and impressive stands at Roker, costing perhaps two to three million pounds’. Collings, who privately disagreed with Cowie, remained tight-lipped. A wary chairman, cautious after rebuttals from Clough and McMenemy, lowered his sights on the recently installed Wolves boss John Barnwell. When he was at Peterborough he had applied to replace Adamson, but Collings, then chasing bigger fish, judged his status as a Third Division manager unworthy of consideration. Barnwell, now invigorating Wolves despite only a short time there, promptly rejected Sunderland’s offer. Ian Greaves at Bolton followed suit. There was criticism when Collings turned to Len Ashurst, one year into an assignment at Fourth Division Newport County. Ashurst, the former long-standing stalwart, unexpectedly asked for time to consider Roker’s approach before incredulously deciding to remain in Wales. The impressive 35-year-old Ken Knighton, not long first team coach at Roker, attracted attention from managerless Blackburn Rovers. Detecting support for him from the players, Collings awarded him a two-year contract and by doing so brought an end to what was becoming an embarrassing soap opera. Knighton appointed Frank Clark as his assistant. Clark had climaxed a lengthy playing career by recently winning a European Cup medal with Nottingham Forest in the May final against Malmö. Favourably viewed as a fresh, dynamic management duo of contrasting personalities, they drew comparison with a younger version of the Clough and Peter Taylor partnership.

Money was available. On the strength of his display for Sheffield United at Roker Park, Sunderland agreed a club record £560,000 for midfielder Alex Sabella. Although local radio reported his arrival as a done deal, Sabella backtracked when he puzzlingly deferred to his wife’s wish not to relocate further north. Bryan Robson however made a popular return from West Ham. Sunderland also signed the highly rated goalkeeper Chris Turner from Sheffield Wednesday.

15

GOING UP IS THE EASY PART

1979-80 to 1980-81

In August '79, Gary Rowell returned to first team action in the opening goalless draw at Chelsea but was used sparingly as Brown initially partnered Robson up front. Clarke and Elliott formed an effective centre back line alongside right back Steve Whitworth who, although unfairly singled out for criticism from the crowd, would prove the only ever-present. The season progressed with a clear dichotomy between home and away results.

Sunderland overcame Newcastle on penalties at St. James' Park in a League Cup tie after both legs were drawn. This was the only away success until the end of the calendar year. Robson scored a splendid goal from 18 yards out to defeat Manchester City on a misty night in front of over 33,000 at Roker before West Ham ended Cup interest at Upton Park on bonfire night. Sunderland were in mid-table; John Hawley, purchased from Hull, had scored a hat-trick on his debut but was now sidelined with injury. After four successive away defeats more cash was splashed. Stan Cummins signed in November from Middlesbrough for a record fee of £300,000 and shortly afterwards this figure was slightly exceeded with the exciting capture of Claudio Marangoni from Argentinian club San Lorenzo. The ball control and eye for goal of Cummins led Jack Charlton, his manager then at Ayresome Park, to predict he would become the game's first £1 million player. At only 20 years old he had fallen out of first team favour on Teesside. Standing a fraction short of 5'4", some clubs were reluctant to take a chance. Knighton, with characteristic candour, called him 'an absolute bargain'. Marangoni, typically adept, accustomed to the rock-hard pitches and sunshine of South America, made his debut on 8th December in a 2-1 home win against Cardiff watched by a sizeable pre-festive crowd of 25,000. It was a culture shock. In one telling incident he collided with a team-mate, almost knocking himself out cold.

However it was Marangoni, netting from all of 25 yards at Craven Cottage on the last Saturday of the year who was responsible for a first league away win. Sunderland had kept in touch with the leaders in their two previous games through late goals at Roker Park. The Shrewsbury fixture was brought forward a day to avoid the traditional low crowd on the last weekend before Christmas; on a bitterly cold Friday night before 21,237 a Kevin Arnott goal two minutes from time secured two points. The icy weather was no inducement for fans. Even though the thirty-four rescheduled matches included First Division fixtures at Arsenal and Wolves, the Roker gate was far and away the best. On Boxing Day with the Fulwell End as a backdrop, Arnott preserved the unbeaten home record by sublimely bending a free kick over the Wrexham wall. Sunderland, fifth in the table, were four points behind leaders Newcastle, whom they visited on New Year's Day. Despite an early lead through Stan Cummins they were overrun 3-1. Anyone within the 38,322 present would have been hard-pressed to correctly guess the divergent fortunes of the two clubs in the second half of the season. Newcastle, falling away badly, only won a further two matches as Ken Knighton's team found their form, only losing once in 18 remaining league outings.

Yet the immediate aftermath of the derby debacle was not encouraging; a third round FA Cup defeat by Bolton Wanderers preceded a match against Oldham when Sunderland, watched by a season's low of 19,456, returned to the dressing room one down. Alan Brown saved face with a second half hat-trick. Stan Cummins then scored four times in a 5-0 home win over Burnley. The defeat at Preston in the next game on 16 February '80 proved the last of the season. When teenager John Cooke, standing in for Brown, scored a late goal to defeat Luton it sparked an unbeaten 14-match run. The sun came out, figuratively and literally. A two-yard tap-in from Cummins won a scrappy derby with Newcastle on a warm Easter Saturday. A banner tied to the Main Stand paddock proclaimed, 'Red Knight On Target'. Away victories at Wrexham and Shrewsbury on consecutive days hoisted Sunderland to the summit of the division. The resurgence attracted 33,000 for the visit of Orient on another sunny afternoon. Arnott struck a wonderful trademark free kick but a tentative performance allowed a point to slip away. There were no such doubts however when Robson and a marauding Shaun Elliott shared four goals for the main Match of the Day slot that captured a 5-0 romp over Watford.

With two matches remaining Sunderland, in third position, were in control of their destiny and looked forward to an intriguing, rearranged fixture with FA Cup finalists West Ham, to be played after the Wembley appointment. Before that Sunderland were at Ninian Park. If Sunderland equalled Chelsea's result the last game would not matter. The travelling support of 12,000 were within a crowd of 19,340. Congestion delayed the kick-off by twenty minutes. Cardiff City took a lead only for Robson to equalise with his 20th goal of the season. Leicester and Birmingham were definitely promoted and Sunderland, still playing, knew a further goal would take them above Chelsea, who had defeated Oldham. Jeff Clarke was stretchered off with a knee injury. It remained all square, therefore only a draw was required against West Ham who looked forward to a Wembley final. The following Monday, a testimonial for Mick Docherty proved low-key and attracted 4,000. West Ham became the third Second Division side in eight seasons to win the FA Cup when they defeated fancied Arsenal; understandably at Roker Park 48 hours later they were relaxed and in party mood. Surprisingly, it was deemed unnecessary to make such an important game all-ticket; five thousand unsold tickets for the Easter derby perhaps influencing the decision. On a fine May afternoon crowds poured into the town for an evening kick-off. Gates were shut on 47,129 with a conservative police estimate of 7,000 locked out. David Cross threatened twice in early exchanges as West Ham, expressing themselves freely, enjoyed the occasion. Kevin Arnott settled Sunderland's nerves near the interval before Stan Cummins made it 2-0 with his twelfth goal of a productive season. After the final whistle Roker Park was bathed in twilight as the players circled the pitch. As in their previous promotion of 1976 Sunderland remained unbeaten in home matches, the only two instances since the late nineteenth century that this has occurred.

The players were rewarded with a fortnight in Miami. Robson, the top scorer with 20 goals, in a nod to his FA Cup winning former colleagues commented, 'At this stage of my career it is no use looking back at the medals I might have won with West Ham. I am just glad to have won promotion with Sunderland and the First Division is certainly the league to play in'. Ironically, when Robson was transferred to Roker from Upton Park for the first time in 1974, the West Ham side he left won the Cup that same season. With an average of 27,119 Sunderland were the ninth best supported in England. Knighton, untouched by failure in an embryonic management career, was typically bullish, 'Now we want to build long-lasting success here. If I don't do this job inside three seasons I will get out of football. When I think what has happened in the past two years I can hardly believe it. I have crammed in more experience than some bosses pick up in a decade'.

Tom Cowie became chairman on 26 June '80. Cowie, who watched the great thirties' team, was born and bred on Wearside and had built a huge and expanding car dealership, now quoted on the stock market. When opened in 1959, his Scotswood Road, Newcastle building was acknowledged as the largest motorcycle showroom in the world. Considered extremely wealthy, Cowie was originally accepted to the Roker boardroom in the early seventies, from when he quietly bought into the club, becoming a majority shareholder. That a high profile, local and respected businessman should spearhead Sunderland into the new decade, corresponding as it did with the return of top-flight soccer, instilled optimism. Cowie however was not Ditchburn. His programme notes before the first game against Everton offered a clue, 'Sunderland football club is just over 100 years old. I should like it to continue for another century. But it can only do that if we are prudent. The challenge ahead is enormous. But with good housekeeping and shrewd management we shall survive these difficult times and emerge a stronger and more successful club'. He announced an 80% increase in admission prices, which coincided with rising unemployment as an economic recession bit. His parsimony eventually would stretch to cancelling the players' end-of-year turkeys.

With centre half Clarke missing for a lengthy spell, Knighton signed Sam Allardyce from relegated Bolton as a stopgap replacement. A dearth of transfer activity did not prevent an explosive start in August '80. Everton were beaten 3-1 and in midweek a John Hawley hat-trick sealed a stunning 4-0 win at Manchester City. On the second Saturday Kevin Keegan, new in the colours of Southampton after his continental foray at Hamburg, was a major attraction for a 41,141 Roker crowd who were looking down on the other 91 clubs. Despite an equalising header from Allardyce, the Saints eased to a comfortable 2-1 victory. After losing to Fourth Division Stockport in the League Cup, Sunderland resumed their encouraging start by overcoming Leeds at home 4-1, to climb to sixth after eight games. Robson, shortly out of favour, scored twice and Rowell, coming into form after his long layoff, found the net for the first time in 18 months. The season started to unravel at Aston Villa when a 4-0 reverse commenced a shocking sequence of one solitary point from twelve away games. Knighton's brand of attacking football was attracting praise from everyone bar those connected with the club. He deflected criticism commenting, 'I want my teams to attack, at home and away. We have a duty to be entertaining. Maybe it will cost us goals. But it will also get us goals'. Such talk was out of kilter when the reward of only two points for a win designated a draw a desired commodity. In November Stoke, who were managed by a pragmatic, defensive-minded Alan Durban, showed mettle when they held Sunderland to a turgid goalless draw. The crowd, down to 21,483, vented anger on Durban, taunting him with a recent statement when he inferred that a circus with clowns was a more appropriate venue to guarantee entertainment than a football match. At the end of the month, early snow brought the first chill of winter to Roker Park; Sunderland were comprehensively outgunned by an all-yellow Liverpool who led 4-0 before conceding twice in the closing stages.

A rift developed between Cowie and the manager. Knighton complained that the three quality signings he hoped for at the start of the season had not materialised; he bemoaned a lack of bargaining power. Despite this, decent home form kept the wolf at bay with a stupendous thirty-yard strike from John Hawley and ice-cold composure from Arnott overcoming Arsenal 2-0. When new players finally arrived it was an underwhelming balancing-of-the-books exercise. The majority of Marangoni's fee was recouped when he returned to his former club, the proceeds part-funding Tom Ritchie from Bristol City and Ian Bowyer from Forest. Neither made an instant or future impact. Joe Hinnigan, an overlapping full back, arrived from Third Division Wigan and his goal at Crystal Palace ended the away hoodoo before he eased relegation fears by scoring twice in the next game, a 3-0 win over Coventry. A 1-0 home setback against Wolverhampton Wanderers, on an afternoon when a radio commentary of the Grand National was of more appeal than the dire fare on the pitch, pushed Cowie to the brink. Following another defeat at Stoke, it was no great shock when Ken Knighton and his assistant Frank Clarke were relieved of office, giving coach Mick Docherty four games to secure safety. Cowie later contended that Sunderland lost a great deal of money backing Knighton's judgement in the transfer market. A rare contribution from Ritchie of a hat-trick against Birmingham on Easter Saturday diluted end-of-season worries until fellow strugglers Brighton rocked Roker Park with a 90th minute winner in the final home game. That left Sunderland having to beat Liverpool to avoid another quick return to the Second Division unless Norwich were unable to take the points from an already relegated Leicester. League Cup winners Liverpool were focused on a European Cup final with Real Madrid. The champagne Bob Paisley made available if Sunderland stayed up was not wasted. A Stan Cummins goal gave the huge away support cause for celebration but ironically, the victory proved academic because Norwich unexpectedly lost.

16

ALL UPHILL FOR DURBAN

1981-82 to 1983-84

Now it was Tom Cowie's attempt to land the high-profile name that Sunderland yearned for. He aimed for the number one choice of everyone. Bobby Robson, raised in Langley Park, County Durham, had built unfashionable Ipswich into a major force. In the season gone they finished four points behind champions Aston Villa having beaten the Midlanders twice and dismissed them from the FA Cup. Villa, singularly focused on the league, used only 14 players, seven of whom were ever present. Ipswich, in chasing three trophies, encountered problems similar to those that had plagued Revie's Leeds a decade earlier and, burdened with 20 matches more than the modest number of their rivals, were damned by a fixture pile-up. Cowie made his move with a reported ten-year contract worth £1 million after Robson had rejected Manchester United, who were looking to replace Dave Sexton. Robson was sorely tempted to Roker but announced his decision to stay at Portman Road at a civic reception that toasted Ipswich's UEFA Cup win. Paul Hetherington in the Evening Chronicle quoted Robson, 'Despite what most people may have thought, it was not the glamour and glitter of Manchester United that came close to luring me away. The club I had set my heart on joining was Sunderland. The chance to go back home to the Northeast and make them the great club they were in my youth was almost too overwhelming to resist'.

Where Collings had failed, Cowie succeeded in landing one of his targets. The sought-after Alan Durban, holder of an impressive CV, who had consolidated Stoke in the First Division, eventually said yes, although initially there was uncertainty as West Bromwich Albion hovered in the background and his assistant from the Potteries, Richie Barker, let it be known he was unwilling to relocate. Durban played under Clough at Derby before guiding

Shrewsbury to promotion as their player-manager. He was just short of his fortieth birthday, grammar school educated and accredited as one of the brightest managers in the game. He excelled at individual sports, in particular tennis. Much later in life he would be a Shropshire Senior's Doubles Champion. Before appointing Adamson, Leeds fancied Durban but were unconditionally blocked by the Stoke chairman. Asked if he was dismayed at losing the opportunity of such a high-profile job Durban's response was refreshing. Having spent seven months at Stoke, he would have been disappointed if the board of directors had been willing to release him after such a short time. When appointed he somewhat predictably called the potential at Sunderland unlimited. Cowie, delighted with his arrival, claimed he was Sunderland's most important signing in recent history. Unfortunately for Durban, excellent though his judgement at buying players was, he was hampered by strict financial limits as the club wrestled with a legacy of the previous regime's spending.

The commencement of Durban's reign coincided with the widespread trend of reduced attendances throughout the country. Sunderland suffered more than most clubs as their supporters were employed in the very sectors being decimated by a deep recession; traditionally well-paid manual jobs such as coal mining, shipbuilding or steel. A growing problem inside and outside football grounds was social disorder, covered in the media by a catch-all word 'hooliganism'. Exacerbating this were the slum conditions of most grounds, poor sanitary conditions and a lack of spectator comfort that bordered on a basic lack of safety. Sunderland received a sum of money from sportswear manufacturers Le Coq Sportif that was used for a long overdue modernisation of toilets. The club's side of the bargain was a two-year substitution of their red and white stripes for a series of two narrow red lines on a predominately white shirt. The accompanying red shorts represented a further break from tradition. The hardcore who remained on the thinning terraces were horrified at the sight of their team kitted out in something resembling a pyjama top.

Alan Durban initially received a generous budget. Days before the commencement of the 1981-82 season, a club record £350,000 was spent on an 18-year-old part-time forward from second-tier Scottish club St. Johnstone. Ally McCoist, with 22 league goals in his first full season, had started the current campaign with a goal against Celtic in the group stages of the League Cup. Durban, paying for potential, later admitted that McCoist was 'the right player at the wrong time'. The other newcomer at £150,000 was Iain Munro, an experienced full back from Stoke.

The new season heralded a change from two points to three points for a win. Durban's first game in charge, a 3-3 draw at Ipswich after leading 3-1, really did seem like two points dropped in old money. Two goals from Eric Gates rescued the Suffolk club. Nick Pickering, from South Shields, made a first team debut and whilst at Sunderland achieved a full England cap against Australia. Aston Villa, reigning league champions, were then vanquished on a Wednesday evening in front of 29,372 at Roker but the flying start was dashed by a newly promoted West Ham side who triumphed 2-0 on Wearside before 28,347. Whether it was second season syndrome or not the campaign again unravelled as the days shortened. Sunderland waited until 10th March for another home win. A run of eight goalless games was ingloriously ended by a 5-1 defeat by Manchester United before three wins from four away trips took Sunderland out of January with hope of avoiding relegation. One of those games was made memorable through 17-year-old Barry Venison, who came off the bench eight minutes from time at Maine Road on the Saturday before Christmas. With his first touch he created an equaliser for Rowell then sensationally snatched a late winner with his 20-yard drive. On a day when only six of 46 league fixtures survived the wintry weather, the Wearsiders climbed off the bottom above Middlesbrough.

McCoist had ability but his slender frame should have had the help of a powerful, experienced striker. He scored his second and last goal of the season with a superb curling shot against Southampton, warming those present on a cold March night to secure only a second home victory of the season. Shortly before this game only 12,910 watched Sunderland labour to a draw with Notts County. Fewer were present when Bobby Robson's second-placed Ipswich visited on a fine April evening days before Easter. Supporters had given up the ghost after a Tees-Wear derby defeat the previous Saturday, when a Middlesbrough victory returned Sunderland to bottom spot. Durban took McCoist from the firing line, replacing him with Colin West, a teenaged local lad from Wallsend whose father was a dockworker on the Tyne. The tall centre forward had sporadically appeared earlier in the season, albeit mainly from the bench, but now he provided a focal point for the forward line. Against Ipswich his goal rekindled faint hopes of redemption, only for Kevin Steggles to equalise on 85 minutes. There was an immediate change in fortune. Sunderland bagged 20 points from their final 10 games; West scored a further five goals, with Rowell's six taking his season's tally to nine. A 3-1 win over Everton in April gave home supporters a first Saturday afternoon victory in a period of one year. The customary last day drama was enacted when Manchester City visited Roker. Four clubs other than the Wearsiders were in realistic danger of joining already relegated Middlesbrough and Wolverhampton Wanderers. Sunderland, watched by 26,167, successfully defended an early Mick Buckley goal but uncertainty unfolded at the final whistle. Birmingham, Leeds United and West Bromwich Albion all won and with only Stoke losing, it was initially assumed by some attending Roker that Sunderland could be overtaken, due to three of the clubs below them having remaining fixtures. Before the ground emptied, relief came with the realisation that those clubs were scheduled to play each other and would inevitably drop points between each other. Sunderland were to finish one above the three relegation places, with the worst goal difference of four clubs all on 44 points. They were two points ahead of Leeds, the third team to suffer demotion.

Once more there was little or no progress in the senior cup competitions. It was a different picture in the FA Youth Cup. Sunderland, including goalkeeper Mark Prudhoe and full backs Barry Venison and Nick Pickering, played Manchester United in a two-legged semi-final. The first encounter at Old Trafford was lost 1-0 before a sparse 1,541. In contrast, at Roker Park, the main stand was swamped with 6,174 spectators, forcing the club to hastily open both ends of the ground therefore admitting an extra three or four thousand without payment. 15-year-old Paul Lemon, who would make almost 100 senior appearances, put Sunderland level on aggregate before Norman Whiteside and Mark Hughes, later to become household names, scored as United won 3-1 overall.

Relief at the last-gasp escape was tempered when it was discovered that the tall concrete pillars, which thrust the huge, uncovered Roker End terrace skywards, had deteriorated beyond repair. In one fell swoop the capacity of the ground was temporarily slashed from 46,833 to 29,683 before increasing to 36,000 when the end reopened in a truncated form. The projected cost of £200,000 placed an unwelcome further strain on finances.

On the eve of the 1982-83 season Cowie was effusive in his praise of Durban, stating he had worked ‘splendidly within the Board of Directors’ and ‘kept us up by his calm and sensible approach to the trickiest of situations’. In another thinly-veiled swipe at Knighton, he said that Durban had saved the club thousands of pounds and moved out of Roker Park players who should never have been bought in the first place. ‘I expect this club to make steady progress from now on. We have the right manager and players who want to play for the club.’ On 28th August after going in behind at the interval, goals from West, McCoist and Pickering gave Sunderland an excellent opening day victory at the home of newly crowned European Cup winners Aston Villa. The attendance of less than 23,000 was a stark illustration of a growing apathy towards football. A win and draw from two home fixtures, with Rowell scoring the only Sunderland goal in each of those games, meant seven points from the opening three games and the kind comments from Cowie seemed apt. However when a crushing 8-0 defeat from newly promoted Watford followed in short fashion it was obvious that strengthening was required.

Durban, as always, encountered a reluctance from transfer targets to move north. He was not interested in the low-hanging fruit of those in the twilight of a career, looking for an easy final pay day. He yearned for seasoned campaigners with something to prove, good professionals who remained hungry. They were well known within the game but attracting them was difficult. He came agonisingly close with Mick Mills. Terms were agreed but the highly rated Ipswich defender reneged on a verbal agreement once he became aware of Lawrie McMenemy's eleventh-hour interest at Southampton. Dave Watson, the 1973 hero, came close to a Wearside return. Ian Atkins, a talented versatile defender, who Durban signed from his old club Shrewsbury for a modest fee, proved to be an excellent addition. A breakthrough was made when the experienced right back Jimmy Nicholl agreed to sign from Toronto Blizzard having been on loan at Roker from Old Trafford the previous season. In December Durban managed to prise the enormously talented and well-travelled 34-year-old forward Frank Worthington from Leeds. Worthington's extrovert character had restricted him to only eight caps for his country. Arriving for an international get-together in a Stetson and cowboy boots was never likely to impress Sir Alf Ramsey. Contrary to his image, Worthington played all his football for provincial clubs shunning the bright lights of London. Despite scoring on his debut against Ipswich, on an afternoon when the reduced Roker End reopened, goals from Brazil and Gates helped the visitors to a 3-2 victory.

When Sunderland entertained Arsenal on a bitterly cold last Saturday before Christmas, their league position was precarious. Facing difficult fixtures ahead, Durban's side were rock bottom having taken only fourteen points from eighteen games. They were already six points behind Luton who were lying nineteenth, one place above the three relegation spots. Only 11,753 were present to witness a Gary Rowell hat-trick in circumstances far removed from his achievement at St. James' Park. Sunderland, wearing flat soles minus studs, managed a better grip on the icy surface than Arsenal and the 3-0 victory allied to the introduction of Worthington instigated an unbeaten run. On Boxing Day a goalless draw was secured at Old Trafford; the following afternoon, as the mercury climbed to 15°C, the arrival of Liverpool attracted a capacity crowd. Their captain Graeme Souness, a ferocious competitor, described decades later as 'filthy' by a reminiscing Martin O'Neill on the radio station talkSPORT, may or may not have been aware of remarks made pre-match by Shaun Elliott, who said he had nothing to fear from the league leaders. The defender's throwaway comment returned to haunt him in the 32nd minute of a tight contest. Souness, extremely lucky to only receive a booking, maimed him with an outrageous over-the-top foul near the main stand touchline. Elliott was ruled out of action for three months but his words proved prescient. A battling Sunderland took no prisoners as they held Liverpool to a goalless draw. Durban, mindful that the introduction of Atkins and Nicholl had tightened his defence, added brush strokes. Veteran Welsh winger Leighton James arrived from Swansea on a free transfer. The manager squeezed the best football of his career from a player known to be temperamental and a challenge to authority. Mark Proctor was loaned from

Nottingham Forest shortly afterwards. Sunderland took 29 points from 14 games, only losing once. Disappointingly, the upsurge was not met with significantly higher attendances; back-to-back wins over Manchester City and Everton attracted an aggregate of barely 30,000. Gary Rowell scored twice in both games with each marked by a trademark penalty. In the next outing a single Rowell strike at Stoke earned three points. Supporters were growing disillusioned with a club who had fallen into a pattern of striving for promotion or struggling to preserve top-flight status. They were baffled at the relative success of traditionally smaller, stock unfashionables such as Watford, Swansea, Norwich and Brighton.

Sunderland, having played 30 matches, were only four points off seventh position when Tom Cowie gave a withering and controversial press release. In acknowledging the progress Alan Durban had made he justifiably said that the team deserved bigger support. Cowie then said he would never have visualised a time when Newcastle United, in the Second Division, would consistently draw 'much bigger crowds than a Sunderland side playing so well in the top-flight'. Fans, already annoyed by Cowie's perceived economy measures, were enraged. The fact that crowds at United were deemed artificially high because of Kevin Keegan did not mitigate feelings; indeed it led supporters to question why Sunderland, with a better squad of players, were unwilling to speculate in similar fashion to mount a challenge for honours.

The season petered out to sixteenth position, which at least represented a slight improvement. Again, there was no progress in either of the domestic Cup competitions. A third round FA Cup tie with Manchester City attracted 21,518 to Roker, only bettered by league visits from Liverpool and Manchester United. The replay was lost. There was one unusual aspect to an April evening match with Brighton. With the advance consent of the Football League, both teams agreed to fulfil the fixture despite a floodlight at the Fulwell End being temporarily out of use.

Durban's third term commenced with Paul Bracewell and Mark Proctor on board. After Proctor's loan spell ended, a fee of £250,000 was agreed with Nottingham Forest for a permanent deal. Bracewell, a highly promising 21-year-old from Stoke, able to win and pass the ball in midfield, was signed for a similar amount. To recoup part of the outlay Durban was obliged to accept a bid for McCoist from Glasgow Rangers. Detecting a change in the mood music from Cowie, the Sunderland manager suspected his days in the Northeast might be numbered and with his timespan to develop the career of McCoist in doubt, he advised the youngster to pack his bags. Although never a prolific goalscorer at Roker, McCoist had been bought as a future investment. Sunderland stood a loss of £100,000 on the original fee paid to St. Johnstone.

The attendances during September and October '83 were the lowest early season figures since before the outbreak of the First World War. The image problems within the sport and the poor seasons since promotion were to blame. More than just a couple of good results were required to attract fans back. A miserable rainy day for the visit of unglamorous Coventry, who were beaten 1-0, may in part have excused a meagre crowd of 11,612 but another sub-12,000 crowd at the next home game against Stoke was disappointing. Granted, Midland sides never amounted to attractive opposition but Sunderland were returning from a superb victory at Liverpool, courtesy of Gary Rowell's twentieth consecutive successful penalty conversion. Liverpool were en route to a third consecutive title. Against Stoke, in an unusually entertaining encounter, Sunderland took the lead twice to share four goals.

The few fans who kept the faith and been rewarded with mediocrity for their loyalty were now sensing an improvement. Those who had stopped going were in denial. When word spread of Sunderland's renaissance it often descended on deaf ears

On 5 November '83 goals from West and Atkins defeated Arsenal at Highbury, a game in which Tony Adams debuted for the Gunners. Sunderland then earned a midweek League Cup draw at Norwich before sweeping aside Watford 3-0 at Roker. The size of the crowd of 15,407 was encouraging, as was a tremendous attacking performance by West and James. Indeed, Durban commented that the acquisition of Leighton James must have been one of the best free transfer signings anyone had made. Roker was buzzing for the visit of second placed West Ham. With its reduced footprint, 20,000 fans made the old ground seem almost full but despite noisy encouragement, Sunderland failed to capitalise on their positive start to the game. West Ham weathered the tempest and imperceptibly gained a foothold before David Swindlehurst unearthed a late winner. The opening twenty minutes was a rare occasion when crowd and team fused as one. It marked the high point of the Durban era. A League Cup replay defeat by Norwich dulled expectations before comprehensive home wins over West Bromwich and Luton propelled Sunderland into the New Year with their tally of 30 points from 21 games representing more games won than lost. The signing of Lee Chapman from Arsenal for £150,000, who Durban had brought through the ranks at Stoke in similar fashion to that of Ian Atkins when commencing his managerial career at Shrewsbury, provided further evidence that he was building a squad of players that could compete at the right end of the table. The five supporters' letters that appeared in the Saturday evening Football Echo, a week after Sunderland had triumphed 3-0 at Bolton in a third round FA Cup tie, were an accurate gauge of feelings. An excerpt from each reveals the positive vibes around the club. 'Indeed there is a general feeling that Sunderland really are a team worth watching … Progress is slow at Roker but who would deny the fine job Alan Durban is doing … However, he (Durban) now seems to have got his team to look like a quality First Division side with excellent away form … there is a wind of change blowing through Wearside, it should sweep Sunderland up Division One to higher achievements … With the season now at the halfway stage, Sunderland are in a comfortable position in the table, and the time has come for an assault on the top six places.'

Less than two months later Alan Durban was manager no more. An eagerly anticipated Cup run was arrested with a fourth round home defeat by Birmingham City. There was a testing set of seven winless league fixtures, only two at Roker, where Liverpool were held to a goalless draw and Nottingham Forest avoided defeat through an 85th minute Viv Anderson equaliser. The lack of Cup success and a run of poor results against difficult opposition did not justify Durban's abrupt sacking. Although Cowie commented that the club were in a 'precarious position just above the bottom three', the fact remained that on 2nd March, the day of his departure, Sunderland were lying sixteenth, four points ahead of twentieth placed Stoke having played a game less. In addition, they were no less than eleven and thirteen points clear of Notts County and Wolverhampton Wanderers respectively who occupied the places behind Stoke. This, by the standards of recent seasons, in fact any season, was hardly terminal.

Alan Durban's last waltz was at Old Trafford. Lee Chapman opened the scoring before Manchester United prevailed with goals from centre half Kevin Moran either side of half-time. The game was dogged by roughhouse play from 18-year-old Norman Whiteside that prompted the Sunderland defender Gordon Chisholm to comment, 'He's getting away with murder. He goes in with everything, elbows, feet, the lot'. Durban directed anger towards his own team without mentioning Whiteside. In a rare and unexpected public outpouring, probably precipitated by the growing pressure he was under, the Sunderland manager divulged he had told certain players that they were a 'disgrace' and added that without Paul Bracewell the side would collapse. Cowie's less than appreciative programme notes written for the Queens Park Rangers game after the appointment of Len Ashurst are worth relating: 'As you will know, Alan Durban was dismissed from his position as manager last Friday. He had been with us since June '81 and I'm sure that he is sincere in his belief that he has done a worthwhile job … The facts are that under Alan's direction Sunderland played 112 League games, winning 31 and losing 47'. He then disclosed that Durban had described as insulting the offer of a one-year contract that had been made early in the New Year. There was no common ground between the pair; Durban was never likely to sign a mere one-year extension and his decision not to do so had given Cowie a weak green light to propose the motion for his dismissal. Cowie felt he had backed him enough in the transfer market and results were slow in coming. Patience is not a virtue of chairmen and major shareholders of football clubs. The board's decision however was not unanimous.

A day after Bryan Robson took temporary charge to steer Sunderland to a welcome point against Arsenal, Len Ashurst resigned his position at Cardiff and on the Monday morning he was appointed manager. The quickness of Cowie's action suggests Ashurst had been notified of the club's intention some time before Durban left.

After refusing the Sunderland job in 1979, Len Ashurst achieved promotion with Newport County and Cardiff from the Fourth and Third Divisions respectively. His success at winning the Welsh Cup at County qualified them for the Cup Winners' Cup where they narrowly lost a quarter-final against Carl Zeiss Jena from East Germany. He had assumed an almost legendary status in Wales. His appointment at Roker stirred mixed emotions. In accumulating the highest number of outfield appearances for a Sunderland player and forever associated with the 1964 team, he was held in high esteem. His character reference within the game was impeccable. And yet his managerial career, including stints at Hartlepool, Gillingham and Sheffield Wednesday, had not provided him with any exposure of working with top-division players. There was a suspicion that unlike Durban, he would readily accept Cowie's economy measures. This feeling was reinforced when John Aldridge, a player who Ashurst had developed at Newport, wanted to rejoin him at Sunderland. Cowie, only prepared to meet the modest £75,000 fee by the method of instalments, lost out to Oxford United who offered to pay the full amount up front. Later in his career Aldridge became a leading marksman for Liverpool. Lee Chapman, desperate to escape reserve team football at Arsenal, had, without due consideration, jumped at the opportunity to rejoin Durban. He soon discovered a startling difference between life at Highbury and Roker Park. Although he considered it a pleasure to be amongst the Sunderland folk, who possessed a 'genuine warmth and good nature' he observed that everything at the football club, 'had the appearance of being second-rate, with cost-cutting economies apparently seeming to be of paramount importance'.

There was little doubt the new manager would have his work cut out. Of the players inherited from Durban, it remained to be seen who wished to remain on board and, if results were not acceptable, how much the goodwill arising from Ashurst's stellar reputation as a former servant of the club would stretch.

Three consecutive defeats in April were followed by a lethargic draw against Tottenham; both goals were scored in the first half. A lack of action on the pitch and the warm, still weather did not fully account for the crowd's indifference. In one particular moment, the quiet of the afternoon was pierced by the rhythmic hum of a distant aeroplane. There was a feeling an era had ended, a new one yet to emerge and that Cowie, at the very least, had been peremptory with Durban. Regardless, Ashurst, without a contract and seemingly in little hurry to finalise one, managed to put a few wins together although a remote threat of relegation lingered on the last day. This was removed when Leicester were beaten at Filbert Street 2-0 courtesy of Chapman and a 38-year-old Robson, pressed into action in lieu of coaching duties. Those points lifted Sunderland to thirteenth, only four points above relegated Birmingham but the highest league finish since 1956; this only served to underline the underachievement over the years. In the wake of this match, an impromptu champagne celebration was organised and hosted by the directors. It proved less than sparkling and fell flat in similar fashion to the season that had promised so much back in November.

17

A SEASON TO FORGET

1984-85

Alan Durban had modified Knighton's team in a patient, considered way. Ashurst, partially without choice, rang the changes overnight. Everton, rather than being guilty of daylight robbery, benefitted from Sunderland's inability to value the true worth of the unsettled Paul Bracewell and Ian Atkins. Accepting £250,000 and £60,000 respectively for Bracewell and Atkins was a travesty, notwithstanding that both helped the Merseysiders to a league title the following year with the former, a future England international, only missing five games. Atkins, bought as cover, featured six times. In his autobiography 'Gray Matters', Andy Gray recalls the reaction of the whole Everton squad when news broke of Howard Kendall signing Bracewell. They were 'taken aback' and thought it impossible that anyone could be an improvement on the prevailing midfield four of Steven, Sheedy, Reid and Richardson. Gray and his team-mates quickly realised that the young, relatively unknown newcomer was 'a terrific, neat and tidy, no-frills pro'. Lee Chapman, only at Roker a few months, was sold at a loss to Sheffield Wednesday. He later became the leading scorer in a Leeds team who won the last First Division title before the birth of the Premier League. Leighton James had also played his last game in a red and white shirt. Gary Rowell, at an age of only 27, given a free transfer to Norwich became another telling departure. Admittedly, Rowell had only managed five goals from open play in 31 full appearances but in the previous season his record was 14 in open play from 35 appearances. Of his Roker career record of 88 league goals, 85 came from 229 full appearances and 3 from his 25 introductions as a substitute.

Immersed in an overhaul of the playing squad Ashurst had little time for summer recreation. He signed Gary Bennett, an athletic centre half from his old club Cardiff, for a tribunal fee of £65,000. Bennett became a cult figure, eventually to be rewarded with a deserved testimonial against Glasgow Rangers that attracted 20,000, an indication of his popularity. Two dashing forwards Clive Walker and Howard Gayle arrived in the close season from Chelsea and Birmingham respectively and when the tricky, skilful forward David Hodgson signed from Liverpool in August for a cut-price £125,000, supporters were heartened that Ashurst's brand of football would prove entertaining. Hodgson, who commenced his career at Ayresome Park, had been an expensive buy at Anfield but was unable to secure a regular place. Other signings such as Steve Berry were not so well known. He was implausibly plucked from Portsmouth who, in their attempt to offload him, had sent him on loan to Fourth Division Aldershot. Berry, who established himself as a first choice for Ashurst, did not miss a game in the subsequent League Cup campaign but, unable to sustain his early promise, eventually drifted to lower-league football with Newport County.

The Ashurst purge showed promise. Durban's deferred gratification was history. Attendances increased; a revolving door of new faces and the Cup run brought excitement. A direct, off-the-cuff style of play prevailed. Ashurst commented that, 'there would have to be a few bookings, bloodied noses and bruised shins'. An opening day 3-1 win over Southampton, varnished by debutant Gary Bennett scoring past Peter Shilton, set Sunderland up for a splendid start of 20 points from 13 games. Over 23,000 saw Nottingham Forest overcome after extra time in a League Cup (renamed the Milk Cup and sponsored by the Milk Marketing Board) replay; there were over 27,000 at Roker for the fourth round tie with Tottenham. The goalless draw prefaced a magic night at White Hart Lane where an inspired goalkeeping performance from Chris Turner and goals from Walker and Chisholm realised an unexpected victory. Days after the first Tottenham encounter, Walker was prominent in a 3-2 success over Manchester United at Roker as his first half hat-trick, including two penalties, produced a remarkable turnaround. United cruised into a two-goal lead within a quarter of an hour; seven seconds from the resumption Walker pulled one back and then, less than a minute later, Hodgson and Mark Hughes were sent off after raising their hands at each other. Cup progress convinced Cowie to secure Ashurst's signature on a three-year contract. Before the ink dried, a heavy 4-0 defeat by Leicester was suffered at home, notable for Alan Smith and a 24-year-old Gary Lineker sharing the spoils. Portentously, the following two Roker league games were also lost.

Stan Cummins, released to Crystal Palace without a transfer fee during Durban's reign, reappeared on the scene, albeit for a short time. His return on a free from Palace, where he was indistinguishable in a struggling Second Division side, smacked of financial expediency. He had moved to Selhurst Park after asserting his right to leave Sunderland at a Football League hearing, because the new terms offered were inferior to his original contract. As poor league results continued, confidence drained and mid-season signings Reuben Agboola and Ian Wallace were thrown in. The New Year derby at Newcastle was a horrid affair. The black players Howard Gayle and Gary Bennett were continually the victims of racial abuse from a minority within the home crowd. In such an atmosphere it was no coincidence that they were both dismissed from the field of play, Gayle for contesting the award of a penalty and Bennett for a heavy tackle. Peter Beardsley's hat-trick ensured a 3-1 victory for United. Mark Proctor, a key midfield player, sustained a bad injury that ruled him out for the remainder of the season. In the League Cup at Watford, on a freezing January evening, a Clive Walker goal was sufficient as Sunderland, again upsetting the odds, marched into a semi-final against Chelsea over two legs. Form in the league was now of concern. Going into February, the defeat of rock bottom Stoke ended a run of seven defeats out of eight. The attendance of 14,762 indicated all was not well.

Football management is unlike any other job. There is no recognised learning curve. Results, or the lack of them, is the signifier of competence; a few months of misfortune or questionable judgement can tarnish all the experience and goodwill a manager has accumulated. Ashurst's honeymoon period was over. However as befitting a Cup night, Sunderland produced a spirited performance in blustery conditions to take a two-goal advantage to Stamford Bridge. Colin West emerged the hero. He scored from one penalty kick and missed another but reacted quickly to net after Niedzwiecki had pushed the ball against a post. Only six minutes into the second leg a David Speedie goal gave Chelsea hope but Clive Walker, energised at his old stamping ground and cutting a devastating figure, equalised then scored a match defining second on 70 minutes to put Sunderland 4-1 up on aggregate. All hell broke loose. Hundreds of Chelsea fans burst onto the pitch, some tearing seats from the stands, as mounted police charged to restrain them. Sunderland players reported attempted personal attacks from the frenzied mob. In total, 24 police were hurt with 104 arrests made in and around the ground. The match restarted in farcical conditions after a brief delay. There were police on the pitch when West scored a third, before Pat Nevin replied to reduce his side's overall deficit to 5-2. All of the four First Division teams Sunderland dismissed from the competition would finish in the top half of the table.

Chelsea chairman Ken Bates was acknowledged as the villain of the piece. Unforgivably, he decided not to make the match all-ticket therefore risking inadequate segregation or a wasted journey for those travelling from the far north. Unfortunately, some Sunderland followers were discomfited by finding themselves in a seated area occupied by home support and others, on arrival at the ground, were locked out. Bates, noted for relishing confrontation to get his own way and a controversial figure in the game since the mid-sixties when he threatened all manner of upheaval at Oldham Athletic after buying the nondescript Lancashire outfit, was unable to agree a fee for the highlights to be shown on television and then attempted to block coverage of the anarchy, which had been filmed a video company. As his High Court injunction against Thames Television failed, the video was relayed on the following night's national news. Unfortunately a great occasion had been tarnished. Sunderland's Wembley opponents Norwich were not quite mid-table. Destiny decreed that they were due to meet at Carrow Road only eight days before the final, an encounter in which Sunderland managed a vital and what seemed at the time a hugely significant win. Ian Wallace, replacing the injured Colin West, scored one of the goals in the 3-1 victory. Wallace, who played abroad before signing, had only featured in the Milk Cup once as a substitute but now he was primed for the competition's showpiece.

Ashurst was not dealt a good hand. The build-up to the final was riddled with problems. Off the field there was unease from the players, who perceived a stingy stance from the club regarding ticket allocation and money donated to their pool. More damaging was a suspension to captain Shaun Elliott, their most experienced defender, who had picked up bookings in the return leg at Chelsea and then Carrow Road, the former at Stamford Bridge having cost him a Wembley appearance. His replacement at Wembley, David Corner, was making only a fourth senior appearance. A settled Norwich forward line included the highly rated Asa Hartford and Mick Channon.

After an undistinguished 45 minutes the beginning of the second half at Wembley was calamitous. 18-year-old Corner was caught in two minds on the byline as John Deehan bore down on him. He neither shepherded the ball out of play or booted it into touch, therefore allowing Deehan to cross into the penalty box for a Hartford shot to be deflected off Gordon Chisholm past Turner. Minutes later, a Clive Walker penalty struck the base of a post. Although a deflated Sunderland allowed Norwich to dictate, the Canaries' central defender Steve Bruce was named man of the match. That decision perhaps summed up an unusually flat final. On the London Underground Norwich fans sang 'we won the Cup', which was met with the retort of 'we scored the goal'. From a Sunderland perspective the only positive aspect from Wembley was the good behaviour between the rival supporters, an example being an impromptu car park kickabout. Both clubs agreed to compete for 'The Friendship Trophy' whenever they were in direct opposition. Quite possibly, a few of those East Anglians were present on an October evening in 1956 when the visitors, featuring Len Shackleton, honoured an invite to mark the inauguration of the Carrow Road floodlights. Although an uncharitable Sunderland prevailed 3-0, it proved a rare highlight that season for Norwich who finished bottom of Division Three North and were forced to apply for re-election.

The blame for the defeat was pinned on Ashurst's decision to select Ian Wallace and not to reinstate a fully fit Colin West to the forward line. West was transferred on deadline day to Watford where Graham Taylor rejuvenated his career. In open play he scored in seven of the remaining games, becoming leading scorer the following term, before a deserved move to Glasgow Rangers.

There was no post-final joy for either team. Sunderland, increasingly jaded, won only one of twelve remaining games to finish with 40 points. Norwich, suffering unspeakable misfortune, joined them in a descent to the Second Division. Everything went wrong for the East Anglian club and their wonderful supporters. Coventry City were centre stage again but on this occasion without Jimmy Hill, now a director of Charlton Athletic, their great escape owed more to good fortune than any intimation of culpability. When Norwich completed their season Coventry needed to win all three remaining games to overtake them. The first of those was at an already relegated Stoke where they duly led through a first-half Stuart Pearce penalty. Six minutes remained when a penalty was also awarded to the home side. Ian Painter's shot thudded off the underside of the bar and may have crossed the line, although the referee was unconvinced. A reprieved Coventry took the points at Luton by scoring five minutes from time. Fifteen days after the official end of the season, runaway champions Everton fielded a shadow eleven that surrendered 4-1. Norwich, even with 49 points, had been pipped on the line by a Coventry team better versed in escapology than Houdini himself. As if this wasn't cruel enough, it remained for UEFA to flourish the coup de grâce. In the wake of Heysel (mentioned in the following chapter) English clubs, including Norwich, were banned from European competition.

18

A FALSE MESSIAH

1985-86 to 1986-87

Tom Cowie's response was immediate. The contract he had taken so long to finalise with Ashurst was ripped up and appropriate compensation amicably agreed. Sunderland's quest for the Holy Grail was over. After years of rejection, their craving for a big managerial appointment was sated. Gateshead born Lawrie McMenemy, at 48, was at the peak of his career. The imposing grammar school-educated, former Coldstream Guard had cut his managerial teeth in the lower divisions attaining promotions with Doncaster and Grimsby. His biggest achievement was winning the FA Cup with Second Division Southampton before transforming them into one of the leading clubs in the country. McMenemy acknowledged the former Sunderland manager Alan Brown as his mentor. Brown had contacted him to offer a coaching job at Sheffield Wednesday. His authoritative and engaging television personality made him popular with football fans and housewives alike. At Southampton McMenemy attracted a host of top-class players at the end of their careers. Respected more as a great man-manager and motivator than for his coaching acumen, he utilised the knowledge of his players on the field and entrusted them to behave responsibly off it. His approach worked. At Roker however there was no former World Cup winner Alan Ball to direct and influence operations on the field; there was no former England captain Kevin Keegan to energise and set an example to younger team-mates. In contrast to the tranquil Dell there would however be pressure to get results from day one.

Before global multi-billionaire investors transformed the Premier League into their personal plaything, money has always talked loudly. Cowie, in order to prise McMenemy away from his comfort zone, agreed a king's ransom of almost £4,000 per week wages. At that time no manager or player in the English game was on anything like that, let alone someone employed outside the top division. Billy McNeill for example, was managing First Division Manchester City on a salary slightly more than £25,000 per annum; a season later he moved to Aston Villa for £35,000. Lew Chatterley, the coach who accompanied McMenemy, was rumoured to be on a better package than the departed Ashurst. The new man was greeted as a messiah when he drove into Roker Park on 11 July '85. Cowie hung his hat and future on McMenemy.

For all the bravado there were heavy dark clouds. The national game was halfway through a year now looked back upon as an annus horribilis. At the end of Ashurst's regime when Sunderland bade a timid goodbye to the First Division, a tragedy unfolded at the home of Bradford City when a fire ripped through the main stand killing 56 spectators. At the Liverpool versus Juventus European Cup final at the Heysel Stadium Belgium, 39 Italians died as a consequence of hooliganism, inadequate segregation and crumbling terracing. Football was out of fashion. It was in danger of disappearing from the consciousness of the nation when the Football League was unable to agree a joint deal with the BBC and ITV for broadcasting rights. From August '85 to the end of the year no televised football, either live or highlights, was broadcast. Frank McAvennie, a West Ham signing from St. Mirren, was leading scorer in the opening months yet remained unrecognisable to the general public until he appeared on the prime-time BBC 'The Wogan Show'. Attendances dropped to a new post-war low with champions Liverpool, the second best supported club in the country, averaging a modest 35,271.

McMenemy aimed to replicate the system he used at Southampton. The principle may have been the same but some of the goods were of inferior quality and perhaps purchased in haste. The first two signings, Eric Gates and Frank Gray, costing £250,000 and £100,000 respectively, although both in the twilight of their careers, were nevertheless of unquestionable ability and bore the stamp of the manager's modus operandi. Cowie may have previously hesitated at spending on older players without a reasonable chance of any sell-on residual value but this was a brave new world with his dream appointment in place. Gates, a creative forward player, was a regular in a very good Ipswich team; Gray, a left-sided defender, possessed a wealth of experience from Leeds and Nottingham Forest. They were fully capped for England and Scotland respectively. Gates initially had talks with Newcastle boss Jack Charlton at Scotch Corner, a clandestine North Yorkshire rendezvous before the time third parties became involved in transfer talks, but Charlton, as ever notoriously frugal, was unwilling to meet his demands. McMenemy, realising Gates' availability, then intervened offering a basic wage of £600 per week. Although that was the going rate for a player of his pedigree, the extra carrot of an additional £11,000 each year as a loyalty payment tempted him to drop a division. Gray and Gates proved worthy acquisitions; few others met expectations.

With four debutants opening the 1985-86 campaign, Sunderland were well beaten at Roker by Blackburn. Despite unbridled optimism on a sunny day, the attendance of 21,202, although comparing favourably with most games that afternoon, was an indication of the low esteem in which football was now held. The first five games were lost without a single goal. A win finally came at Shrewsbury in the eighth game. More money was spent, again on older players. Alan Kennedy, 31 years old, had played in Liverpool's first eight fixtures and arrived at Roker in a £100,000 deal. Newcastle again were unable to compete when Kennedy refused the opportunity of returning to his former club. His disappointing performances under McMenemy might have suggested why Liverpool offloaded him. As later disclosed in the Evening Chronicle, he received a generous £25,000 signing-on fee.

In the same week George Burley, with over 500 games for Ipswich in his legs, joined Kennedy in a full back pairing. The team sheet was evolving quickly. No less than four goalkeepers had swapped the green jersey by March. Sunderland benefitted from a dead cat bounce with a move from the bottom three to mid-table before it slowly dawned that McMenemy had left his magic wand behind on the south coast. Two wins in seventeen games left the club scrambling for safety as the humble manager waved his white handkerchief after a last-game victory over Stoke that left them four points above relegated Carlisle. This match marked the end for Barry Venison and Shaun Elliott in a red and white shirt; Nick Pickering had already departed amongst a revolving door of coming and goings. It seemed that those leaving had more to offer than the older players who remained. Gates, although only scoring nine goals, was the leading scorer and had a habit of finding the net in tight games when it mattered.

The FA Cup almost brought a smile. Roker was packed with 35,484 when Manchester United arrived for a fourth round confrontation. It was the last occasion in history that some fans were locked out of a game on Wearside. Howard Gayle missed an absolute sitter near the final whistle that would have won the tie at the first attempt. Barry Davies opened his MOTD commentary by stating that, 'For the most passionate and arguably the longest-suffering supporters in the land, today is a day when there is hope of jam for tea'. There was stale bread at Old Trafford.

The bold appointment by Tom Cowie was going awry on all levels. He expected the increased turnstile revenue to cover the large increase in outgoings. For a side with only 13 victories, the best average attendance in the division by a long chalk would ordinarily be considered healthy. Yet with Eric Gates not the only player on wages beyond the affordability of most clubs in the First Division and an average attendance of 16,052, some 2,295 less than the relegation season, it did not require an accountant to deduce that the break-even figure was nowhere near being met. A loss of almost £600,000 was reported. The money accumulated throughout Ashurst's League Cup run had been frittered away. Tom Cowie gave McMenemy the extra role of Managing Director. This only served to embroil the manager within the internal politics of a divided boardroom, to the detriment of day-to-day team affairs. There was constant tension between the Financial Director Barry Batey and Cowie. Batey made it plain from day one he was not in agreement with either McMenemy's methods or his salary and vehemently voiced disapproval when Cowie gave him shares in the club to go with the position of Managing Director. A personality clash between Batey and Cowie developed into open hostility; whilst the Sunderland chairman did not exactly represent 'old money' he identified in his adversary something of the arriviste. Within months of McMenemy's appointment Batey was stripped of his finance position. Cowie, with the express intention of voting his nemesis off the board, wanted to go further and schedule an extraordinary general meeting for April. He was unable to do so as Batey had acted quickly, having succeeded in safeguarding his position on 21st March with a High Court injunction. Cowie's enthusiasm for running Sunderland was weakening. In the April meeting he offered to sell his shares provided Batey did the same. It elicited the comment from Batey of, 'Mr. Cowie is taking the soul out of the club. There is no heart left in the place'.

As Cowie presided over a disintegrating club, both on and off the field, never would the idiom from an ancient Greek storyteller 'Beware of what you wish for' be so apposite for Cowie. With Sunderland plunging into debt, McMenemy was forced to swallow his principles and abandon a policy of signing quality players slightly past their best. He had always believed that in the lower divisions 'you are 90% a coach and 10% a manager, because you don't have the players'. The top players he reasoned, were the opposite and needed managing not coaching as they 'had been around the world and played international football'. He bought Steve Hetzke from Blackpool, a 30-year-old centre half who had never performed beyond the third tier. At the end of McMenemy's first season Tony Ford, with over 300 games for Grimsby to his name, commenced a short loan spell. Increasingly, McMenemy relied on his acknowledged coaching limitations.

On 11 August '86, less than a fortnight before the start of McMenemy's second year in charge, it was announced in a completely unexpected development that Bob Murray had taken over as chairman from Tom Cowie, having acquired almost enough shares for a controlling interest in the club. The episode opened a window on a football club riven with revolt. A meeting had been convened earlier to enable Cowie to take control of Sunderland by purchasing the shares of Barry Batey for a figure of £350,000. There was disagreement over a minor detail. Batey asked for £3,000 that Cowie presumed was for the legal expenses of the transaction and therefore of no concern to him. Both parties had it seemed, on a point of principle, decided they were unable to go ahead. Cowie seized the impasse as an opportunity to significantly reduce his involvement with the club. Without seeking a profit, he transferred all his shares to Murray whilst at the same time stepping down as chairman. His main motive however was to ensure Murray's shareholding increased as close as possible to the key figure of 50%, which once attained ensured he could not be outvoted on an ordinary resolution. Cowie claimed that the swing in boardroom power had reduced the worth of Batey's unchanged holding to around £50,000. Batey of course shed a different interpretation on the insignificant cash amount that scuppered the deal. He claimed it was money owing to him from the High Court injunction and by asking for it he had prompted Cowie to pull out of the agreement to buy his shares and also influenced his decision to resign as chairman. Batey said, 'I think I have done the football club and the town a huge favour. He was offered the bait and he fell for it, hook, line and sinker'. Murray, delighted at becoming the central figure and rising above the internal politics, commented, 'All in all, it's a tremendous challenge but I have to say I'm looking forward to it. I was born and brought up in the Consett area and my dad first took me along to a game when I was nine years old. I stood on a wooden box in the clock stand and have been smitten ever since'. Murray, featured in the Sunday Times Rich List through wealth accruing from his Spring Ram kitchen manufacturing enterprise, was worth an estimated £30 million. He had only been a board member for two years, during which time he had built a minority shareholding commencing with the 250 shares transferred to him by Cowie.

By 25th October Sunderland had climbed to fifth position after two goals from Gray and David Buchanan defeated Birmingham. There had however, been an embarrassing two-legged League Cup knockout from Third Division York swiftly followed by a 6-1 collapse at Blackburn. Buchanan, plucked from Northern League Blyth Spartans, represented a desperate throw of the dice. He initially thrived, netting eight goals in his first fourteen league and Cup games but soon wilted. Terry Curran was a gifted, unpredictable forward who befitting his explosive temperament never stayed anywhere long enough to make an impact. He played with some success under McMenemy at Southampton before falling out with the big man who he later said, 'could not run a fish and chip shop'. Curran was shocked when McMenemy offered him a one-year contract at Roker. The reunion was short-lived. Curran, his father terminally ill with cancer, was allowed compassionate leave only to be unconditionally ordered back within a fortnight to appear in a reserve game in order to regain fitness. Curran, his mind elsewhere, stuck two fingers up in anger at those in the two hundred crowd that he deemed were harshly barracking a young team-mate.

Results soured and the club were braced for another relegation scrap. In February '87 Tom Cowie, disillusioned at the lack of progress in a proposed rights issue of shares, severed his long association with Sunderland when he resigned his position as director. Murray now bore the brunt of the intrigue and innuendo within the inner sanctum. The departing chairman said, 'Bob Murray is a good man and I wish him every success'. In time, the relationship fractured. Barry Batey, who had previously refused to sell his shares to Cowie, was a dyed-in-the-wool Sunderland fanatic and a former England schoolboy international. Most newspaper articles prefaced his name with the description 'property developer' or less flatteringly, 'property speculator'. This was well before an era when half of the general public appearing on Channel 4 property programmes were enthusiastically describing themselves in those terms. Batey was gaining in notoriety. It was alleged that his hardline stance was starving Sunderland of much needed internal investment. Despite not possessing anything like the financial clout of Murray he owned 25% of the shares, a proportion that entitled him to a significant degree of influence in determining club policy and therefore enabled him to block a special resolution that was essential for a rights issue. A rights issue impels all board members to buy extra shares in proportion to their current holdings; a failure to do so leaves any current holding at risk of dilution. Batey, by preventing a £1 million plus injection for the cash-strapped club, indicated he was either unwilling or not in a position to buy shares up to the value of those he held. The latter was probably the case. Batey's previous injunction had only won him a stay of execution. The club's Articles of Association stipulated that each year, through a process called 'retirement by rotation', the longest-serving director would have to request re-election. In the wake of his opposition to the share issue he was voted off the board. Batey was now on the outside of the tent, potentially posing a greater threat.

Early the following month Sunderland were lying fourteenth, preparing to play at Birmingham City. McMenemy's policy of buying established players was now dead in the water. He said he was aware at the season's start that no money was available for players and that the situation had not changed. He also commented, 'When I came here I inherited a team relegated from the First Division on Division One-related wages. It takes time to change things around, and also time for young players to come through'. The development of young players was not McMenemy's forte and not the prime reason why Cowie had wanted him. He expected an instant turnaround with oven-ready players. McMenemy's new arrivals of Gates, Gray, Kennedy and Burley, to name just four, were certainly receiving 'Division One-related wages' and if anything were paid appreciably more than those under the austere regimes of Ashurst and Durban. It seemed that McMenemy was not fulfilling his side of the bargain and after eighteen months, in response to growing pressure, he took a pay cut that reduced his annual salary to £125,000.

The Midlands trip was aborted due to heavy snowfall. Sunderland suffered their fourth consecutive defeat in the rearranged midweek fixture with only 5,563 dotted around the vast St. Andrews ground. A 2-0 lead at West Bromwich was then squandered before a visit from Sheffield United on 11th April proved the last straw for Lawrie McMenemy, no longer defended by a departed Cowie. In the wake of a 2-1 defeat watched by 8,544, the lowest Saturday afternoon attendance since 1933, McMenemy gathered his belongings and in the early hours fled south. Seven games remained when Bob Stokoe, already alerted by Murray of the impending change, returned on a short-term rescue mission. A miracle was not required from the authentic messiah as Sunderland were not in the bottom three but with one point from six games they were on a downward trajectory. Stokoe, who always looked older than his years, was now 56, and since the sad circumstance of his Wearside departure had anonymously shuffled around the lower leagues, accepting managerial jobs for a second time at former clubs Blackpool, Rochdale and Carlisle, before cramming in a third spell at Brunton Park. He was well suited to those unpretentious outposts; they fitted him like a well-worn glove. Roker was a different proposition. Notwithstanding an intense media spotlight and unrealistic expectations, Stokoe inherited a first eleven that had been continually chopped and changed. At Bradford City in his first match Sunderland lost to two late goals despite being 2-1 ahead through a Mark Proctor brace. They were now in the bottom three, albeit briefly. In his emotional homecoming on Easter Monday evening, a point was taken against Leeds who had Billy Bremner in the opposite dugout. Shrewsbury were then overcome at Gay Meadow as the club moved up to eighteenth. With three home matches remaining from the final four, safety was scented and over 16,000, the largest crowd since October, were present for the return fixture with Bradford City. Proctor again scored twice but the Yorkshiremen again prevailed 3-2. Undeterred, in their next match Sunderland grimly held on to a 12th minute lead against Crystal Palace.

A glut of midweek fixtures remained before the final Saturday. However, for some clubs there would be a final twist. It had been decided to reduce the number of clubs in the First Division from 22 to 20. Consequently, the Second Division would take up the slack by a compensatory increase from 22 to 24. The straightforward solution of relegating as many as four clubs and promoting only two was deemed unfair, therefore a convoluted, compromise play-off method was devised. Instead of the usual three up and three down, the team finishing fourth bottom in the First Division competed with the teams that finished third, fourth and fifth in the Second Division. Both the semi-final and final were contested on a two-legged basis. The winner would either retain top flight status or claim what, in a previous season, would ordinarily be the third promotion spot. This method reduced the number of First Division clubs by one each year. In the first season of transition, it created the anomaly of an odd number of teams in both divisions, therefore rendering Newcastle United and Reading as unemployed on the opening weekend of the 1987-88 season. The meddlesome Football League, in their wisdom, imposed play-offs throughout the four divisions therefore leaving the third bottom side in the Second Division the task of defeating two Third Division sides to ensure safety.

After 40 games Sunderland were fifth from bottom, holding a two-point advantage and better goal difference over Huddersfield and Shrewsbury. Sunderland, through Gordon Armstrong, took a point at Millwall to reach 48 points but were caught by Huddersfield and Shrewsbury who both won. With Brighton and Grimsby already doomed, it boiled down to Sunderland needing to beat Barnsley to secure safety, regardless of results elsewhere. Neither Shrewsbury nor Birmingham, who played each other, were safe. At Roker Keith Bertschin, another of McMenemy's imprudent forays into the transfer market, opened the scoring before Frank Gray added another. The 2-0 lead should have been unassailable against a team with nothing to play for but Barnsley reduced the arrears before half-time. A Mark Proctor penalty was then saved. The visitors anguished a 19,000 crowd by scoring twice to record a shock 3-2 victory. Huddersfield claimed safety with a third consecutive win. Shrewsbury defeated Birmingham 3-0 to climb above Sunderland whilst the Blues, sweating on events at Roker, were relieved to maintain their flimsy two-point advantage.

Gillingham were the opponents in the play-off semi-final. At Priestfield Stadium, Tony Cascarino completed a hat-trick inside half an hour after a Mark Proctor penalty had opened the scoring. A late Proctor effort reduced the arrears. The Sunderland goalkeeper Iain Hesford should have prevented at least one of the goals, especially a soft overhead kick from Cascarino. The second leg on Wearside was difficult to keep abreast of as Sunderland chased a 3-2 deficit. Gillingham struck first before Gates cancelled their aggregate advantage by scoring twice in quick succession. Mark Proctor yet again missed a penalty. Then Hesford faced a penalty. He palmed Greenall's kick but Cascarino, the scourge, forced the ball over the line in an ensuing melee. The unrelenting, miserable drizzle mirrored the resignation of most of the 25,470 present. They were ready to leave until Gary Bennett, thrown forward in desperation, headed an 88th minute goal to level the aggregate at 5-5. There was delirium as he stood motionless, arms aloft facing the Fulwell End. Extra time brought a mere stay of execution. Tony Cascarino, with his fifth goal of the tie, sucked the air out of Roker Park when he nudged Gillingham ahead overall and level in the game. There was deflation, a stunned silence and confusion as supporters grappled with the arithmetic of the 'away goals count double' rule. Two goals were required for victory. Again Sunderland responded. When Bertschin put them 4-3 up to level the scoring at 6-6, a quarter of an hour remained. More drama seemed likely. Instead, minutes slipped away and the game ended with the hollow consolation of a Pyrrhic victory. Their manager Keith Peacock rated the second leg as the 'most astonishing' game of his life. That was until much later in his career, when it was eclipsed by a particular Wembley play-off final when he was part of a Charlton Athletic coaching staff. Sunderland were no longer part of a select group of clubs who had never played below the top two divisions. The group comprised: Arsenal, Birmingham City, Chelsea, Everton, Leeds United, Leicester City, Liverpool, Manchester City, Manchester United, Newcastle United, Tottenham Hotspur, West Bromwich Albion and West Ham United.

19

UP, UP AND NOT AWAY

1987-88 to 1990-91

Bob Murray, finding his feet as chairman, threw himself into restoring Sunderland's fortunes at their lowest ever ebb. The Third Division club grappled with a combined debt and bank overdraft approaching one million pounds. In the summer of '87 he approached York City and took manager Denis Smith and his assistant Viv Busby from Bootham Crescent. Smith was one of the best uncapped defenders in the country in a long, distinguished career as a resolute centre half with Stoke. He has an entry in the Guinness Book of Records as a footballer who has sustained a record number of injuries. All told, by his own reckoning, he had endured at least 28 breaks or major operations and a cumulative 200-plus facial stitches. He won a League Cup winner's medal but lost twice to Arsenal in consecutive FA Cup semi-finals, only denied victory through the award of a last-minute penalty that earned the Gunners a replay after they trailed 2-0. His commitment to the cause at Roker was exemplified when he agreed terms with Murray. Sunderland were unwilling to pay York £20,000 compensation, so Smith managed to halve their demand to £10,000. Murray, aware of Sunderland's precarious financial position, wanted reassurances, so Smith offered to personally reimburse the compensation to Murray if he failed to win promotion at the first attempt. Barry Batey hovered menacingly in the background and often in the foreground of Murray's thoughts. In November '87 six 'rebel' shareholders including Batey were granted a High Court action on the basis that Cowie had acted illegally by transferring shares to Murray and McMenemy, without the knowledge and approval of board members. Four long years passed before the slow and expensive wheels of justice ran their course, long enough to ramp up the pressure on Murray.

John McPhail was 31 when Smith recruited him from Bristol City to play alongside Gary Bennett. McPhail had played for Smith at York. Also purchased was right back John Kay from Wimbledon who, likewise, would give excellent service to Sunderland. The capture of teenager Marco Gabbiadini from York towards the end of September was a brave call from Smith. Sunderland parted with almost £100,000 for a player who in his eight starts that season wearing the number nine shirt for the Minstermen only scored once. He had previously made over 50 league appearances and found the net 13 times. His debut in a disconcerting 2-0 home defeat by Chester did not augur well as Sunderland languished in twelfth position after nine games. Then Gabbiadini, benefitting from the wily Eric Gates, made an impact with two goals in each of his next three games to spark a run of six consecutive wins. He was a strong, confident forward whose quickness and bravery found scoring positions. Almost 20,000 turned up to witness a 4-1 victory over York. Southend were beaten 7-0 on a Tuesday night, a revitalised Gates scoring four. There was another hat-trick from him before New Year. Smith disclosed that two young prospects, Gary Owers and Richard Ord, had signed contracts tying them to the club for three years. Ord had made his first team debut against Southend. Sunderland turned the Third Division into a procession. With 30,000 packed into Roker Park, Northampton were beaten 3-1 and the championship trophy paraded. Included within the tally of 92 goals, Gabbiadini scored 21 goals in his 35 games, Gates 19 goals in 42 games and McPhail, a revelation in the opposition box, 16 goals including 10 penalties. 93 points provided a nine-point cushion from second placed Brighton. Not since 1936 had Sunderland scored as many in a season. Away supporters enjoyed the novelty of quaint, characterful, and ramshackle grounds. They particularly cherished Springfield Park in Wigan, unaltered since Northern Premier League days. An eventful afternoon was spent taking turns to slide down an increasingly muddy grass bank. Roker Park support was impressive. An average of 17,424 was only bettered by Aston Villa in the Second Division and ranked fifteenth in the country.

Many supporters were unhappy at the reluctance to splash out in the transfer market, attributing Murray's accountancy background as the explanation for his prudence. For Murray, promotion was tempered by the increasing cost of maintaining a dated stadium, his inability to advance the rights issue and the potential liabilities of the High Court action. Denis Smith's first taste of managing in the Second Division was without any addition to the players who romped away with the Third Division. Early results were moderate; Murray sanctioned the signing of Billy Whitehurst, a bustling old-fashioned forward of the type that tyrannised defenders. Sunderland were sixth in January but subsided to mid-table. Uniquely in post-war times, two consecutive home crowds numbered less than 10,000. In an unsettled forward line Gabbiadini, a firm favourite, scored a goal every other game despite disadvantaged by Gates no longer being first choice. The club transfer record was breached when Welsh goalkeeper Tony Norman signed from Hull in a £400,000 deal that involved Iain Hesford and Whitehurst as part-exchange; for the next three and a half seasons the reliable Norman and understudy Tim Carter were familiar figures. Sunderland's 63 points from 46 matches comprised 16 wins and 15 defeats.

Two excellent signings made a difference the following season. In readiness for 1989-90, Paul Hardyman, an accomplished left back arrived from Portsmouth. Paul Bracewell, previously a Durban signing back in '83, returned to Roker on loan from Everton. He made a second debut for Sunderland in an early-season victory over Middlesbrough. In the next home game, Gabbiadini managed a hat-trick against Watford. Bracewell, controversially sold by Len Ashurst in his first spell at Roker, had proved a success in Everton's midfield and when Smith offered £250,000, persuading him to sign a permanent deal on the 28th September, it was a major coup. It was also a calculated gamble by Smith. Still only 27, Bracewell's career was blighted by an ankle injury that it took specialists eighteen months to diagnose and cure and had prevented him adding to his three England caps. When he failed a medical the Sunderland manager was undeterred. A decent crowd of 24,075 saw Gabbiadini secure the points against Oxford on Boxing Day before a trip to Reading brought another dispiriting third round FA Cup exit. Progress however was made in the League Cup and 18,000 witnessed a 5-2 replay victory over Exeter. A home quarter-final tie with First Division Coventry was the reward; except for the Tyne-Wear derby, the gate of 27,218 was the largest of the season. A goalless draw was enlivened by a flashpoint between Gary Bennett and David Speedie, Coventry's combustible Scottish striker. There had been bad blood between them in past encounters. On this occasion, Speedie deliberately aimed a kick at Bennett's leg and the Sunderland defender grabbed him by the throat shoving him into the Clock Stand paddock where he landed, crumpling advertisement boards. Both received marching orders. The replay at Highfield Road, lost by five clear goals, coincided with a poor run of results as Sunderland slipped from third to tenth. A home defeat by Leeds that meant only two out of twelve league outings had been won, prompted the Football Echo to call play-off chances a forlorn hope. Leeds and Sheffield United were clear at the top with Newcastle who were lying third benefitting from the division's runaway leading scorer Micky Quinn.

The arrival on the scene of young, talented Glaswegian Kieron Brady proved a game changer. He was the architect of a thrilling 4-3 victory over West Ham, scoring one and making two. The following Saturday he struck the only goal at Bradford City when he weaved past two defenders before finishing sublimely. Smith commented, 'Of course young Kieron's goal at

Bradford was right out of the top drawer, and there is no doubt he has added an extra dimension to our play'. Sunderland's late surge booked a play-off match against Newcastle who, despite Micky Quinn being handicapped with a hamstring strain, were clear favourites to reach Wembley when they escaped from Roker Park with a draw, courtesy of a last-minute penalty save by John Burridge from Paul Hardyman. The Sunderland defender was then sent off when he followed up with a reckless challenge on Burridge. Five United players were booked in a feisty game. An incident at the end of the second leg overshadowed that. At St. James' shortly after Mark McGhee hit a post, Eric Gates opened the scoring and towards the end, a second goal from Gabbiadini triggered a pitch invasion in an attempt to get the game cancelled. Fortunately over 500 police were present and those on duty within the ground quickly intervened. The referee George Courtney, determined to overcome mob rule and ensure completion of the game, detained the teams in the dressing room for twenty minutes until order was restored. The 2-0 victory booked a final against Swindon, managed by Ossie Ardiles. It was another Wembley disappointment. In the first half Gabbiadini, racing the goalkeeper for a loose ball, sustained a twisted ankle and with his sharpness blunted Sunderland failed to make an impression. Swindon enjoyed better possession, created a host of chances and the inevitable goal, scored by Alan McLoughlin, did not reflect their dominance. Hanging over Swindon was a Football League inquiry into illegal payments that was only concluded a week after Wembley. The guilty verdict voided their win over Sunderland and sparked a fierce debate over the vacant promotion berth. Newcastle, who finished third in the Second Division, and newly relegated Sheffield Wednesday both pressed strong claims. Ron Atkinson at Wednesday expected an occurrence from the Third Division in 1968 to take precedence when relegated Mansfield earned a reprieve at the expense of Peterborough, demoted after making illegal payments. A decision to promote Sunderland was made on the basis that the play-offs were sacrosanct once the normal league season was over. It is understood that the Northeast clubs received two votes each before the Football League president Bill Fox cast his deciding vote. Wearside rejoiced and considered the outcome partial recompense for the dark events at Highfield Road in 1977.

Bob Murray imposed a strict budget of £500,000, despite protests from Smith that this was inadequate for a club entering the First Division. Half was spent on Peter Davenport at Middlesbrough, a forward Manchester United had expensively signed from Nottingham Forest, but who failed at Old Trafford to replicate his form with Brian Clough. Attempting to recycle and rejuvenate a player is a gamble but Smith had little option. The pedigree of Kevin Ball, the other signing, was beyond doubt. He had relished his defensive role for Portsmouth, a team universally recognised as being able to handle themselves and get their retaliation in first when the going was tough. Ball, comfortable at centre half or as a midfield destroyer, made over 350 appearances for Sunderland before becoming a valuable member of the management team. To many supporters he is a living legend. A decision was made to release Eric Gates based on his age and being the club's highest-paid player. With the squad short of experience this was a judgement call. John McPhail, who had formed an effective pairing with Bennett, appeared alongside the centre half for the first game at Norwich but was then offloaded to Fourth Division Hartlepool, who he then steered to promotion as player-coach.

Two players in and two players out left a frugal Murray open to criticism. Later in the season he released further funds but Sunderland no longer possessed the appeal of a newly promoted club and furthermore, it was a seller's market with clubs unwilling to release anyone of worth. Smith was compromised. He hastily paid Preston £225,000 for an overpriced Brian Mooney, who only featured in four games before being released on a free transfer, never to appear again in English football.

When August arrived, the first three games suggested that the windfall arising from Swindon's misdemeanours should not be feared. At Carrow Road, in their opening fixture, Sunderland fought back from a two-goal deficit before a third Norwich goal proved decisive. Tottenham were held to a goalless draw at Roker Park before a capacity 30,000 crowd eager to see the talented Paul Gascoigne, who was fresh from England duty in the World Cup where he made front and back-page news. The following Saturday, a late Gary Bennett goal dramatically earned three points against Manchester United.

Frustratingly, there were too many occasions when Sunderland's impressive travelling support witnessed their team throw away a lead with careless abandon as if it were confetti. The Robert Louis Stevenson phrase, 'to travel hopefully is a better thing than to arrive' came to mind. Instead of having enough points in the bag by Easter, Sunderland were unable to avoid a last-day dénouement at Maine Road. In September, a late penalty from Dennis Wise at Chelsea denied Sunderland a point after Kieron Brady had equalised. Three drawn games stand out, in which strong positions were squandered. The first of those was two weeks later at Plough Lane, when Wimbledon took a share of the points with two goals in the last quarter of an hour. Then, at Tottenham in December, after relinquishing a 2-0 lead, a Colin Pascoe goal seemed to guarantee an unlikely victory before Gary Lineker fashioned a 90th minute equaliser. In a festering festive period, six valuable points were frittered away, commencing with a Boxing Day defeat at Selhurst Park when David Rush put the visitors ahead, only for Crystal Palace to turn the tables with goals on 78 and 84 minutes. Three days later Sunderland led Queens Park Rangers 2-1 before conceding on 63 and 78 minutes. The third of those costly draws was at the Baseball Ground in March, against a Derby side propping up the division. Sunderland let slip a 3-0 scoreline, a capitulation that sucked them into a relegation position. A week later Sheffield United, who had only managed four points in their first sixteen fixtures, arrived on Wearside chasing a sixth consecutive victory, in the midst of a revival that would propel them to mid-table. Their manager Dave Bassett had previously piloted the infamous 'crazy gang' of Wimbledon from the Fourth to First Division and signed a number of their current and former players for Sheffield, including the self-styled hard man Vinnie Jones, who although a very good professional making the most of his ability, possessed a bark worse than his bite. A 55th minute error from Gary Bennett that allowed Ian Bryson to score separated the teams; the defender stated, 'I felt sick about the goal – the ball hit some mud and skidded past me'. That was their only effort on target. The spoiling tactics from the visitors continually annoyed the majority of a 23,238 crowd and as the referee lost control, John Gannon and Kevin Ball were sent off after a coming together. On the final whistle there was a serious flash point when the visitors' on-loan Glyn Hodges, having been substituted, suddenly emerged from the dugout to head-butt Gordon Armstong, an offence judged so serious that the FA deemed it worthy of a six-match ban. Denis Smith commented, 'I have never seen anything like this in all my time in the game. What Hodges did takes some believing'. On an afternoon such as this, it didn't require a huge leap of imagination to grasp that the 'sport' in its infancy throughout the medieval years was knowingly violent, and that some places in England introduced anti-riot laws to combat it. Ball, coincidentally, had also been dismissed the previous season for an offence involving Gannon, when playing for Portsmouth.

A siege mentality of conceding fewer home goals than all but three clubs in the division had enabled Sunderland to prolong their relegation fight to the bitter end. The first three Roker Park games of the New Year were won 1-0. Derby were already doomed before Sunderland eked out consecutive goalless draws in their final two home outings to find themselves locked on points and goal difference with Luton on the last day of the season. In order to stay up they had to better the Bedfordshire team's result and ensure that if both sides won, their winning margin was one goal better. Luton, in free fall, were fortunate to entertain Derby and were able to end their depressing sequence with a 2-0 victory. The Sunderland fans descending on Maine Road like a plague of locusts provided Manchester City with a gate of 39,914, their highest of the season and around 15,000 up on the four previous matches. The joy when Gabbiadini and Bennett put the visitors 2-1 up towards the end of the first half proved short-lived and premature. Before Sunderland reached the sanctuary of the dressing room Niall Quinn equalised. When City's David White secured the points with an injury time goal, Sunderland's relegation was already sealed. The Manchester Evening News obviously rated Quinn, scorer of two goals, the man of the match but the Irishman, in acknowledging the performance of his opponents, thought his young goalkeeper Martyn Margetson deserving of it. Peter Reid, manager of City, was unstinting in his praise for a Sunderland team that but for missed chances, should have triumphed: 'Sunderland made a great fight of it. I am disappointed for them and their great fans. But I am sure they will return. A club with their tradition and support do not deserve to be in the Second Division'.

20

THE NATIVES ARE RESTLESS

1991-92 to 1993-94

If only Tom Cowie had been patient with Alan Durban, Sunderland may not have suffered the turmoil of the Ashurst and McMenemy regimes. If only Bob Murray had allowed Denis Smith one more signing it may have been enough to preserve the advantage in the closing stages of a couple or more games and squeeze more mileage from Marco Gabbiadini and Peter Davenport's haul of nine and seven goals respectively. The ifs, buts and maybes that haunt the destiny of any football club can stretch beyond the horizon. At Sunderland, seven seasons containing two promotions and three relegations hinted at something other than those vagaries and chance factors. The sudden conclusion of a legal action sugar-coated the bitter pill of relegation in dramatic fashion. In London on 11 June '91, the rebel shareholders spectacularly failed in their High Court action, a Trojan horse for their hopes of taking control of the club. They withdrew their action on the second day of the hearing. The Journal quoted Murray, 'My family and friends have had privately four years of intense stress. At times I've worried about the safety of my family and friends'. Michael Crystal QC referred to the allegations as baseless. Crucially, Murray was allowed the opportunity to purchase 209 shares from one of the rebels Allan Martin, who by agreeing to sell avoided court costs. This relatively small transaction pushed Murray's shareholding to 53.6%. This was of immense significance as it was only a month later when Sunderland finally succeed in executing a rights issue. Following legal advice, the club secured their objective by virtue of an ordinary resolution that only required a 50% vote in favour, as opposed to the 75% pertaining to a special resolution. Brian McNally explained in the Journal that existing shareholders were able to purchase shares on a 'two for one' basis, in proportion to their holdings. He wrote, 'The anti-share issue vote represented about 25.3% and matched almost exactly the size of rebel shareholder Barry Batey's stake in the club'. Batey, deciding not to purchase the extra shares he was entitled to, allowed his proportion to reduce and he eventually sold out to Murray. The issue raised £2 million; Murray's grip on the club was now appreciably strengthened and his personal commitment in excess of £1 million. No sooner had this major impediment to the club's progress been removed, Sunderland were impelled to address the ramifications of a report from Lord Justice Taylor.

A report by Taylor had been published in January '90, which detailed an inquiry into the 1989 Hillsborough FA Cup semi-final disaster, when 95 Liverpool supporters and two in later years, lost their lives resulting from negligent overcrowding in a section of terracing. The prime recommendation of Taylor, to avoid the possibility of future tragedies, was for all major stadiums to be converted to all-seater. The accumulation of safety regulations deriving from Taylor were difficult and costly to implement. Having resolved the uncertainty over his influence in the boardroom, Murray now wrestled with the dilemma of refurbishing Roker Park or rebuilding from scratch on a greenfield site. The double-decker main stand and newer Clock Stand predated the war. A temporary solution before a decision was arrived at involved removing seats from the rear of those stands, widening gangways and constructing external stairways that allowed a safe exit to the paddock areas below. The numbers permitted on the terracing were gradually reduced. The Fulwell End capacity of 12,500 on the 1980 West Ham promotion night was downgraded to 7,216, a figure although meaning it was the largest remaining terrace in England, merely served to highlight the extent to which the club were lagging behind the prevailing all-seater trend. The Roker End, packed with over 20,000 in its heyday, had remained untouched since its drastic surgery of 1982. However, once Sunderland complied with Taylor's stringent measures, fewer than 4,000 were allowed to sample the delights of its lack of protection from a stiff North Sea breeze. During the 1973 Cup run the Clock Stand paddock alone held over 4,500. The final capacity of Roker Park settled at 22,000.

Denis Smith's hope of funds to mount a promotion push were dashed again. A large chunk of the £2 million rights issue was earmarked to repay a £750,000 bank loan and cover £650,000 spent on essential safety modifications at Roker Park. At least Smith was able to keep the players that came so close to staying up. Even that modest comfort unwound when, realising his side needed fresh impetus, he reluctantly parted with Marco Gabbiadini. After scoring a hat-trick at Charlton, a home defeat by Grimsby proved Gabbiadini's last game. Crystal Palace signed him in September; the fee of £1,800,000 dwarfed Roker's previous highest sale of £275,000. A third of the proceeds were spent on left back Anton Rogan from Celtic and forward

John Byrne from Brighton. Byrne scored twice on his home debut against Watford in a 3-1 win but with no discernible uplift in results, Smith gave Third Division West Bromwich Albion £900,000 for their leading striker Don Goodman, whose previous season's tally of 21 goals in 39 games had come in a relegated side. Gabbiadini's cut-price replacement, who was Cup-tied, managed 11 goals from 20 matches and his wholehearted approach made him a worthy successor. In the league campaign Sunderland were inconsistent throughout. The spectre of relegation hovered briefly in April but by then all and sundry were captivated by an enthralling FA Cup adventure.

Denis Smith had promoted reserve team manager Malcolm Crosby to be his assistant and ended a partnership with an aggrieved Viv Busby, who filed for wrongful dismissal. Between Christmas and New Year, on the back of consecutive defeats that left Sunderland in seventeenth position, Smith himself was shown the door by Murray. After two promotions and coming close to preserving top-flight status on a shoestring budget, many supporters and critics presumed his sacking unfair. Neil Warnock, impressive at Notts County after a lengthy non-league managerial apprenticeship, was the preferred candidate at a club counting the pennies. Before Murray acted events overtook him. Crosby's first game as caretaker manager was a 2-0 victory over Barnsley on 1 January '92. His second, against Port Vale, secured a comfortable passage into the fourth round of the FA Cup. A Don Goodman hat-trick helped take care of Millwall 6-2, followed at Derby by a third consecutive league victory before Sunderland claimed a place in the last sixteen by beating Oxford United at their tight little ground. Less than a month earlier at the very same venue, Denis Smith's side had capitulated 3-0 beside the dreaming spires. The self-effacing Crosby was thrust into the spotlight.

Against top-flight West Ham, on an afternoon marred by gale-force gusts, a John Byrne equaliser propelled Sunderland into the last-eight draw where they were provisionally paired with Chelsea. Getting past two First Division clubs, both of whom possessed home advantage, was a big ask for a team whose recent league form of two draws and two defeats represented a regression to the mean. On a memorable night at Upton Park, two early goals from Byrne were cancelled out by Martin Allen either side of the interval before David Rush, with twelve minutes remaining, ensured a shock 3-2 victory. The Chelsea quarter-final, played on a Monday night, was slipping away until Byrne's equaliser maintained his record of scoring in every round.

Not since 1973 had Roker Park been besieged with fans queuing for tickets on a Sunday morning. On the Wednesday evening as the Sky cameras rolled, Peter Osgood and Jim Montgomery, former players from the opposite teams, sat together in genial fashion whilst Steve Cram performed to perfection his role as a famous fan, probably because he genuinely was. Ian Porterfield, who in a different guise might have been asked to sit with Osgood and Cram, was in the away dugout as Chelsea manager. Peter Davenport put Sunderland one up early in the game and against the run of play was denied a second by Dave Beasant. The clock ticked slowly; the advantage was defended, sometimes desperately. Chelsea, unrelenting, came in waves. Paul Bracewell twice cleared off the line and Townsend headed against a post; the fear of a late equaliser hung heavy in the night sky. Norman the Sunderland goalkeeper made a reflex save from Dennis Wise to turn his header over the bar. With five minutes left, three-quarters of the ground were silenced when Wise burst into the penalty box and equalised. The momentum surely was Chelsea's. Not on this occasion, as time remained for Brian Atkinson to swing in a right-wing Roker End corner in front of the jubilant away fans. Gordon Armstrong's head connected and with no defender positioned on the post the ball flew into the net. Vinnie Jones, playing for Chelsea, wrote later, 'I had heard stories of the Roker Roar but, Jesus, only hearing is believing. What a bloody din they made'. The closing scenes were a fitting last hurrah for a ground on borrowed time.

At Hillsborough, Sunderland were marginally better than Norwich in a scrappy, fraught semi-final. John Byrne, again the talisman, headed in from three yards after a rare bout of accurate passing. For the likeable 37-year-old Crosby, a local lad from South Shields, the victory drew him comparison with Stokoe. This side were not however, of a certain vintage. Five defeats in a row bookended the game at Sheffield. Owers, Rush and Atkinson were never destined for stardom. There was less than overwhelming conviction that the club were on the threshold of a historic moment. Only five points separated them from relegated Plymouth Argyle. And yet, Sunderland may well have lifted the famous trophy a third time. Opponents Liverpool were in transition and only won nine of their first 30 league matches the following season. The final was nearly an unprecedented all-Second Division affair. In their semi-final replay at Villa Park, Liverpool scraped past Portsmouth 3-1 on penalties after narrowly surviving the first encounter at Highbury through an equaliser four minutes from the end of extra time. At Wembley, chances fell to Sunderland in the first half. Byrne with perhaps the best opportunity of the match failed to make clean contact with the goal at his mercy. Bracewell hammered in a shot from close range that deflected off a defender, zigzagging to safety. Liverpool imperceptibly took control; McManaman out on the right started to assert himself and shortly after the break delivered a perfect cross that Michael Thomas converted. With the silverware's destiny no longer in doubt, Ian Rush scored a second.

The newly formed Premier League, containing sought-after broadcasting rights, commenced in August '92. During a lucrative five-season contract with Rupert Murdoch's Sky, top-division clubs were eligible for a share of £304 million. Regardless of league position and number of matches screened, each club was guaranteed an equal share of half the windfall. The initial agreement made provision for 60 live matches and seemed huge. In one fell swoop, top-flight clubs derived most of their income from broadcasting rights and sponsorship, the latter turbocharged by increased exposure to the cameras. Gate receipts, traditionally the major source of income, were less important with each passing season. There was an increased urgency for Sunderland to claw themselves out of the second tier, now renamed the First Division.

Crosby's position was made permanent when Sunderland reached Wembley. In readiness for a first full season, he attracted the former Ipswich manager Bobby Ferguson as his chief coach. Ferguson, in turn, helped to persuade his former centre half Terry Butcher, now a free agent following a sacking from his player-manager role at Coventry the previous January, to join Sunderland. Butcher, a former England captain venerated as the head-bandaged, bloodstained warrior on national duty during a World Cup qualifier in Stockholm, had competed in three World Cup final tournaments. The signing of the 33-year-old was lauded a major coup, despite a knee injury that had excluded him from competitive football for six months after his release from Coventry. There was £650,000 splashed on Shaun Cunnington from Grimsby and £250,000 on John Colquhoun from Hearts. The trio made debuts in an opening day defeat at Swindon. Paul Bracewell, surprisingly without the offer of a new contract, departed for Kevin Keegan's Newcastle. John Byrne, the clever forward, but now suspected of not giving his all for the cause, was shipped out to Millwall with the campaign barely under way. Arguably, the playing squad was no stronger. Results were poor and fans were restless well in advance of a 6-0 Sunday afternoon rout at West Ham on 11th October. The attendance of just over 10,000 to watch the promotion-bound Hammers seems inconceivable now, as were similar crowd figures for the two previous games at Upton Park, which unlike Sunderland's visit were not broadcast live. Nowadays at their new Olympic Stadium home, West Ham possess over 50,000 season ticket holders. A week later Sunderland lost 2-1 before a capacity 28,098 in the Tyne-Wear derby. Keegan's team recorded their eleventh win out of eleven, courtesy of a Liam O'Brien free kick that he struck shortly after a Gordon Armstrong equaliser. Newcastle, anointed 'the entertainers' by the media, were bankrolled by John Hall's limitless ambition. To the south on Teesside, the plans of Middlesbrough owner Steve Gibson for a new stadium were well advanced and when realised, it would welcome world-class imports from Brazil and Italy. Drastic action was required to prevent a perfect storm scenario of Sunderland being squeezed in the middle.

The game was undergoing huge changes. Hooliganism was retreating. For so long a sporting pariah, there was a groundswell of goodwill towards football after the nation had been captivated by Italia '90, through the tears of the no-longer-clowning Paul Gascoigne and the heartbreaking penalty shootout England suffered in the semi-final. Because of growing commercialisation within the game and a rebranding of spectators as consumers, it was apparent that the whole match day experience was changing and that, in order to entice a new breed of supporter, stadium facilities would have to be radically improved. Slowly, a realisation dawned that Roker Park might not be for ever. There were now too many truths to turn a deaf ear. The debate was shifting from rebuilding the Roker End to knocking down the whole edifice. It was a start.

One of football's enduring myths is that when it comes to a derby match, form goes out of the window. This does not seem to be the case. Taking results from the Tyne-Wear games as an example, it seems there is evidence to suggest that the opposite is true and that the better team nearly always prevails. From 1953-54 to 2011-12 there were 29 seasons when Sunderland and Newcastle shared the same division. On only five occasions has the lowest finishing side in the final table taken most of the available points from their meetings. Sunderland failed to register a single victory in their previous five relegation seasons that have included derbies. That lengthy period also, strangely, reveals a lack of home bias. Sunderland's recent streak of six wins in a row is hardly anomalous; neither club had distinguished themselves in the league over that period. It may be that psychological factors have some bearing on explaining this. In the days before a derby, both teams are subject to an intense scrutiny and the profile of the game is higher. Perhaps a team that would ordinarily underestimate weaker opposition and therefore produce a sub-standard performance are less likely to do so when local bragging rights are at stake. In addition, as both are effectively performing in a location where their support overlaps, home advantage may not be as important.

After yet another home defeat in January '93, the fifth in thirteen matches, the long shadow of Butcher eclipsed Crosby. He was appointed player-manager at a salary of £70,000. The veteran Mick Harford joined for the closing months but form did not improve and after a run of two points from the twenty-one available, the club seemed destined for another taste of third-tier football. On the penultimate Saturday they faced Portsmouth at Roker, to be followed by two remaining away games. Portsmouth had climbed to the top of the table by winning 11 games out of 12 with the other drawn. Sunderland earned a stunning 4-1 victory assisted by two finely placed Goodman penalties. The first, after 35 minutes, resulted from the visitors being reduced to ten men when Guy Butters was dismissed for handling a goal-bound Armstrong shot. There was more misfortune for the massed ranks of the 6,000 who made the long journey from Hampshire as they witnessed a second sending off, courtesy of Paul Walsh, who elbowed Martin Gray in the face. Sunderland then lost at Tranmere. At Meadow Lane Butcher hauled his tired legs into the last game knowing that even if his team lost they would stay up provided Brentford and Cambridge succumbed at difficult away venues. At half-time Sunderland were three down at Notts County but other results were favourable and remained so. Portsmouth rued that awful afternoon at Roker. Despite a winning finale they finished third on goal difference behind West Ham, failing to advance in the subsequent play-offs.

Reluctantly and unavoidably, a heart-wrenching decision was arrived at to leave Roker Park. The tight warren of terraced streets that gave the ground's location so much character over the years, that pulsed with the seething masses agog for Buchan, Halliday, Carter, Shackleton, Hurley, Baxter et al, was now culpable in signing its death warrant. There was no room for expansion. Sunderland raised their sights. The ambition to develop a 287-acre site in Washington, lying west of the large Japanese Nissan car manufacturing plant, crystallised into consultations and architectural designs. A 40,000 all-seater stadium comprising four separate stands would sit alongside a smaller arena, surrounded by a multiplex cinema and retail outlets. The lavish scheme was costed at a prohibitive and perhaps optimistic £76 million, given the likelihood of an expenditure overrun in a capital project of this ilk. Unless large-scale private investment was attracted, some of whose motives may necessarily not have chimed with the football club, Murray required a novel approach to realise his dream. He mulled over the tantalising, although risky, possibility of a public share offering. In 1983 Tottenham Hotspur had become the first sports team in the United Kingdom to become a public company when they listed on the London Stock Exchange. It was not until 1991 that football was tempted again. Manchester United's share issue to the general public was met without enthusiasm; half the shares were unsubscribed.

After he walked away from Sunderland, Tom Cowie constantly sniped at the board's lack of investment in the team. Newspaper speculation of him returning, either to take complete or partial control, lingered. Murray considered disposing of his majority shareholding and Cowie, sensing an opportunity, had a tentative offer of £500,000 dismissed as derisory by the Sunderland chairman. A war of words between them reached its apogee in June '93 when the Sunderland Echo revealed Cowie's intention to buy the entire club. The two parties were poles apart in their valuations. Allegation and counter-allegation followed; nothing concrete happened. Cowie was scathing of the Washington move, stating that the prime objective was that of a property development and not the progression of the team. He likened it to, 'building a £120 million stable in which to place a dead horse'. Murray retaliated by claiming Cowie's intentions were never serious, 'The board finds Sir Tom's actions inexplicable and can only assume he was trying to achieve favourable publicity through them'.

Sunderland were in dire need of strengthening. Murray, perhaps stung by the criticism, gave the manager a sizeable kitty. At a cost of around £2 million, four players were signed in what became known as Butcher's summer of reconstruction. Derek Ferguson, who played with Butcher at Rangers, was signed from Heart of Midlothian. In addition to Phil Gray and Ian Rodgerson a large amount was spent on centre half Andy Melville from Oxford. An unexpected incident dashed prospects for the 1993-94 season. Following a friendly game at Middlesbrough, Ferguson was driving away from Roker Park when he hit a car on a roundabout. His three passengers, the aforementioned signings, were all hospitalised. Butcher pressed a patched-up Ferguson and Melville into action for the opening fixture at Derby, lost 5-0. Although Charlton were beaten 4-0 in the next game the tone was set for another inauspicious season as the club drifted without purpose. Against expectations there were home and away leg League Cup victories over Leeds that then gave Sunderland a fourth round Aston Villa tie. The First Division opposition attracted 23,692, an attendance that Roker Park never again surpassed, given the increasing restrictions on capacity. Ron Atkinson, the visiting manager, readily admitted after the game that without a world-class display from his goalkeeper Mark Bosnich, 'Sunderland would have murdered us'. Villa in fact triumphed 4-1. Atkinson was impressed by teenager Martin Smith, a precocious but unpredictable talent, who made his first team debut a week previously. An immediate, unconditional offer from Atkinson of a million pounds was briskly rejected. After Smith later won an England under-21 cap, his career ebbed and in similar fashion to the talented Kevin Arnott before him, he dropped down the leagues.

When Sunderland lost a home match in November against Southend to record a fifth consecutive league defeat the mood turned ugly; Butcher's expensive recruits were not proving value for money. An angry mob outside the Roker Park boardroom was dispersed by mounted police. Bob Murray, anointed public enemy number one now that Cowie had faded from prominence, responded. He sacked the beleaguered Butcher and his number two Ian Atkins; the parting was acrimonious. News broke on 26 November '93, the eve of Nottingham Forest's match at Roker, and coincided with Bob Murray's announcement to stand down as chairman and intention to reduce his 68% shareholding. Although he intimated that his energy was better deployed in the quest for a new stadium, privately he felt that the toll taken on his well-being by the terrace unrest and boardroom turmoil was becoming too much to bear.

John Featherstone, whose 12% stake made him the second largest shareholder, deliberated for a fortnight before almost reluctantly agreeing to become the new chairman. Butcher claimed his working relationship with Murray had been strained for some time but did not use this as an excuse. He acknowledged his time at Sunderland as a failure, adding that this was a second management failure, following his only other job at Coventry. The players he left behind were not sad to see the back of him; one reportedly punched the air in joy. After the Southend game he had committed the cardinal sin of criticising them in public. Dave Bassett and Steve Coppell were considered for the managerial position before Butcher. Both at the very least would have made a better fist of spending the funds Murray had made available. Years later, in an autobiography written with Bob Harris, Butcher provided a clue to why a team that should have been in the top half was struggling. Within days of Sunderland avoiding relegation the previous season, he advised six players including Owers and Armstrong to look for another club. None were able to quickly move on. When circumstances forced Butcher to select those players, it created tension with both them and their displaced team-mates.

Mick Buxton, the chief coach and brought up in Ryhope, was a supporter of Sunderland and was as surprised as anyone to be given charge of the side until the end of the season. If anything, this pound shop appointment stemmed from the precarious financial position the club were in, a combination of managerial upheavals, a ground with limited revenue potential, the wasteful summer outlay by Butcher and the uncertainty over the proposed relocation. For now however, Buxton had to get by on a shoestring. His background as player at Burnley and manager with Huddersfield and Scunthorpe suggested that he was able to do so. After Buxton's first match, a 3-2 defeat by Forest, more or less the same set of players took 37 points from 19 games. The evidence that Butcher had lost the dressing room was plain to see. Sunderland rose almost without notice to the lofty heights of mid-table obscurity, finishing with as many wins as losses. Buxton took the highly rated Polish born right back Darius Kubicki on loan from Aston Villa before securing a permanent move at the end of the season. Kubicki made 123 consecutive league and Cup appearances falling just short of George Mulhall's record of never missing a game from September '62 to April '65.

In March, Murray was encouraged by a decision from Sunderland City Council to grant the Nissan project outline planning permission. This was likely to have been the start of a long and tortuous process, inevitably encompassing a full public enquiry. The productivity of Nissan's car assembly lines was driven by a process called 'just-in-time manufacturing', whereby inventory levels were maintained at an absolute minimum to reduce the outlay on working capital. Despite concessions by Murray, at one stage reportedly offering the football club to the Japanese for £6 million, the manufacturing giant argued with some justification that the extra match day traffic would threaten the timely inflow of components to their production lines. The scheme reached an impasse. It was dead in the water when the enticing prospect of utilising the brownfield site of the exhausted Monkwearmouth Colliery, without any apparent objections, presented itself. Time was of the essence as Sunderland were fearful of the FA removing their permission to permit standing at Roker Park. The threat of a reduced capacity to 16,000, due to having to bolt benches onto terracing, galvanised action.

21

MURRAY'S VISION

1994-95 to 1996-97

At the start of the 1994-95 season Sunderland only lost twice in their opening fifteen fixtures but nine draws prevented a promotion push. At Roker, only one of the first ten league matches were won. There was then the damp squib on Wearside of a live BBC broadcast of the fourth round FA Cup tie with Tottenham, lost 4-1, as Sunderland played most of the second half without the sent-off Gary Bennett who handled a goal-bound shot. The uneasy ceasefire in hostilities from fans towards Murray for this one-off glamour tie was resumed with a vengeance the following week when Port Vale came to Roker. On the eve of the match, the directors released a contentious statement offering to resign en masse provided suitable investors came in to take the club forward. It was no coincidence that they went public 24 hours before an independent 'Sunderland Supporters Action For Change' group were ready to pounce at the Vale game. They managed to poll 8,247 fans within the 13,000 crowd and a staggering 98% declared a vote of no confidence in the owners. Before and after the game demonstrators screamed for a conspicuously absent Murray to sell up. On that February day of disquiet and disorder, the football team slipped into a relegation berth when they only managed a draw. Removed from the toxic atmosphere at Roker, solitary strikes by Craig Russell and Steve Agnew earned six points in four days at Watford and Southend respectively, only for a meagre 12,043 to witness the next home discomfort, a defeat by Tranmere on 5th March.

Buxton had reshuffled his playing squad to no effect. Don Goodman and Gary Owers, both dependable servants, moved to Wolves and Bristol City respectively, the latter deal earning Sunderland a decent fee plus the worthy acquisition of full back Martin Scott in part-exchange. In a last throw of the dice £600,000 was spent on the Everton striker Brett Angell, formerly of

Southend. Angell, a failure at Goodison only finding the net once in twenty games, was destined to become merely another name on a long list of ill-judged signings since Denis Smith's sacking. He was a characteristic panic buy to cheat the deadline cut off, ineffectively thrown in on a Friday night at Barnsley where Sunderland lost 2-0. Murray, no longer chairman but pulling the strings in the background, acted decisively. Realising the gravity of the situation, he made an appointment that was met with unanimous approval. Buxton was relieved of his duties and replaced by the former Manchester City manager Peter Reid, initially on a short-term basis with a bonus available provided he kept Sunderland in the division.

The garrulous, quick-witted, Huyton-born Reid was well known within the game. His credentials were first class. After showing character to overcome career-threatening knee problems and resolve in evaluating his own worth at Bolton during a contract dispute, he progressed to Everton under the astute Howard Kendall, where he won two league championships and 13 England caps. His self-deprecating humour, a trait of someone comfortable in their own skin, was evident on those occasions when he berated himself for allowing Maradona, the flawed Argentinian genius, who some might more accurately have described as a cheat on the field and drug taker off it, to ghost beyond him and score that wondrous goal in the famous 'Hand of God' Mexico '86 World Cup quarter-final. As a player manager and then manager at Maine Road, Reid guided City to two fifth placings followed by ninth, only to be abruptly sacked by Peter Swales after four games of the '93-94 season.

At Everton, Kendall encouraged and actively participated in a drinking culture in order to instigate team spirit. Reid, like no Sunderland manager before him, embraced his mentor's style of man management, not uncommon in the English game until Arsène Wenger's continental influence at Arsenal called time on last orders. Reid introduced himself to the Sunderland squad at a local restaurant and spared no expense with the wine. Murray's change of direction at this late stage of the season was a gamble but he called it right. Reid claimed his place in the dugout for the visit of Sheffield United. His infectious, fist pumping demeanour galvanised Sunderland to a 1-0 victory as young Craig Russell came from the bench to net a scrappy goal. Martin Smith scored in each of the last three matches to secure vital points; twelve points in Reid's seven matches guaranteed safety with something to spare.

Peter Reid negotiated a permanent two-year deal on a promise that £1 million was made available to strengthen the playing squad. Bobby Saxton was appointed chief coach. Saxton's down-to-earth, old-school manner disguised a sharp, bright football brain. Paul Bracewell, at 33 years old, was available on a free transfer after his sojourn with Keegan. Reid, familiar with Bracewell having occupied midfield with him at Goodison, was delighted to grant him a third career at Roker and entrust him with the additional responsibility of Assistant Manager.

The Sunderland board relented when Reid threatened to walk out on his freshly signed contract if £750,000 was not forthcoming to purchase David Kelly from Wolves. Reid had won an important victory and also drew a line in the sand; he was nobody's puppet. The board members, including John Fickling, a new director and second largest shareholder, turned out their pockets. They believed in Reid. They took the unprecedented step of awarding him a 5% stake in the club, valued at around £300,000. Reid possessed the unlearnt knack of being able to converse with everyone everywhere, from tea lady to chief executive, whilst if the occasion demanded, to upset the peace and then rebuild bridges. He was accustomed to giving players both barrels in the privacy of their dressing room. When his Manchester City team sheepishly returned at half-time after a pasting from Blackburn, an irate Reid opened his team talk by saying that in Shearer and Sutton Blackburn possessed the SAS, and then pointing to the City strikers, mocked them with the riposte 'and we have the SAS also: soft as shite'.

The beginning of 1995-96 brought five points from five games and threatened a fifth season of anonymity. The on-field influence of Bracewell ensured otherwise. The standard-bearer for Reid's instructions, acquainted with every blade of grass, he dictated and prompted play by dominating the ball with a series of short, quick passing movements. Such an environment was conducive to the development of youngsters. Richard Ord from Murton had matured into a fine versatile defender and other local lads Michael Gray and Craig Russell emerged. Gray a left-sided winger, was an ever-present in Reid's first full season, before converting to an effective attacking left back, a position from where he won three England caps. He appeared in over 400 games for Sunderland, a worthy achievement in the modern game when there are no restrictions in the freedom to move between clubs. Russell, who came through the youth team, competed for a place with expensive signings Angell, Phil Gray, Stewart and Kelly and eventually moved to Manchester City. On a December afternoon against Millwall, his four goals propelled Sunderland to the First Division summit; one week before arriving at Roker, Millwall had been in pole position. The Roker public were slowly stirring after the stagnation of recent seasons; the game attracted almost 19,000 but a severely limited capacity prevented them flocking back in large numbers.

When the Premier League became established in the nineties football fans lost their unconditional love for the FA Cup. However, when Sunderland were paired with Manchester United at Old Trafford there was a clamour for tickets. Despite an early Nicky Butt strike, Agnew and Russell put the Wearsiders ahead before Eric Cantona spared Alex Ferguson's blushes. The replay was sandwiched between two Sunday afternoon televised appointments that delivered an underwhelming defeat by Norwich, before 14,983 at Roker, and then a goalless draw at Leicester. Sunderland, stalling in the promotion race, were able to give United another fright. Michael Gray thrilled a 21,000 crowd before Paul Scholes equalised and as United took control, Andy Cole spared extra time with a 90th minute decider. Sunderland had showed their mettle to the Premier League champions-elect.

Shay Given, 19 years old, fresh from Blackburn on loan, had been responsible for the clean sheet at Leicester. The Irishman was a revelation; Sunderland simply stopped conceding goals. Given managed 12 clean sheets in his first 14 appearances until conceding two against Huddersfield. The visitors were unable to hold their 2-1 lead. Another teenaged talent Michael Bridges, from Whitley Bay, burst forward with two late goals to enhance his super-sub reputation as Sunderland chalked up a ninth consecutive victory. Bridges, his career plagued by injuries, would eventually be sold to Leeds for £5 million. The highlight of that run was an emphatic dismantling of leaders Derby when Craig Russell netted twice. The performance served as a fitting tribute to Alan Brown, who at the age of 81 had passed away in his retirement spot in the West Country that week; there was classical music rather than the traditional one-minute silence before kick-off. One point from the last three matches signified that the foot was off the pedal, but Sunderland were excused as they still finished a comfortable four points ahead of second placed Derby. The famous First Division Championship trophy, albeit no longer representing the ultimate achievement in English football, was held aloft at Roker Park for the first time since 1936. Under Reid the club only conceded 33 goals in the 46-match season; this was remarkable considering that Charlton Athletic were ranked next with 45 conceded.

The brave new world of the Premier League beckoned. A rapidly changing landscape half a mile from Roker Park in the direction of the city centre told of a bolder journey. On the site of the exhausted colliery, the groundwork for a 40,600-seat stadium would soon be completed to allow the emergence of a vast steel skeleton from a subterranean base. Bob Murray, after writing off £850,000 on the ill-fated Nissan venture, was determined to bring the new project in at a competitive cost. To keep a lid on outgoings, he micromanaged the purchase of everything from office furniture to the procurement of cement. The projected construction costs of the new stadium, variously reported as between £14 million and £20 million, although always likely to prove a bargain, threatened a legacy of potentially crippling debt. Sunderland, in order to minimise costs, cleverly employed the same contractors and design team responsible for Middlesbrough's Riverside Stadium. They had already received substantial assistance from a Development Corporation who covered the £2.5 million site preparation and infrastructure costs. Murray pledged a contribution in the region of £2 million and not much less than £1 million accrued from the sale of Roker Park to a housing company. Murray's strategic masterstroke, over and above the painstaking day-to-day number-crunching, was his momentous decision to launch Sunderland on the stock market. The announcement in November '96 of a Christmas Eve listing was perfectly timed, either accidental or deliberate. The square mile was infatuated by the sudden surge in the game's popularity and were unrealistically bullish of high returns within the sector. In becoming only the sixth club to go public since Manchester United in 1991, the club profited handsomely from the prevailing zeitgeist. The shares were initially priced at £5.85, valuing Sunderland at £47.7 million, but within days had climbed to £7.50 thereby increasing that valuation to £61 million. Reid's personal holding at this juncture was an astronomical £3 million. The directors, especially Murray who was now reinstalled as chairman, saw their wealth, albeit on paper, increase if not exponentially then certainly beyond any initial expectations. The major beneficiary was Sunderland plc. The share issue was a game changer. The remaining costs of guaranteeing completion of the stadium were met in full from public and institutional investors. Sunderland were debt-free. As the millennium approached, stock market sentiment altered. The football industry, where a fortune from burgeoning broadcasting rights could be frittered away on the whim of chancers and narcissists, or by inflated players' wages or even a single refereeing decision, would be acknowledged an unsuitable investment vehicle. Brian McNally must have felt vindicated. Writing for the Sunday Mirror, just before the flotation, he advised fans not to purchase the shares. Nine months hence, when the virgin stadium hosted its first league visitors, the price had already drifted below £3.40 and McNally, for his trouble, was an outcast. He was banned from the press room and reduced to covertly compiling a match report, surrounded by the hoi polloi. By July '04 with Sunderland's shares a depleted sixty pence, the club returned to private ownership.

The Stadium of Light was designed with easy provision for expansion. In the summer of 2000, at a cost of £7 million, 6,000 seats were added on a tier rising above the North Stand. A year later Newcastle increased their capacity by 16,000 at a cost of £42 million. Arsenal completed their bespoke, opulent, 60,000 capacity Emirates Stadium in 2006 initially with a budget of £170 million, which through unforeseen circumstances and enhanced specification, ballooned to £390 million. Sunderland and Middlesbrough were trailblazers in showing that large clubs were able to eschew tradition by leaving behind dilapidated, run down premises. The grander stadiums developed afterwards, for example the new White Hart Lane, were futuristic in design and boasted interiors resembling a luxury hotel. None would come anywhere close to the Stadium of Light if value for money was used as a criterion.

Peter Reid was allowed a substantial, although not over-generous, slice of the new money from the share issue that was expected to wash through Wearside. A club record fee of £1.3 million was paid for Manchester City forward Niall Quinn, who Reid managed at Maine Road. A million pounds prised Alex Rae, a tenacious but skilful midfield player from Millwall. During August '96 a three-game unbeaten opening included two goals from Quinn in a 4-1 victory at Nottingham Forest and a goalless draw at Anfield. Resources were then stretched. Quinn, a long-standing totem pole of the Irish Republic national side, was presumed to be in the veteran stage of his career. His signing was criticised after he snapped a cruciate and missed a huge chunk of the Premier League campaign. Rae, battling personal problems, was either out of favour or twelfth man. Quinn's belated return caught the end of a relegation scrap. Had the pair appeared in a majority of games there is little doubt that Premier League football would have distinguished the Stadium of Light's grand opening. Even without them, as January was left behind, Sunderland seemed secure in eleventh place. There had been another remarkable substitute cameo by Bridges when his two late goals defeated Everton at Goodison. A 3-0 victory over Chelsea had lit up a dank Sunday in December. An early FA Cup defeat by Arsenal was of little consequence; the overriding priority was consolidation.

Insidiously a threadbare squad was dragged into trouble. Leicester and Derby, the other newly promoted sides, were enjoying their ride without the worry of preventing what would be England's second largest club stadium from hosting second-rate fare. Despite goals from Michael Gray and John Mullin earning an unexpected home victory over Manchester United, Sunderland were in familiar territory. This was the only win in a twelve-match sequence. Chris Waddle, a 36-year-old former England forward, was persuaded to join for the remaining seven games of the season. At the same time Allan Johnston, a talented Scottish winger, arrived from the French club Rennes. A point earned at Champions League-bound Newcastle and a vital win at fellow strugglers Middlesbrough opened a route to safety. With three games remaining Sunderland were above Nottingham Forest, Middlesbrough and Southampton. The latter, two points adrift, were the last ever visitors to Roker Park for a competitive evening fixture; a draw to preserve the status quo would have been acceptable. Urged on by an emotional crowd who were witnessing the end of an era, Sunderland spurned a succession of corners and chances. Egil Østenstad's early goal had proved decisive.

With two fixtures left Sunderland, who were lying third from bottom a point below Southampton, West Ham and Coventry, faced Everton in their last ever league match at Roker Park. The all-ticket crowd numbered 22,108; the lowest crowd that season had been 18,642. Everton, after a lively opening marred by missed scoring opportunities, unravelled when Paul Stewart converted a soft penalty. In the second period Chris Waddle lashed in a free kick that was needlessly given away by goalkeeper Neville Southall, before Johnston safeguarded the game to ignite a prolonged farewell party. At the end cheers turned to tears as fans lingered, many of whom took a last nostalgic look at the aged stadium's corrugated iron roofing, concrete terracing, accumulation of clumsy modifications and distinctive main stand balcony, regrettably disfigured by advertisement hoardings.

Sunderland, two points ahead of Middlesbrough and Coventry, required a final day victory at Wimbledon's temporary Selhurst Park home to guarantee safety. Nottingham Forest were already down, a mere three years since their previous demotion when a florid, maudlin Brian Clough said his goodbye to football. Sunderland, rarely threatening to score in an unexpectedly low key game, were defeated by a Jason Euell goal five minutes from time. At White Hart Lane, Coventry and Tottenham kicked off 15 minutes late. Away fans were delayed in motorway tailbacks, caused by an accident. As Middlesbrough's fate had already been decided by their draw at Leeds, an agonising wait remained until the final whistle in North London. Coventry, aware that preserving a 2-1 lead would suffice, withstood late drama when their goalkeeper, Steve Ogrizovic, denied the Spurs substitute Neale Fenn, with a point-blank save from seven yards. Sunderland finished a mere three points short of thirteenth position. In an echo of 1977, albeit less controversially, Coventry had again escaped at Sunderland's expense.

Middlesbrough's relegation came only two years after their Riverside relocation. Plagued by injuries and illnesses in December, they decided not to fulfil a fixture at Blackburn and were penalised three points. Defeats were suffered in both major domestic cup finals, despite owner Steve Gibson's blank chequebook enabling Bryan Robson to sign the expensive and highly-paid foreign players Ravanelli, Juninho and Emerson. Peter Reid had not been permitted such luxury because of the financial straitjacket imposed by the ground relocation, but the climate was changing. His work at Roker Park was noticed; in addition to his shareholding windfall, a BBC fly-on-the-wall, warts-and-all documentary series titled 'Premier Passions' inestimably lifted his profile and that of the club. The darkest part of the night had passed. Despite relegation, Reid's future was assured. Fears that the new home would be a white elephant were banished. A healthy demand for season tickets vindicated Bob Murray's bold decision to leave Roker Park. Ajax were invited to christen the Stadium of Light and a competitive 'friendly' ended goalless before a capacity crowd of 40,000.

22

IS THIS REALLY HAPPENING?

1997-98 to 1998-99

Peter Reid's biggest summer outlay, as he planned a quick return to the riches of the Premier League, was controversial. A club record of £2.5 million was spent on former England schoolboys captain Lee Clark, a dyed-in-the-wool Geordie, who had only ever known senior football at Newcastle United. Clark, a creative and combative midfield player, had been prominent in a Keegan side pipped to the title by Manchester United. The arrival of Kevin Phillips barely registered.

Phillips was 21 years old when Watford took him from Baldock Town, where he had retreated after a rejection from Southampton. At the very modest part-time Beazer Homes League club, whose status dictated they were only eligible to join the FA Trophy at the qualifying stage and would have five rounds to negotiate before reaching the first round proper of the FA Cup, he started as a full back before being pushed into a forward role. From there, he scored 29 goals in season '93-94 before moving to Vicarage Road part way through the following season. His goals ratio in League football was initially impressive but he was dogged by injuries and in the '96-97 campaign when playing in the third tier, he only managed four in 16 matches. Although Phillips was under the radar of the bigger clubs, Ipswich offered £300,000 and agreed personal terms. Watford wanted another £50,000 and as the move fell through, Sunderland, with Alan Durban following his progress in a scouting role, stepped in with an accepted bid of £350,000 that was subject to future enhancements.

The opening day loss at Sheffield United did not deter anyone on 15 August '97 when Sunderland welcomed Manchester City for the first Stadium of Light league fixture. The start was delayed as almost 39,000 saw Quinn, alongside new boys Phillips and Clark, feature on the scoresheet in a 3-1 victory. The next two games were lost, the following three won. Form was patchy. After a terrible 4-0 defeat at Reading in October, speculation surfaced regarding Reid's position. In mitigation, Quinn was undergoing another spell out and the manager was searching for a settled eleven. The centre forward was on the brink of calling it a day. His knee had not mended and he intended to return a pension form to the Professional Footballers' Association to confirm his retirement. In a last desperate throw he endured another operation. The cruciate had in fact healed but the surgeon discovered a minor problem of two bones fused together. When Quinn's plaster was removed he was a new man, or as he disclosed in his autobiography, 'I started to run. Wow! I'm like a foal'. When he returned to first team action in the autumn, Sunderland were stirring. Reid had made changes. Andy Melville was replaced at centre half by summer signing Jody Craddock. Richard Ord was no longer a first choice. Young Darren Holloway appeared at right back. Allan Johnston, predominately right-footed, was granted a regular run on the left wing, aided in a supporting role by left back Michael Gray. This allowed for the arrival of right winger Nicky Summerbee from Manchester City in a straight swap with Craig Russell. His father Mike had won a First Division championship medal with City back in 1968. Sunderland were transformed. A resurrected Alex Rae claimed a regular place alongside Clark in the middle. Phillips benefitted from the aerial dominance and hold-up play of Quinn. Defences were unable to cope with Sunderland's two wide men. There was no better crosser of a ball than Summerbee and this, allied to his positional awareness, made him a valuable part of the forward line. Reid, never one to complicate a simple game, instructed him to find the head of the reborn Quinn; a chance operation had given the Irishman a heaven-sent opportunity to transform the Stadium of Light's steel, plastic and brick into a spiritual home, deserving of a great football club. Quinn later said, 'I learned my trade at Arsenal, I became a footballer at Manchester City but Sunderland got under my skin'.

After their humbling experience at Reading, Reid's newly shaped side did not lose in their next sixteen outings. Phillips was on his way to 29 league goals from his 42 appearances with Quinn, Clark and Johnston in double figures. Clark, who proved one of Reid's better signings, was the only ever-present outfield player and a 13-goal haul was his riposte to the nickname of 'Jigsaw' he brought from Tyneside, where it was unfairly said that he 'fell to pieces in the box'. His time and abrupt departure from the Stadium of Light lends perspective to the rivalry between Sunderland and Newcastle United. Despite his consistently good performances that won over a partisan crowd, Peter Reid reluctantly decided to sell Clark after he was photographed at Wembley in 1999 during Newcastle United's FA Cup Final against Manchester United, wearing a tee-shirt emblazoned with the slogan 'Sad Mackem Bastards'. A contrite Clark defused the situation, by claiming a friend had thrust it on him in a moment of light-hearted fun. However, more pertinent years later, was an admission in his autobiography, 'Black Or White, No Grey Areas', in which he claimed that joining Sunderland was the biggest mistake of his career and that when they were on the brink of joining Newcastle in the Premier League, he approached Reid to inform him that if selected to play against them the following season, he couldn't guarantee to give 100%.

The Boxing Day win over Bradford City was watched by a capacity 40,055. After the stuttering start to the season, there was ground to recover on frontrunners Nottingham Forest and Middlesbrough and it took a further string of results to push Sunderland into an automatic promotion place before the visit of Queens Park Rangers on a wet, cold Good Friday. Two goals from Niall Quinn that were cancelled by Mike Sheron, who scored twice in the last fifteen minutes, meant that instead of being seven points ahead of third-placed Middlesbrough, their closest rivals, Sunderland were five and had now played a game more. Middlesbrough, who had just lost a second successive League Cup final and their two latest league matches, were about to throw the towel in and their manager Bryan Robson wanted to rest his star performer, the mercurial Paul Merson, for the play-offs. Merson would have none of it; Boro revived and achieved five wins and a draw from six remaining fixtures. Coming into the last home game, Sunderland nevertheless remained favourites alongside Forest to go up. The clamour for tickets for the visit of Stoke was unprecedented. At the rear of the East Stand 600 permanent seats were installed enabling 41,214 to witness 'Super Kev' Phillips score twice as Sunderland signed off with a rousing 3-0 win on a sun-drenched day. Two away games were left. Holding a slightly better goal difference, two wins out of two were needed to make sure of promotion. In the field of sporting endeavour, a superhuman effort to come from nowhere to within grasping distance of the prize can often be undone by one freak moment. This was patently not the case at Portman Road but Sunderland were still derailed. After a cagey, dour first half Ipswich gradually took control, completing a routine 2-0 victory. Middlesbrough were only able to draw the following evening but that sufficed to ensure a decisive one-point advantage on the final day and render Sunderland's victory at Swindon academic. Gallingly, the defeat by Ipswich had only been the third since the Reading game way back on 4th October; an impressive accumulation of 90 points from 46 was not enough. A play-off semi-final against Sheffield United beckoned. Nevertheless, Sunderland were short-priced favourites to join Middlesbrough and Forest in what would be the first occasion all three newly relegated clubs returned to top-flight football within a year.

The first leg at Bramall Lane was lost 2-1. The return game was a night to remember as Sunderland's new home came of age. A veil of mist hemmed in and amplified a deafening roar. The all-seater crowd produced a din to rival Roker Park. An own goal and a thirty-fourth of the season from Phillips ensured a 3-2 aggregate and a passage to a Wembley confrontation with Charlton Athletic, who finished a mere two points behind Sunderland in the final table and remarkably had not conceded for nine matches. Unless present in the north London postcode HA9 0PQ on bank holiday Monday 25th May, only the possession of a graphic imagination can come close to capturing an occasion that is regarded as the most enthralling play-off final of all time. The bald facts on their own form a compelling narrative. Charlton's first-half lead was overturned shortly after the restart by Quinn and Phillips. Clive Mendonca equalised on 71 minutes before Quinn retaliated within two minutes to put Sunderland 3-2 ahead. Five minutes from the end, the Charlton centre half Rufus equalised again. In extra time, Summerbee put Sunderland ahead a third time on 99 minutes before Mendonca completed a hat-trick when he made it 4-4 within four minutes. Both teams scored their first six penalties in the shootout. Charlton edged ahead 7-6. The fourteenth penalty kick of the match, taken by Michael Gray, was saved by Saša Ilić. There was no Phillips or Clark to take a penalty; both had departed injured. Charlton were promoted. There would always be next season. Ironically, the Charlton hat-trick hero Mendonca, born in London, had moved to Sunderland as a young child; he supports the Wearsiders and at this current time is an employee of the Washington Nissan car plant.

Little adjustment was required as Reid sought to dispel the bitter disappointment. A new, highly rated Danish goalkeeper Thomas Sørensen impressed. Paul Butler, a young centre half, was signed from Bury for £1 million and established himself as first choice. Sunderland, off to a flying start during 1998-99, rose to the top of the table with 22 goals from 8 matches including a 7-0 win over Oxford. Danny Dichio and the promising Bridges, who had found it difficult to force himself into the first team, both scored twice. This unlikely partnership had replaced the injured Quinn and Phillips, who were not reunited until 9 January '99; they both found the net in a 2-2 draw at QPR, by which time Sunderland were nine points ahead of their closest pursuers. The duo were therefore ready for a League Cup semi-final with Premier League Leicester City. Notwithstanding the overriding priority of promotion, knockout domestic competitions had become devalued since Rupert Murdoch's annexation of the game to enhance his broadcasting empire. The competition was unappealing in the early stages, with two-legged ties against York and Chester negotiated before a rare highlight when Everton were beaten on penalties at Goodison. Leicester dominated at a slightly less-than-capacity Stadium of Light. A bizarre 45-yard free kick from Gavin McCann maintained hope for the away leg, on a night when earlier the visitors had established a deserved two-goal lead through Tony Cottee. At Filbert

Street it was nearly a different story. In a highly competitive encounter, Niall Quinn levelled on aggregate before Cottee edged Leicester through.

Having suffered a customary early-round exit in the FA Cup there was a clear run in the League. The final 17 fixtures produced 14 wins and three draws. Phillips, despite making only 26 league starts, found the net on 23 occasions; Quinn scored 18 from 36. The club scored 91 and conceded only 28. Sørensen kept a remarkable 29 clean sheets. Butler, the newcomer, and Andy Melville, the veteran in his last season on Wearside, only missed two league games each in an effective central defensive pairing. Sunderland, whose progress resembled a lightly handicapped horse on firm ground in the five-furlong Epsom Dash, ran away unencumbered to the Championship, finishing 18 points ahead of second placed Bradford City. Kevin Ball, already proving a great ambassador for the club, fittingly lifted the trophy in his last full season for Sunderland. The 105 points from a 46-game season was a record, only surpassed since by Reading who managed one more during 2005-06. The average attendance of 38,724 was the highest since George Hardwick's temporary tenure 34 years earlier.

23

TWIN PEAKS

1999-00 to 2000-01

Peter Reid wanted an experienced defender to help the club acclimatise in the Premier League. Steve Bould was 36 years old when he made his debut at Stamford Bridge on the opening day of the season. Alongside Lee Dixon, Nigel Winterburn, Tony Adams and Martin Keown he had been an integral part of George Graham's mean Arsenal backline. Bould extended his career long enough for his new colleagues to benefit from his organisation and know-how. Stefan Schwarz, a much-travelled Swedish international who enhanced midfield, came from Valencia for a record-breaking £4 million.

Despite the signings who proved their worth, there was a constant traffic in lesser-known players; many were older, foreign acquisitions who did not meet expectations. At considerable expense, Helmer, Roy, Fredgaard, Núñez and Di Giuseppe all passed through the club during that first season of Premier League football. Except for Roy none made a mark, with only Helmer managing so much as a full league appearance. Two years previously, Zoetebier, a Dutch goalkeeper, had been given a three-year contract after £350,000 was paid to the selling club. He did not appear in the league and his contract was cancelled after six months. Fredgaard, rated an exciting prospect in Denmark, cost £1.8 million but after one substitute league outing eventually moved back to Scandinavia with only a fraction of the outlay recouped. The strange case of Milton Núñez shone a light on the haphazard nature of the transfer market around the turn of the century when clubs, flush with easy money through lax lending from banks and an overvalued stock market listing, were persuaded to pay extravagant prices for some unknown foreigner, based purely on a grainy video of his best moments that had been put together by a mercenary agent. When Sunderland announced the signing of Núñez for an initial fee of £1.6 million, they presumed him to be a player from Nacional in the Uruguayan First Division. They were unaware that Núñez was merely a journeyman from a third-tier Uruguayan side. It is alleged that Núñez's agent Pablo Betancour, in the course of finalising negotiations with Sunderland's client Paul Stretford, had stealthily changed fax references to read Montevideo instead of Nacional, to the point where it was presumed the two clubs were one and the same. Núñez made less than one full league appearance for Sunderland. Stretford took Betancour to the English High Court accusing him of fraudulent behaviour but the judge ruled there was no evidence against him. There is more than one version of the complicated story attempting to explain how Sunderland ended up with a player who may have struggled in the Conference, but there is no escaping the wider truth of a football club, not alone in that era, who failed to exercise due diligence concerning the exchange of such astronomical amounts of money.

Results wise, Sunderland were thriving. Despite what proved to be an opening day baptism of fire for Bould at Chelsea, the 4-0 setback soon looked a mere blip. In the same month there was a biblical downpour at St. James' Park on an electrically-charged night as Newcastle fans, soaked throughout and lacking a roof over their heads in a half-developed Milburn stand, witnessed a shift in the balance of power between the major Northeast clubs. As the pitch grew waterlogged, Quinn and Phillips scored second half goals to earn a 2-1 victory. The elements were not conducive to the 'sexy' football with which the Newcastle manager Ruud Gullit always thought himself associated. He was sacked shortly afterwards with fans critical of the Dutchman for starting the game without Alan Shearer. Sunderland's next two away games were won 5-0 and 4-0 at Derby County and Bradford City respectively. Such are the rare gifts that are bestowed on football fans without rhyme or reason. Excluding penalties, the hat-trick achieved by Phillips at Derby was the first by a Wearside player in a top-flight game for seventeen years.

There was an extraordinary Sunday contest against West Ham at Upton Park when Sunderland, standing fourth in the table with 23 points from 11 games, were chasing a sixth consecutive victory that would place them at the very top of the Premier League. The two points Leeds United dropped, whilst sharing eight goals with Everton in an earlier kick-off, provided the opportunity. That seemed to have vanished when Steve Bould was dismissed very early, until Kevin Phillips shocked all by heading home a Quinn cross, leaving the visitors to withstand a second half onslaught. The post twice denied Paolo Di Canio before Trevor Sinclair equalised on 89 minutes. The Premier League was not to be feared. On a crisp December afternoon, following a string of impressive away performances, another capacity Stadium of Light crowd watched in awe as Quinn and Phillips pulverised Chelsea with two goals each in an opening 45 minutes en route to a 4-1 win;

this was a game more than any other which has come to define the Stadium of Light's formative years. Supporting Sunderland was not supposed to be like this. Phillips repeated his feat the following Saturday against Southampton. He had taken two goals from each of his last three games; his 19 goals from 18 games had helped Sunderland to 37 points.

On Boxing Day, Peter Reid's team shorn of an injured Kevin Phillips were thrashed 5-0 at Everton. The following fixture ended controversially when Sunderland, leading Manchester United 2-0, were denied victory by a Nicky Butt equaliser after the award of a disputed free kick with only minutes remaining. A further nine league matches passed without a victory. Buried within that period was a moment to remember in the inaugural Tyne-Wear derby at the new stadium. Kevin Phillips crowned mounting pressure to complete a comeback, scoring his second goal of the match against Newcastle in a 2-2 draw. The barren 11-match sequence ended when Phillips scored a late winner against Everton but there was thinly-veiled criticism from the crowd as Sunderland struggled to break down the visitors. Reid wondered if expectations were becoming unrealistic. A return to form was not enough to secure European football but it established a final seventh placing, the highest since 1955.

Kevin Phillips became the only Englishman to win the European Golden Shoe (Boot) and retains the distinction to this day. When Ally McCoist had earlier scooped this honour twice in a row while playing in Scotland, no allowance was made for the divergent standards of each domestic league; a goal in Wales was of equal worth to a goal in Italy. This accounts for the relatively unknown David Taylor of Porthmadog winning the award in 1993-94 with 43 goals and why the accolade evaded Alan Shearer, for whom Newcastle had paid Blackburn a world record £15 million. Phillips ended with 30 league goals. His versatility was evident throughout; either a spectacular strike from 25 yards, a Johnny-on-the-spot tap-in, a header defying his slight stature or a one-on-one with the goalkeeper. More often than not it was Quinn the provider, leaving him to find a yard of space to guide the ball over the line. On Match of the Day over Easter Gary Lineker, after witnessing another Phillips double that sank Sheffield Wednesday, rated the Sunderland striker a certainty for the forthcoming European Championships in Holland. Despite ticking all boxes, Phillips was completely ignored by Kevin Keegan, who neither started with him for any of the three group games nor summoned him from the bench. England, relying on Shearer and Michael Owen, failed limply to reach the knockout phase. All told, Phillips made eight England appearances without scoring. In mitigation, he never played a full ninety minutes and his body language betrayed him as an outsider looking in, not accepted by the established order.

Sunderland were not stationary, either on or off the field. The North Stand extension permitted 47,121 to be present for the 2000-01 curtain-raiser against Arsenal. Despite Sunderland being second best for long periods, a Niall Quinn goal separated the teams. The flattering reviews of debutant centre half Stanislav Varga were attributable to a host of simple chances the visitors spurned rather than any resemblance of him to Charlie Hurley. The onion bag-count distorts and colours judgement. Towards the end of the contest, Patrick Vieira was adjudged to have hit Darren Williams in the face and received a red card. Williams and Peter Reid exonerated Vieira afterwards by claiming it was accidental. With the season in its infancy, Don Hutchison, the Brazilian Emerson Thome and the Argentinian Julio Arca were signed from Everton, Chelsea and Argentinos Juniors respectively for combined fees of over £10 million. Hutchison, from Gateshead, captained Everton and had started his career at Hartlepool before progressing to Liverpool, West Ham and Sheffield United. He came with a reputation as a player who could take control of midfield and neither be beaten nor duck a challenge. Thome, belying the reputation of his countrymen, was a blunt, no-nonsense centre half. Arca, in comparison, was a stylish left-sided midfielder who also filled in at full back. The composition of the team altered. Mysteriously, Nicky Summerbee was out of favour and therefore with Quinn in his thirty-fifth year, Phillips enjoyed less support, consequently finishing the season with a reduced tally of fourteen goals. The gifted winger Summerbee was shunned by Reid, banished from first-team training sessions and was relieved to join second-tier outfit Bolton Wanderers in the January window. Halfway through the previous season, following a London match, Summerbee, Machin and Gray were involved in a weekend's harmless entertainment with the 'B' list television personality Melanie Sykes, which was extensively reported in the Monday's edition of the Sun. It proved anything but harmless for Summerbee, who found himself no longer a first team regular before being permanently cast in the wilderness. Whether or not the incident was a major factor in Summerbee's changing fortunes, it shed light on a drinking culture within the club and the propensity of some players to stay over in the capital city after a game.

Undoubtedly, the Sunderland defence had tightened considerably. The side were arguably better balanced in this Premier League campaign. Chris Makin and Michael Gray, an effective full back pairing, compared favourably with Jack Stelling and Arthur Hudgell of the immediate post-war era. After a slow burn in mid-table, another 2-1 win at St. James' Park materialised when Sunderland again reversed an interval deficit, with drama aplenty when Thomas Sørensen dived left to deny Shearer a point-saving penalty in the closing minutes. Three years later Sørensen, in the colours of Aston Villa, again saved a late Shearer penalty, on this occasion to prevent Newcastle taking all three points. The November derby joy commenced a splendid period of eight wins in ten matches. Alex Rae was playing the best football of his career, Hutchison a streetwise man-mountain, and alongside them Reid had the option of Schwarz, Arca and Gavin McCann, the latter a bargain buy from Everton. McCann even managed an England call up, coming on for the second half as one of six changes in a full international against Spain at Villa Park.

A place in the quarter-final of the League Cup was met with an unexpected defeat at the home of Crystal Palace. In the FA Cup hopes were raised after Sunderland returned to Selhurst Park and defeated Palace 4-2 to advance into the fourth round. West Ham however triumphed 1-0 in a fifth round tie at the Stadium of Light. The attendance of 36,005, enhanced by a visiting contingent numbering 5,000, compared unfavourably to a season's league low of 44,526. High on the agenda was the prospect of qualification for the Champions League. The first and second finishers in the League were guaranteed the group stage with the third placed side to face one qualifying hurdle. Bradford City were rock bottom of the Premier League with 15 points from 22 games when they visited Wearside. An expected three points did not materialise. The opportunity of opening a four-point gap from third in the table Arsenal was missed as the game petered out goalless. Sunderland now entertained runaway leaders Manchester United in a game notionally billed as a top-of-the-table clash. It was a volatile affair. Michael Gray, Andy Cole and Alex Rae were given their marching orders as the home side were reduced to nine men, ultimately to lose 1-0 on the wrong side of a series of disputed refereeing decisions. Another tight game at home to Liverpool ensued. There was controversy when Gary McAllister, despite being fouled a good two yards outside the penalty box, managed to stay upright until he theatrically threw himself to the ground once the white line was crossed. The visitors equalised with their convenient spot kick to cancel Hutchison's earlier goal.

In a repeat of the season before, momentum stalled. There was a patchy run of results before a late resurgence lifted Sunderland to another seventh finish, albeit short of European qualification, but an outstanding achievement when assessed within the context of the previous four decades. Standing still is akin to going backwards in a competitive environment. The Quinn-Phillips axis was on borrowed time. Would Sunderland stick or twist? Reid was aware of the cost involved in turning the club from the best of the also-rans to one capable of realistically challenging for honours. In his autobiography 'Cheer Up' he claimed Murray did not share his ambition. Reid however confessed to mistakes with the limited funds available. The statistics indicate he had developed a cautious, almost negative stance. Over the 2000-01 campaign 38 league games produced 46 goals with only 41 conceded, far removed from the vintage of his early time at Monkwearmouth. The public were undeterred; the ground expansion enabled them to attend in ever greater numbers. The average attendance of 46,791 was the third best in the country and only one thousand less than the all-time 1949-50 Wearside high; astonishingly each one of the last eight home games attracted at least 47,000.

24

NOT SO CHEERFUL

2001-02 to 2002-03

As the 2001-02 season evolved it was obvious that the wrong players had been signed and the wrong players let go. Reid admitted to a lack of homework on the 'character' of 29-year-old Lilian Laslandes, a French international signed from Bordeaux for £3.5 million. A generous contract may have been his prime motivation for signing. Compromised by personal and fitness problems, he failed to score in his twelve league appearances, seven of which were from the bench. Two years later, after a series of underwhelming loan spells on the continent with Sunderland subsidising his wages, he was a free agent. Reid had little option but to nurse Quinn through the season. The oldest member of the squad, he remarkably featured in every league game, even though he played the full ninety minutes in only a third. The supply line to the once prolific Phillips was fractured.

Complicated negotiations to import Nicolás Medina were concluded. Medina, who arrived from Argentina in another £3.5 million transaction, was lauded as one for the future but his period at Sunderland was a non-event; his solitary first team appearance was a Cup tie. The sudden departures of Hutchison and Rae were damaging developments considering the season was less than a month old. Rae, content on Wearside, was puzzlingly sold to Wolves whilst Hutchison with three years left on his contract demanded a 100% wage increase from his reported £14,000 a week package. Hutchison had outperformed expectations in the year since his arrival. Bob Murray refused to negotiate; high-principled Sunderland lost a key player to West Ham for the insubstantial compensation of £5 million. There was a further setback when Peter Reid failed to persuade the Arsenal midfielder Ray Parlour to move from Arsenal, despite offering to almost double his weekly Highbury wage of £20,000. Parlour, aka 'the Romford Pelé', a label befitting his popularity at Highbury rather than a likeness to the sublime Brazilian, was open-mouthed at the numbers thrown at him when he met Reid, but his polite refusal underlined the difficulty of persuading players to move north.

In a disappointing campaign, only in December did Sunderland achieve consecutive victories. This was shortly after the urgent quest for a quality midfielder was met with the arrival of the American Claudio Reyna, for a club record £4.5 million. By now, an increasingly injury-prone Stefan Schwarz was missing games with Thome, the previous most expensive signing, sidelined from New Year's Day for the remainder of the season. The second of those back-to-back victories was a surprising 3-0 Boxing Day win at Blackburn when Niall Quinn peeled back the years to score twice. This pushed Sunderland up to eleventh with a ten-point buffer from third bottom Derby, who in turn were a single point above Ipswich and Leicester. The respite was short-lived. In a game at Portman Road, the East Anglian club were four up at half-time against Sunderland, then five at full-time. Three narrow victories were hollowed out in the second half of the season against Derby, Bolton Wanderers and Leicester. The bottom three positions remained unchanged. The Wearsiders finished on 40 points with four to spare over relegated Ipswich. Sunderland only managed 29 goals with Phillips contributing a modest 11.

Peter Reid knew he was under pressure. Reports suggested that the Swede Zlatan Ibrahimović had been the subject of a failed £6.2 million bid and that Sunderland were not prepared to continue discussions with Ajax. The young Leeds forward Robbie Keane was targeted to provide fresh impetus for the impending 2002-03 season. Leeds, having gone for broke under their chairman Peter Ridsdale, failed to qualify for the Champions League and, desperate to sell, agreed a £9 million fee. Keane, who had joined Leeds after a short stay at Inter Milan, seemed reluctant to leave Elland Road but there was no hesitation when Tottenham called. Again, the club had failed to land a prime target. With Thome persistently absent with a series of injuries, Sunderland signed Phil Babb on a free transfer from Sporting Lisbon. Reid was aware that right back Chris Makin had never been adequately replaced. Perhaps the Liverpool manager Gérard Houllier was of the same mind. In a conversation with Reid, he casually mentioned that he was open to offers for full back Stephen Wright. Reckoning that Wright was worth having, having broken into the Anfield team with a dozen or so appearances after a loan spell at Crewe, the Sunderland manager took the bait with a seven-figure bid. The club's transfer policy was becoming reactive as opposed to proactive.

The mood on Wearside altered over the summer as signings did not materialise. It was no longer the impatient minority who were setting the agenda. With potential successors George Graham and David O'Leary hovering in the background, a majority of supporters wanted a change in management. On a warm-up tour of Belgium, in an incident that attracted widespread publicity, Peter Reid had a beer thrown over him by a fan. On the eve of a season that commenced with a goalless draw at Blackburn, Reid commented, 'There is no way I'm going to walk away. It doesn't matter how much lager is thrown over me, I will not walk out on this job'. The attendance of 37,698 for the first home game against Everton, lost 1-0, gave a clear indication of markedly reduced season ticket sales. The lowest attendance the previous season had been over 43,000 with the first home game against Ipswich attracting 47,370. Deadline-week desperation unfolded when Reid smashed the club transfer record by paying Glasgow Rangers £8 million for tall Norwegian striker Tore André Flo, who in receiving £42,000 per week became the highest earner at the Stadium of Light. Rangers did not dissuade him. Earlier, a five-year contract was handed to Matt Piper, a Leicester winger of raw potential. The East Midlands club, newly relegated and facing administration, were pleasantly surprised to receive £3 million for a player not established in their first eleven. Those deals took Sunderland's market expenditure well past £20 million inside a year. At the same time, writing in the match day programme, Reid asked supporters for a sense of perspective by comparing Sunderland's recent league positions with underachieving Tottenham and Everton. That may have been a valid point, as over the previous three seasons Spurs and the Merseysiders had never finished above ninth and thirteenth respectively. He used the word 'fantastic' in describing the finances at Sunderland, saying that '90% of football clubs would like to be in our financial state'. Bob Murray may have begged to differ.

Flo proved a colossal waste of money despite his debut equaliser in a turbulent encounter at the Stadium of Light against Manchester United. Their leader Roy Keane lost his composure in a slanging match with Jason McAteer, lashed out and was dismissed. This occurred months after an infamous incident in Saipan when Keane walked out on the World Cup tournament, understandably aggrieved after a public dressing down by the Republic of Ireland manager Mick McCarthy in front of the whole squad, of which McAteer was part. This was in response to an interview between Keane and Tom Humphries in the Irish Times, in which the Republic's captain blamed the Football Association of Ireland and McCarthy for poor facilities at their pre-tournament training base. Keane, despite a stinging foul-mouthed tirade across the room in reply to McCarthy, received private support from some of his team-mates as he packed his bags and was later exonerated by the FAI.

Any belief that the spirited show against Manchester United represented a turning point dissipated with consecutive 3-0 defeats, the latter by Fulham on Wearside. The gate of 35,432 was the lowest league attendance since promotion. There was a home win over Aston Villa then a stunning 7-0 win at fourth-tier Cambridge in a second round League Cup tie before a defeat at

Arsenal signalled the end for Peter Reid. Bob Murray decided enough was enough. Sunderland, with eight points from ten matches, were nineteenth in the table, one from bottom. To quote the politician Enoch Powell in one of his less controversial utterances, 'All political lives, unless they are cut off in midstream at a happy juncture, end in failure, because that is the nature of politics and of human affairs'. A football manager's existence is far more precarious.

If longevity in the hire and fire culture of football is a worthwhile performance indicator then Reid, who had been in charge for no less than seven and a half years, was a success. Only Bill Murray of the post-war managers has endured a longer uninterrupted spell. Consecutive seventh-place finishes allied to the wonderful attacking football his teams played in rising twice from the second tier, cements a worthy place in Wearside history. As his reign progressed Sunderland retreated into a shell to become functional and workmanlike. He was the undisputed, key figure off the field within the early Stadium of Light era. His influence was everywhere. This was in an age before the remit of a manager narrowed into a specific coaching role, alongside a greater importance attending to media matters. Areas such as the recruitment of players, disciplinary measures and contract negotiations were increasingly the responsibility of professional specialists. No Sunderland manager before or since has had to deliver promotion and consolidation for a publicly listed company. Murray backed Reid's judgement with significant funds. However, many of Reid's purchases were overpriced with limited, if any, resale value and their generous contracts would eventually prove a financial burden. That scenario has never been unusual in the English game since the abolition of the maximum wage but was, if anything, more common in the formative years of the Premier League when new money flooded in, raising the stakes at some clubs to the height of recklessness. Bradford City, owned by Geoffrey Richmond, promoted with Sunderland in 1999 and relegated within two years, were the classic example. The most ill-considered signing of all time must surely have been their acquisition of the 32-year-old Italian free agent Benito Carbone, given a four-year contract worth £40,000 per week. Richmond's brand of fantasy football took them down a cul-de-sac to administration. Sunderland were not there yet but Murray was looking over his shoulder. The annual accounts revealed that in the year to 31 July '03, wage costs increased from £23 million to £30.5 million and as a percentage of turnover from 59% in the previous year to 80%. Reid's removal was expected but the identity of his replacement unexpected. Howard Wilkinson was asked to avert relegation and possible financial meltdown.

Wilkinson had taken Leeds to the last authentic First Division Championship in 1992 by finishing ahead of Manchester United, who by common consent had done a Devon Loch at the winning post. Wilkinson had a reputation for pragmatic football, working the percentages and discovering that tiny bit of improvement overlooked by others, whether it be on the training ground or in a player's head. The 58-year-old former PE teacher was regarded as an intellectual within the game; after leaving Leeds he became an FA Technical Director. At Elland Road he signed the peerless Eric Cantona and then dispensed with his match-winning brilliance when he felt the Frenchman had become a bigger story than the club. Gordon Strachan, his captain at Leeds, rated him highly but claimed that Wilkinson could often be 'idiosyncratic' and go off on a tangent during team talks.

Following a series of substitute cameos, Niall Quinn's final appearance was during a home defeat by West Ham on 11th October, an occasion that coincided with Wilkinson's introduction to Wearside. Awarded a three-year contract, his tenure was short-lived. 'It was the worst decision I ever made. It was for the wrong reasons. I didn't do my homework', he has since said. It may have been a mistake to appoint Steve Cotterill as his assistant. They had never worked together and Cotterill, having briefly managed at Stoke and prior to that at Cheltenham Town, was not cut out to be a number two. For Bob Murray it certainly was an expensive mistake; Wilkinson's 152 days encompassed two wins from 20 matches and a considerable compensation package. The loss of Reyna for the remainder of the season just before he took office was a blow. In the middle of December, Michael Proctor delivered a home win over Liverpool for the first time since 1958. Wilkinson's team had earlier drawn at Anfield to knock them off top spot. Liverpool were in decline; those results were fool's gold. Liverpool remained winless for eleven games. Before the Boxing Day game with Leeds, despite the new spearhead of Flo and Phillips producing a mere six goals between them, the club were lying seventeenth. Had they taken advantage of Proctor's first half strike against the Yorkshiremen they would have gone level on points with their opponents, thereby opening a six-point gap from bottom-of-the-table West Ham. Instead, Sunderland capitulated 2-1, before dropping into the bottom three at Southampton two days later, when the home side unearthed an 90th minute winner only moments after a Flo equaliser. Wilkinson's psychological approach, allied to a greater emphasis on team shape, set pieces and analysis of the opposition, failed to revitalise a team riven with doubt. It was becoming a hopeless crusade for one of football's supposedly deep thinkers, especially when, within seven minutes of a first-half against Charlton Athletic at the Stadium of Light, Proctor twice and Wright inconceivably scored past their own goalkeeper Thomas Sørensen. The season imploded. One point from 19 games with 15 straight defeats led to a then Premier League record low points tally of 19. Kevin Phillips top-scored with six out of a total of 21.

Amidst the carnage, Mick McCarthy had replaced Wilkinson with nine games remaining. Relegation was unavoidable but the appointment gave the former Republic of Ireland manager and centre half time to take stock, restore morale and reshape personnel for a fresh start in the First Division. McCarthy's appointment was welcomed. He was a blunt, imposing Yorkshireman with a playing pedigree at Manchester City and Celtic. Through his ancestry he had amassed 57 Irish caps. Guiding the Republic to the last sixteen of the 2002 Japan-South Korea World Cup was an achievement, more so as it was done after the falling out with Roy Keane. They were edged out on penalties by Spain in the knockout phase.

25

STONY BROKE

2003-04 to 2005-06

The bottom-line financial loss of £20.872 million during relegation was a staggering increase on the 2001-02 season figure of £3.967 million. The balance sheet as at July '03 disclosed that net liabilities (debts minus money owed to the club) had more than doubled to over £55 million. A first parachute payment instalment from Sky of £5.1 million hardly guaranteed a soft landing. Players' contracts bore no resemblance to the diminished status of the club and, as was the norm within the industry then, no provision existed to reduce wages if relegation occurred. Bob Murray concentrated on avoiding administration by planning a fire sale of players and devised creative ways of achieving it. It is instructive that when Kevin Phillips moved to Southampton, he accepted a reduction in weekly wages from £33,000 to £16,000 to comply with their wage ceiling. To gain Phillips' approval Sunderland accepted a reduced fee of £2 million from Southampton, therefore allowing the buying club to pay him £1 million compensation. The decline of Phillips mirrored that of Sunderland. In his first 57 Premier League games he scored 40 goals, the remaining 82 games produced 21 goals. His overall total of 113 league goals places him at the head of the post-war scoring chart. After one season on Wearside, record signing Flo was sold to an Italian club for a mere £1 million. Sørensen at £2.25 million was another departure. Despite the cut-price departures Sunderland still had the highest wage bill in the First Division even though Murray, reverting to his hard-headed prudence of pre-Stadium of Light days, had cut overall expenditure in half and met his admirable objective of avoiding administration. New arrivals received a low basic wage, with higher earnings only achievable through an incentivised package covering appearances and performance bonuses. Dean Whitehead joined a year after relegation and quickly became a first-team regular on a basic wage of £2,500 per week.

McCarthy imposed his will. Michael Gray, another earmarked for a move, arrived for pre-season training in a brand-new Ferrari. With austerity measures in vogue, the manager ruled Gray's indulgence insensitive, promptly fining him two weeks' wages. A loan move to Celtic signalled the end of his long career on Wearside. McCarthy later signed Gray from Blackburn when he was managing Wolverhampton Wanderers.

The first task was to avoid an unwanted record. Back in 1898-99 during their last season as a league club, Lancashire club Darwen lost eighteen consecutive league matches. Since a goalless draw at Blackburn in January, Sunderland, including a new start to First Division life with two defeats, had contrived to lose seventeen consecutive times. A 2-0 win at Preston North End in August '03 prevented an unwelcome entry in the history books. McCarthy was effective in streamlining the squad and the higher wage earners were gradually jettisoned. The veteran centre half Gary Breen arrived on a free transfer from West Ham and was appointed club captain. He had played in all four of the Republic of Ireland's World Cup final games. Initially given a two-year contract, this was later extended with McCarthy eventually naming Breen as his most influential signing. Marcus Stewart and young Scottish forward Kevin Kyle, who between them scored 24 goals, formed an attacking pair of some effectiveness. Tommy Smith, out of contract with Watford, was a typical signing of those straitened times. He came in for one season, did a job, then moved on. Jeff Whitley, in similar vein, found himself unemployed after a spell at Manchester City before Sunderland snapped him up in September. Arca and Wright remained. Mart Poom proved a worthy replacement for Sørensen. George McCartney, a left-sided defender, established himself as a regular and would soon be captaining the side and be worthy of recognition to be chosen for the Football League PFA Championship Team of the Year.

McCarthy, working within severe financial limitations, dragged Sunderland off the floor. Four consecutive wins into January claimed fourth position. The Stadium of Light, hosting a third round FA Cup tie with Hartlepool, was besieged by a largest ever away following of 12,000. The attendance of 40,816 saw a Julio Arca goal overcome the visitors. As the season progressed, with a play-off qualification likely, the prospect existed of two visits to the Cardiff Millennium Stadium, which was being used in place of a rebuilt Wembley. Avoiding the big guns, Sunderland nevertheless knocked out two fellow First Division sides and in a fifth round replay, emerged victorious at Premier League Birmingham, with Tommy Smith scoring twice. In the quarter-final, Smith again obliged in front of over 37,000 against Sheffield United. Millwall, another second-tier side, were the semi-final opponents at Old Trafford. Sunderland were on a winning streak when they faced the mid-table Londoners but lost 1-0 in a desperately disappointing game. The game was underwhelming; almost a microcosm of the Cup run itself. A shadow remained over the club, the swift fall from grace difficult to process. The prospect had gone of Sunderland adding to their visits in '73 and '92 to become the only side outside the top division to reach an FA Cup final for the third time.

Promotion remained viable. Automatic hopes were raised with goals from Smith, Breen and Kyle days after Old Trafford, as Sheffield United were dispatched 3-0 to clock up 23 points from 9 games. West Bromwich Albion however, who were to finish second, emerged victorious in front of 32,201 on Wearside. The play-offs beckoned. Sunderland, in third, faced sixth-placed Crystal Palace in the semi-final. The late drama at Selhurst Park, when Kevin Kyle brought his side back to 2-2 before Andrew Johnson quickly retaliated on 87 minutes, was an aperitif to the controversy on Wearside. Through first-half goals by Kyle and Marcus Stewart, Sunderland were on the brink of Cardiff with 90 minutes on the clock when Poom, impeded from a corner, allowed Darren Powell to head a disputed far-post goal. As Palace had been reduced to ten men during normal time, Sunderland remained favourites but a goalless extra time meant penalties. When Jeff Whitley stepped up after a catalogue of misses from both sides, he calculatedly broke stride, stopped dead, and then lamentably attempted to wrong-foot the goalkeeper with a slow, nuanced strike of the ball, only succeeding in handing Nico Vaesen a task not beyond the capabilities of a seven-year-old. Palace took the game with their next penalty. Disappointment was shrugged off. There was a realism that the club were not ready for the Premier League and that more sacrifice, scrimping and saving was required. Never had defeat in such a vital end-of-season game been met with so much indifference.

The low profile, calibrated signings continued. Steven Caldwell, after a handful of Premier League games for Newcastle, arrived on a free to form an effective central defensive pairing with Breen. Stephen Elliott, released by Kevin Keegan at Manchester City, cost only £125,000 and, replacing Kyle, linked with Stewart up front. Over 2004-05 they contributed 29 goals. Michael Bridges returned to Wearside but beset with fitness problems, was unable to secure a place. Resurgent Sunderland were in third position, three points from top when they suffered a 3-2 Boxing Day setback in front of 43,000 against Leeds. At Preston on New Year's Day, a first-half hat-trick by Richard Cresswell brought another defeat with the same scoreline. Sunderland came back. Only two more games were lost as eight straight wins cemented top position. Promotion was confirmed in the penultimate home game when Stewart and Caldwell overturned Leicester's lead on a day when third-placed Ipswich dropped points. 18-year-old Ben Alnwick, deputising for Poom and Myhre made an assured goalkeeping debut in front of 34,000. Gary Breen was presented with the Championship trophy on the final day, a 1-0 win over Stoke City. The attendance of 47,350 was the largest for a fixture in the second tier since May '79. They had, however, gathered to commemorate the occasion, and there was little of the verve that had swept like a prairie fire through the Stadium's early days. The last few years had exacted a heavy toll. For younger followers, celebrating with unrestrained delight, it was a blessing they were unable to glimpse the immediate future; the following 15 months they only tasted one league win at the Stadium of Light. The average of 29,000 represented a drop of 10,000 on the previous promotion season. McCarthy said, 'We've got everything going for us. We'll be ready tactically, mentally and physically'. His bravado was likely to be short-lived unless funds were advanced for major strengthening. That was unlikely. Murray may have cauterised the haemorrhage of cash but the overall debt, standing at £46 million, included an amount of £30 million that was due within a year and only offset by a mere £3.5 million owing to the club.

The modest purse McCarthy received was mainly used to buy two forwards and Kelvin Davis, a goalkeeper. Jon Stead, who cost £1.8 million from Blackburn, took until April to score his one and only goal for Sunderland whilst Andy Gray, a £1.1 million capture from Sheffield United fared little better, scoring two. His only Premier League contribution was an equaliser in the opening day fixture against Charlton Athletic in front of a disappointing attendance of 34,446, before the visitors ran out 3-1 winners. There was a setback when Alan Stubbs, a vastly experienced defender from Everton, did not establish himself as a first team regular. In the unforgiving environment of the Premier League, a 'make do and mend' mentality was inadequate. Only 31,212 witnessed a 1-1 draw with West Ham. Before Sunderland entertained Manchester United, McCarthy claimed that his side were not being blessed with 'fortune good enough to see breaks go our way' and was reasonably satisfied with performances despite a yield of five points from eight matches. Neither management nor supporters possessed expectations. The encounter with Ferguson's United commenced a run of nine straight defeats. The last home game of 2005 with Bolton was drawn; the club were marooned with a pitiful six points. Only one victory in the next eighteen league games was secured. Third-tier Brentford inflicted a fourth round FA Cup dismissal.

Mercifully, Mick McCarthy was relieved of his thankless task in February. He had given the job his unstinting endeavour and criticism of his poor summer signings should be tempered by the mess he had inherited. Kevin Ball as caretaker manager must have wondered when, if ever, a home win would come. An unusual April snowstorm, forcing an abandonment after 21 minutes of a game that Fulham were leading, came to the rescue. The rearranged fixture, the last home game of the season, saw Sunderland finally win a match at the Stadium of Light. A tally of 15 points from 38 games was the lowest in Premier League history. Sunderland were 15 points adrift of the nearest club West Bromwich Albion, from whom they had taken four points. Strangely, the heaviest defeats were all at home and by a margin of three goals, with no away game producing anything worse than a two-goal deficit. The names of Lawrence, Le Tallec, Miller and Whitehead will not feature in a pantheon of great Sunderland goalscorers but they have something in common with Gurney and Carter. By virtue of their three goals each, those four players share with that fabulous thirties' pair, the distinction of being joint-top scorers for Sunderland in a league season.

26

NEVER SAY DIE

2006-07 to 2008-09

Bob Murray had been chairman of the club and controlling shareholder for almost twenty years. After a second relegation in three years, he was ready to step away. Commendably, his determination to leave the club in responsible hands outweighed thought of personal gain. When Niall Quinn mentioned the possibility of spearheading a group of Irish-based businessmen in a takeover, Murray was confident this would safeguard the future. Quinn had been instrumental in the rise of Sunderland under Peter Reid. During 200 games he had proved a great ambassador; additionally, he had donated substantial proceeds from a testimonial match to charity so setting a precedent that footballers in the future were empowered to follow. To facilitate the takeover Murray, who became life president, allowed Quinn to replace him as chairman. Without profit, he sold his shares to the Drumaville Consortium in a transaction estimated at £20 million. Quinn and six fellow Irishmen, principally involved in construction and hospitality, joined forces with John Hays, a Sunderland resident, owner of the substantial Hays Travel package holiday business. Roy Keane was offered the managerial vacancy following unsuccessful approaches to Martin O'Neill and Sam Allardyce. Keane deliberated. When the new season dawned Quinn reluctantly took charge of the team. Five defeats included a humbling League Cup loss to Bury, the ninety-second placed team in the country. With Quinn on the ropes, his former Irish team-mate decided to grasp the nettle. Keane was box-office. He learnt his trade under Brian Clough at Nottingham Forest before winning just about everything at Manchester United, with the notable exception of a Champions League final. Alongside Paul Scholes, receiving a yellow card in a semi-final second leg at Juventus excluded him from United's 1999 triumph over Bayern Munich. The Juventus game epitomised the fiercely competitive and inspiring leadership qualities of Keane. There were no tears shed when he received his caution for a mistimed tackle. Instead, he gave a performance which Alex Ferguson saw fit to rate as 'the most emphatic display of selflessness I have seen on a football field'. Keane imposed high standards on himself and expected the same of mere mortals. At the Stadium of Light, he would be dealing with a wide range of disparate talents, nowhere near the spectrum he was accustomed to at Old Trafford. For all his aura he was a private person with a small circle of confidants. His appointment, which put Sunderland on the front pages, was extraordinary.

Keane's first appearance at the Stadium was a watching brief. His very presence spurred Sunderland to break their duck at the sixth attempt and beat West Bromwich Albion 2-0. With deadline day fast approaching there was hectic activity as Kavanagh, Connolly, Wallace, Miller, Yorke and Varga were signed, the latter for a second time. 5,000 fans travelled to Derby. Chris Brown, whose father Alan Brown played for Sunderland, and debutant Ross Wallace scored within a minute to earn three points and overcome a half-time deficit. Then fellow newcomers Liam Miller and Graham Kavanagh helped Sunderland to a 3-0 victory at Leeds on the Wednesday evening. Two away wins in four days. Over 35,000 needed little persuasion to attend the next home game, a draw with Leicester City. Keane's signings were players he could personally vouchsafe. A mixture of permanent and loan arrivals mainly comprised Irishmen and Manchester United players, past and present. During the Leicester game Dwight Yorke, in the twilight of a fine career, previously partnering the prolific Andrew Cole at Old Trafford, made a substitute appearance having returned from Australian football. Dropping into a midfield role, he was a valuable part of Keane's set up, both on and off the field.

The initial Keane impact diminished. A home draw against Southampton in November left Sunderland nineteenth in the table with only twenty points from seventeen games. The January transfer window brought in half a dozen new faces. Centre half Jonny Evans, a fine young Northern Irish prospect, was loaned from Manchester United. Instrumental in tightening the defence, Keane wanted to sign him permanently but Ferguson rated him higher than the reported £12 million offered. In addition, the switch of full-back Nyron Nosworthy to central defence proved so effective that he would be voted Sunderland's Player of the Year. The continual tweaks to the playing squad bore dividend. A habit from Old Trafford that Keane instilled in his players was the tendency to keep going until the end and if anything, increase the tempo as the last seconds drained away. At home to Derby and away at Hull, Liam Miller and Ross Wallace came up with winners two minutes into stoppage time. The buzz created by Keane's appointment was evident in the markedly increased attendances. Sunderland defeated Hull in March and climbed to second with 38,448 present; Wolves were dispatched on Easter

Saturday with over 40,000 in the Stadium of Light. The charge up the table was greater than that which Reid had fashioned before the heart-wrenching Charlton play-off game. No less than 42 points from 16 games were collected before a defeat at Colchester in the forty-fourth fixture hinted at a late stumble. The penultimate game against Burnley was brought forward to a Friday evening. Anything less than three points would allow Birmingham and Derby to determine their destiny and expose Keane's team to the play-offs. On an evening of high drama, a penalty miss by David Connolly on 20 minutes prevented Sunderland from adding to an early Daryl Murphy goal, before the visitors stunned a 44,000 crowd to score either side of half-time to go 2-1 up. Their equaliser from former player Andy Gray was a wrongly awarded penalty; goalkeeper Darren Ward did not touch the onrushing Wayne Elliott who conveniently fell to ground. In a further twist, Sunderland were given a second penalty, which Connolly on this occasion converted, therefore setting the stage to chase a winner. On eighty minutes Carlos Edwards, one of Keane's January recruits, lifted the roof when he smashed a glorious, angled drive into the net from 20 yards. Two days later, an unexpected defeat for Derby at Crystal Palace guaranteed Premier League football for Sunderland. There was a perfect ending on the final weekend as a surprising slip at Preston by Steve Bruce's Birmingham allowed a resurgent Wearsiders, 5-0 winners at Luton Town, to claim the title in a carnival atmosphere.

Sunderland entered the Premier League in 2007 at the beginning of an enhanced three-year Sky broadcasting deal that represented an astonishing 70% increase on previous numbers. It basically meant that the reward for finishing fourth bottom was approximate to that which the previous champions Manchester United had earned on the old deal. The payments to each club comprised three elements: 50% represented a fixed amount divided equally between everyone, 25% of the total pot was divided in proportion to the number of live transmissions and the remaining 25% was divided purely by league position. The latter merit payments were worth from £700,000 for bottom position up to a maximum of £14 million for first. The overall distribution was fairly equitable and if anything, the payouts were of greater benefit to those clubs outside the elite.

Little restraint was imposed on Keane. Sunderland's spending, fuelled by an increase from £7.95 million to £35.6 million in TV and media receipts, continued at an upward trajectory. Keane paid £7 million to Southampton for the Trinidad forward Kenwyne Jones. Eyebrows were raised when Sunderland broke the British goalkeeping transfer record, spending £9 million on Craig Gordon, a Scottish international from Hearts. There was another surprise when Michael Chopra, formerly of Newcastle, was signed from Cardiff for £5 million. Although he had finished the season as second top scorer in the Championship, he was unproven at top level. Kieran Richardson, unable to force his way into the Manchester United team, cost £5 million whilst Danny Higginbotham, another former Old Trafford youth team player, arrived from Stoke for £3 million. Higginbotham joined Paul McShane in defence, a cheaper buy from Hull. The priority to buy British was a refreshing counterpoint to the increasing trend of foreign players within the game. From the season's start it was obvious that any Keane eleven would compensate for a lack of quality with 100% effort. A goal three minutes into stoppage time from Chopra brought glee to the Stadium of Light as the bulk of an opening day 43,967 celebrated a winning return to the top-flight. In the first away fixture at Luton, the soon-to-depart Stern John took a point from Birmingham with another 90th minute goal. The Reading game in the middle of September, won 2-1, was a sombre occasion; the crowd and members of the FA Cup-winning team paid tribute to Ian Porterfield, who in his sixty-second year had passed away.

A run of poor results culminating in a 7-1 defeat at Stamford Bridge, took eighteenth-placed Sunderland into a first genuine must-win encounter of the campaign. Derby County, rock bottom, were on their way to eclipsing the Wearsiders' record low number of points and finishing the season on only eleven points, four of those taken from Newcastle. Almost 43,000 at the Stadium of Light witnessed a turgid game lacking incident until, again in time added on, the home side stumbled on a scrappy winner when Anthony Stokes lifted the winter gloom with a tap over the line from two yards. McShane and Nosworthy were struggling with the step-up in class, therefore Keane persuaded Jonny Evans to return after Christmas for his second loan spell. At the same time, Manchester United accepted an offer for their reserve right back Phil Bardsley. The talented, overweight midfielder Andy Reid joined from Charlton for £4 million, coming on from the bench for his debut to provide a superb pass that enabled Daryl Murphy to score in a 2-0 win over Wigan, watched by 43,600. Reid was affectionately dubbed the 'pie-man'. A strengthened defence brought an improvement as Sunderland moved to thirteenth by winning three consecutive matches, including a 2-1 home victory over West Ham, when before a near-capacity crowd Reid crowned an enthralling finish with a late winner. The final position was fifteenth and although there was only a three-point cushion from relegated Reading, once Evans settled the defence, Sunderland were never in serious relegation trouble. An excellent fifth-best English average attendance of 43,344 represented a 35% increase on the promotion figure. The backing of the public and a quick return to Championship fare for Birmingham and Derby justified Keane's transfer activity. However, it would be far-fetched to expect another season consisting of four 90th minute winners in addition to three draws derived from goals scored between 86 and 90 minutes. The 13 goals between Jones and Chopra had not exactly set the division alight. A close-knit, hard-working

British ethos served Keane well in steering Sunderland through perilous waters but in order to progress, a strategy of sacrificing perspiration for inspiration was necessary, with more spending the only certain outcome.

The aim of 'taking the club to a new level' is an impressive-sounding corporate mission target. Apart from a select group of northwest and London clubs possessing global appeal, any level attained will be temporary and illusory unless a wealthy benefactor steps in. A worldwide credit crunch reduced the personal net worth of the individuals within the Drumaville consortium, who were now understandably unwilling to commit more funds. The business interests of those members primarily involved with construction were exposed to a rapidly falling housing market, a situation worse in Ireland than elsewhere. Regardless of economic conditions, the voracious financial demands of remaining competitive in the Premier League dictated that they were unable to help Sunderland evolve. Their involvement had come at a cost. The club's total wage bill after promotion increased from £21 million to nearly £33 million. The expenditure on new recruits was £34 million, notwithstanding small amounts recouped from departures. This was a stark contrast to the straitjacket contributing to McCarthy's failure in keeping Sunderland afloat. A negligible transfer budget and a practically static wage bill of £15 million in the season after his promotion, was out of kilter with an increase in turnover from £25.3 million to £39.3 million. The 80% ratio of wages to turnover in Keane's promotion campaign and the subsequent 50% increase in wages was an indication of Sunderland's renewed ambition after the narrow escape from administration. Ellis Short, holding a personal fortune of over £1 billion and specialising in fund management and bank takeovers, was one of many foreigners looking to buy an English club. After a period of discreet share dealing, he established a majority holding in Sunderland during September '08. The American was following in the footsteps of fellow countrymen who had taken over Manchester United, Aston Villa and Liverpool.

As interest from over the Atlantic hardened during the close season, Sunderland were emboldened. There was a foreign invasion. Steed Malbranque, Pascal Chimbonda and Teemu Tainio were signed from Tottenham, El Hadji Diouf from Bolton and Djibril Cissé loaned from Marseille. The White Hart Lane trio cost £12 million. The gifted, hard-working Malbranque was easily identifiable with his small frame tied to the ball, scuttling crab-like down the right flank before slipping a telling pass inside. After the opening game of the new season was lost at home to Liverpool in August, the players produced a superb win at Tottenham. Chimbonda, a different kettle of fish to Malbranque, displayed behaviour suitable for a morality tale to represent the shifting sands of a game becoming removed from its British roots. Before the short journey to White Hart Lane from the hotel, he appeared late for a pre-match walkabout and that, allied to his laid-back attitude, gave Keane every reason to leave him out of the team at short notice. Anton Ferdinand, brother of the England international Rio, proved the most-expensive signing at £8 million. He was amidst a pay dispute with West Ham, who had offered him £35,000 per week and accused him of demanding more than £50,000. Having turned down Newcastle, he agreed a four-year contract with Sunderland on significantly better terms than those offered by the East London club.

With Chopra returning to Cardiff, initially temporarily, Cissé, the flamboyant Frenchman loaned from Marseilles, took up attacking duties with Kenwyne Jones. In October '08 Sunderland defeated Newcastle on home turf for the first time since '80. A rocket of a free kick from Richardson added to the first goal from Cissé. Three consecutive defeats brought the first murmurings of discontent. Points were lost in the closing stages of games rather than won. Against Arsenal, Grant Leadbitter, an academy product, thought his 86th minute goal had earned three points until an equaliser by Fàbregas dashed hopes. There was little sign of improvement and Keane's recruitment policy was under scrutiny. Chimbonda and Diouf's stays were brief as Sunderland recouped most of their expenditure. The easy, relaxed relationship Keane had enjoyed with his fellow Irishmen was not replicated with the London-based Short, whose negligible knowledge of the game did not prevent him from a more hands-on approach than his predecessors. Short suspected Keane was not spending enough time at his workplace. There is no necessity for a manager to be present 24/7. Brian Clough believed his words possessed more impact if sparingly used. There was tension over living arrangements. Keane continued to rent in Durham whilst his family remained in Manchester. An unwillingness to relocate was interpreted by Short as a lack of commitment.

In November, Sunderland were fourteenth looking ahead to three home games against moderate opposition. All were lost, despite Cissé opening the scoring in two of those. A 4-1 defeat by Bolton was the last straw for Short. Roy Keane left the club by mutual consent. What did for Keane in the end were results; he departed with Sunderland in eighteenth position with 15 points from 16 games. Winning promotion and surviving the first season had been a notable achievement but Keane's latest batch of signings were not providing the expected improvement. Supporters were split in their reaction to his departure.

Ricky Sbragia was promoted from first team coach to caretaker manager, bypassing the head coach Tony Loughlan who was sidelined until he rejoined Keane within a new management structure at Ipswich. There was an instant response at Old Trafford, where only a goal in stoppage time from Nemanja Vidić prevented Sunderland from returning with a point. In

December, Kenwyne Jones found the net twice in a welcome home win over West Bromwich Albion and registered again at Hull as the team scored four times in consecutive games. Sbragia was awarded an 18-month managerial contract on the strength of that upturn. FA Cup interest ended in a fourth round replay at Blackburn after two home ties each attracted barely 20,000. A goalless draw at the Emirates Stadium maintained eleventh position and with more than two-thirds of the season over, a soft landing seemed likely. Sunderland however, only won one of their last thirteen fixtures and that by a 1-0 margin over a Hull City side in free fall. On the final day of reckoning, it was almost too close for comfort. Hull lost to Manchester United, who were assured of the title regardless. Yet even had the Tigers taken three points it would have proved inconsequential because Sunderland, despite losing at home to Chelsea, were guaranteed safety through events at Villa Park, where an own goal condemned Newcastle to a first ever relegation from the Premier League. Middlesbrough and West Bromwich Albion joined them. On Wearside in the nineties, Sbragia had looked after teams at youth and reserve level, later being employed within Manchester United's backroom staff. Never relishing his front-of-shop position at the Stadium of Light, he decided to step down at the end of the season and accept the role of Chief Scout for Sunderland.

27

GOING CONTINENTAL

2009-10 to 2011-12

In the first week of August '09 Steve Bruce said, 'He's everything I want'. It was his reaction to the finalisation of Sunderland's £12 million capture of Tottenham's prolific striker Darren Bent on a four-year contract. 'It is everything I want' may well have been Bruce's reaction to landing the seventh and most lucrative management job of his career when Short gave the wheeler-dealer extraordinaire access to the Stadium of Light Monopoly board and a three-year contract at a reported £60,000 per week. It cost Short £3 million in compensation to secure his release from Wigan. Their chairman Dave Whelan commented, 'Everyone associated with the club is devastated'. Bruce had always been one of those figures in demand from medium-sized provincial clubs, chasing dreams beyond their station. He had captained Manchester United when they knocked Liverpool off their perch in the early nineties. He was earnest and likeable in front of a camera, an approachable players' manager; he left the finer tactical points to his coaching staff and exploited the transfer market with relish. Barney Ronay imaginatively described him in the Guardian as, 'a head that might in another life have belonged to a prosperous family butcher with a secret'. Newcastle fans, irritated that one of their own from Wallsend was managing their bitter rivals, spat out the words 'plastic Mackem' to describe him.

Bruce was pampered by an initially naïve Short, who seemed to think that spending money was the key to success and long-term financial security. The headline capture of Bent, an England international boasting 49 Premier League goals over 128 appearances, confirmed that Bruce was able to deliver a persuasive sales pitch. To bolster the rearguard a reported £6 million was paid to Hull for centre half Michael Turner. World-class Ghanaian defender John Mensah was loaned from Olympique Lyonnais with a view to a permanent deal, despite a career-defining catalogue of injuries. When fit he was outstanding but his outings in a red and white shirt were severely restricted and after two seasons Sunderland decided not to exercise their option to sign him permanently. Lee Cattermole arrived from Wigan for a substantial fee and became an integral part of the club. His enthusiasm, competitiveness and will to win was sometimes not equalled by more skilful but laid-back team-mates. Bigger names than his came and went, leaving Cattermole with the dirty business of firefighting on the pitch. Small amounts were recouped with the departures of Danny Collins and Dean Whitehead, both having been good servants of McCarthy and Keane. Although Bruce's playing squad was in a constant state of flux, this state of affairs now seemed the default position within the Premier League; it was in the interest of avaricious agents to maintain a quick turnover, something readily achievable when foreign imports, who comprised the majority of players within the Premier League, did not possess an allegiance to the part of the country or club where they plied their trade. London of course was an exception. Increasingly, provincial clubs such as Sunderland were finding it harder to attract players of the right calibre and the solution of offering higher wages to ward off competition aroused a suspicion that there was a mercenary motive influencing the decision of any potential signing.

Over 2009-10 Jordan Henderson, an Academy prospect, became a regular first-teamer. At 19 years old, standing six feet, he was a driving force in midfield, possessing a natural stamina that allowed him to cover every blade of grass. It was of scant concern that no single part of his game was exceptional; the overall package of passing, tackling, temperament, leadership qualities and positional awareness more than compensated.

Within four minutes of the new season Darren Bent gave his new team a winning start at Bolton. In October, only a stoppage time own goal from Anton Ferdinand prevented victory at Old Trafford after Bent and Kenwyne Jones scored. The following home game against Liverpool was won by a controversial goal from Bent after only five minutes, owing to an infamous incident that left the visitors furious with a refereeing decision. An away supporter had thrown a beach ball into the penalty area. The goalkeeper Reina was understandably momentarily confused when a weak shot from Bent impacted the large red ball and went in. The visitors were unable to right the injustice in the remaining eighty-five minutes. Against Arsenal, Bent's worth was underlined when his only goal of the match moved Sunderland to eighth with 20 points from 13 games.

However, this was a season in three parts. Remarkably, the next fourteen league matches did not produce a victory. Injuries to Ferdinand and Turner at the heart of the defence may have contributed; both were absent during a 7-2 mauling at Chelsea. At least the club were not embarrassed by non-league Barrow in the FA Cup, whose huge 7,500 following witnessed a 3-0 defeat. The peculiar trade in players from Tottenham continued when loanee Alan Hutton filled in at right back over the closing months. A first-minute strike from Fraizer Campbell that preceded a Bent hat-trick ended the drought as Bolton were summarily dispatched on Wearside. In an extraordinary match with Tottenham, witnessed by 43,184 at the Stadium of Light, Bent took no less than three penalties, only one of which he converted. With proceedings finely balanced, Bolo Zenden magnificently volleyed a right-wing cross from Henderson to secure a 3-1 victory. Wearside marked the last stop for the 33-year-old gifted Dutchman, formerly of Barcelona, Liverpool and Middlesbrough, whom Bruce had signed as a free agent. Darren Bent proved the unequivocal success of the season with his 24 goals ensuring a thirteenth position for Sunderland but although this modest improvement had arisen at a mounting personal cost to Ellis Short, the American was undeterred and he continued to provide the club with interest-free loans.

In readiness for the 2010-11 season, Sunderland broke their transfer record. The £13 million signing of Asamoah Gyan, impressive leading the line for Ghana in the summer's South African World Cup, necessitated the departure of Kenwyne Jones. Even though he was twice voted man of the match by FIFA, there is always a risk in purchasing a player based on his performance in a one-off summer tournament. Bruce, capitalising on his connection with Alex Ferguson, agreed a full season loan for the highly promising Manchester United forward Danny Welbeck. Sunderland possessed a potent attacking trio of Bent, Gyan and Welbeck, backed by the creative Malbranque and the left-sided Bolo Zenden.

Bruce signed his old centre half Titus Bramble from Wigan Athletic. Bramble an impressive figure, complete with a natural ability on the ball, was capable of tackling cleanly and clearing his lines effectively. He was however, never destined for stardom as he lacked concentration and a sixth sense for reading the game. The back four remained problematical. Sunderland attempted to buy Hutton on a permanent basis, but having extravagantly spent on forward power were unwilling to meet Tottenham's asking price. A plethora of attacking talent is a potent weapon but a chain is only as strong as its weakest link. In football it is the least glamorous link, more often than not an unobtrusive defender, who sometimes purchased for a relative pittance, can ensure that the whole is greater than the sum of its parts.

The second season under Bruce started inconsistently. A two-goal lead thrown away at home to Birmingham City preceded a narrow defeat at West Bromwich Albion. At the Stadium of Light Darren Bent created closing time drama against Manchester City and Arsenal. His penalty deep into time added on that defeated City was followed by a 90th minute equaliser against Arsenal. In between those encounters, a goal from debutant Gyan should have earned three points but for a late Wigan equaliser at the DW Stadium. Sunderland were seventh in the table and marginal favourites when they faced Mike Ashley's newly promoted Newcastle at St. James' Park. Not a single Sunderland supporter could have envisaged the Hallowe'en horror show that unfolded on this last afternoon of October '11. At half-time United were three up. Bramble's second-half dismissal helped Kevin Nolan to complete a hat-trick and United prevail 5-1, with only a last-minute intervention by Bent preventing a joint-heaviest derby defeat. Simon Mignolet, signed in the wake of Gordon's persistent injury problems, had previously kept three clean sheets. That derby debacle, never to be forgotten, would always be a convenient source of criticism for Bruce, even though within a fortnight his side delivered the knockout punch of the year to floor Chelsea. In the next away outing after St. James' Gyan earned a point at Tottenham, worthy in itself, before Sunderland shocked the Premier League with a 3-0 victory at Stamford Bridge in a Sunday spectacular only days later. Chelsea were expecting to stretch their lead to six points at the head of the table. The BBC report of proceedings informed that, 'it would have been several more but for the brilliance of Petr Čech. Craig Gordon meanwhile barely had to make a save'. Onuoha, Gyan and Welbeck were the scorers. Injured John Terry and Frank Lampard were omitted. A further contributory cause of Chelsea's capitulation centred on the recent, unexpected departure from the backroom staff of the ever-popular Ray Wilkins. Darren Bent however was missing for Sunderland. The chairman Niall Quinn rated the performance higher than the famous match when he scored twice against the same opposition. He wrote, 'I first came to the club in 1996 and a lot of people rate the 4-1 win over a Chelsea side packed with World Cup stars at the Stadium of Light in 1999 as the highlight of that era. In fairness to everyone involved I have to say that while that day was immense, it was built on a breathtaking opening half whereas last Sunday's performance was for a full 90 minutes'.

The triumphant homecoming was muted. A Monday evening gathering of 37,000 witnessed a seventh-placed side draw with struggling Everton. Sunderland, conceding early, fought back with two Welbeck goals before the visitors rescued a point. Only 35,101 were present against Bolton on a bitterly cold December afternoon, the beginnings of an Arctic winter. They were warmed by a 1-0 win, decorated with a double-stop from the back-in-favour Craig Gordon, a save that received nationwide recognition when it was voted number one in a competition commemorating 20 years of Sky. There was a one-sided game with Blackpool over the festive period. Sunderland created no less than 32 failed scoring attempts; Blackpool momentarily lifted the siege to net twice through D J Campbell. The Seasiders were unexpectedly enjoying their first taste of top-flight football since 1971; this win moved them only two points behind seventh-placed Sunderland and with the luxury of two games in hand. However, as with most surprise packages relying on a nucleus of Championship players receiving Championship wages, their campaign disintegrated into a race to the bottom and they were relegated in May.

In January, after Welbeck, Bent and Gyan had scored in an emphatic win over Blackburn, Sunderland again underperformed in a derby, but on this occasion a late stoppage-time goal from Gyan denied Newcastle three points. Six days later when revenge over Blackpool came with a 2-1 win at Bloomfield Road, Darren Bent did not feature. The Tyne-Wear game at the Stadium of Light had been his last in a Sunderland shirt. It came as a bolt from the blue when Aston Villa, not pulling up any trees in the Premier League, made an unabashed offer of £24 million that encouraged the striker to request a transfer. There was an element of surprise that little was done to dissuade him. Niall Quinn struck an ambivalent stance throughout the quickly resolved episode and there was nothing to suggest Bent was actively seeking a move apart from his reduced goals output, which may or may not have been influenced by the presence of Gyan. Of the eight league goals Bent had scored in 20 games, only five had accrued from open play. The reported £65,000 per week wage from Villa was not met with a counter-offer. Supporters directed vitriol at Bent, questioning his motive at leaving a club, positioned sixth on the brink of European qualification, for a perceived 'smaller club', only separated from eighteenth position by goal difference. Ironically, his last away appearance for Sunderland was the occasion of a 1-0 victory at Villa Park. Asamoah Gyan, discounting penalties, had scored more goals than Bent and was now the leading man. Before the transfer window closed, Bruce paid £6 million for the Benin international forward Stéphane Sessegnon from Paris Saint-Germain. A third round FA Cup capitulation at home to third-tier Notts County hardly merited an inquest: the Premier League was paramount.

At the end of March England hosted Ghana at Wembley in an unusually competitive friendly. Gyan, showing a determination not always apparent when he donned a red and white shirt, was rewarded with a last-minute equalising goal. Danny Welbeck was handed an England debut. Also in the green of Ghana were Mensah and Sulley Muntari, the latter another loan signing who had arrived from Inter Milan in the winter window. Hopes of taking Welbeck permanently were quashed when Ferguson said that he, himself, had more chance of winding up at the Stadium of Light than his protégé. Bent's departure impacted. There was a poor run of nine winless games that was only ended when Wigan were beaten 4-2. Sunderland limped to the finishing line but their last-day defeat of relegated West Ham at Upton Park belatedly pushed them four places up the table. Newcastle, by squandering a three-goal lead at home to West Bromwich Albion, were overtaken. When the wheel of fortune of the richest league in the world stopped on its concluding thirty-eighth spin, Sunderland almost by default it might be said, found themselves in tenth position and Bruce had implausibly fulfilled the owner's ambition of a top-half finish. It was hardly a ringing endorsement of a move to the 'next level' and it would have to be done all over again without Jordan Henderson and Bent. Henderson, who had won an England cap in a game against France, was transferred to Liverpool for £20 million. The fee was considered extravagant for a player with only two senior seasons under his belt; some with valued opinions within the game were unsure if Henderson would realise his potential and were surprised when he and Liverpool progressed to winning the Champions League, Premier League and FA Cup.

An unconventional but compelling book, 'The Numbers Game' by Chris Anderson and David Sally, analysed the impact of strikers over 2009-10 and 2010-11. They assigned a value to each goal based on its importance in influencing the result of a game. Therefore, as an example, a first goal scored in a 4-0 win merited a higher value than the fourth goal. They state, 'the most valuable goal is the second (increasing the team's predicted point value by 0.99). In contrast, going from a likely thrashing to a probable stomping (that is, a fifth goal) is exchanged for only 0.1 points'. Bent is ranked second in each of the two seasons assessed, behind Wayne Rooney and Carlos Tevez respectively. Using this methodology, the 24 goals from Bent in his full season at Sunderland gained the club 20.02 marginal points, which amounted to almost half of the actual points tally of 44. Many Sunderland fans of course would take issue with his contribution in the second season, but that was partially explained by the presence of Gyan on whom hopes were now pinned.

Bruce's Sunderland were a conundrum, on their day beating the best but more often than not, capitulating to modest opposition. Sunderland finishing eight points above relegated Birmingham and Blackpool is an alternative way of assessing their tenth-placed finish. Signing Craig Gardner and David Vaughan from that distressed duo suggested quantity over quality. As Manchester United are a club renowned for releasing players past their sell-by date, the additions of John O'Shea and Wes Brown raised doubt. The versatile O'Shea however, principally a central defender, proved his worth. He shared captaincy duties with Cattermole and gave excellent service. Brown, when selected, was a class act but fitness problems rendered him less reliable than Anton Ferdinand, who was sold to QPR for £3 million after only four appearances at the beginning of the new season. Sunderland were keen to salvage value from a player in the final year of his contract but considering the £44 million received from Bent and Henderson and Short's default tendency to spend, it seemed a strange decision. The arrival of Ipswich forward Connor Wickham for £10 million created headlines. At 18 years old Wickham was the future; Bruce could indulge potential because Asamoah Gyan was the here and now.

Seb Larsson, a newcomer from Arsenal, a wonderful hitter of both a static and moving ball, equalised with a trademark volley at Liverpool to give 1,877 travelling supporters optimism for the 2011-12 season. Sunderland were hopeful of three points from their first home game, an unusually early derby date. Newcastle however edged the Saturday high noon encounter by a single goal to leave Bruce without a success in three derby matches. In less than a fortnight the plans of the Sunderland manager were torn apart. Gyan arranged a one-year loan deal with the United Arab Emirates side Al Ain that was extended to two years before Sunderland reluctantly agreed to make the move permanent. As Gyan had agreed to drop into a significantly lower level of football thereby risking future career prospects, the UAE club dangled an enormous financial carrot. In addition, Sunderland received an unprecedented £6 million for agreeing to the initial release. This was scant compensation for a team that not so long ago had an embarrassment of forward power and were now forced into a short-term fix.

Welbeck had already returned to Old Trafford. Bruce was left with little alternative but to borrow the accomplished but dissolute Nicklas Bendtner from Arsenal. Bruce, when manager of Birmingham, had loaned Bendtner from Arsenal and became aware of the Dane's proclivities. His nocturnal habits were continually at odds with the ethos of Arsène Wenger at Highbury. Bruce's first instruction was for him to keep his distance from Lee Cattermole. This in reality was never likely to happen; the pair teamed up and one of their escapades following a drunken spree involved kicking in the wing mirrors of cars, for which Cattermole was cautioned. At first Bendtner, on realising there was no genuine competition for his shirt, played within his comfort zone. A comfortable 4-0 win over Stoke including three early goals tempered criticism of the manager but the attendance of 32,000 was poor, regardless of the game clashing with the Great North Run. A series of close matches were not capitalised upon and when basement club Wigan arrived on 26th November, Sunderland were five points ahead of their opponents with four clubs between them. Ellis Short commented that there was no reason to panic and gave a positive take on poor results. He pointed out, 'only four teams have conceded fewer goals than us and nine clubs have scored less than us'. Selective or not with his facts Short, who was in the stadium, was unable to ignore the torrent of abuse hurled at Bruce by a significant minority, after a stoppage-time goal from Di Santo earned Wigan victory. Sentiment changed. Short took decisive action and Bruce was reacquainted with the familiar well-paid managerial merry-go-round. His whirl of employment to date stretches over twelve employers, who between them have provided a slew of generous severance pay for a series of jobs carried out with variable degrees of competence.

Martin O'Neill was quickly appointed, to universal accord. As a youngster in Derry, he idolised Charlie Hurley and it was natural he supported

Sunderland. O'Neill had taken Aston Villa to three consecutive top-six finishes, that when added to a couple of League Cup triumphs with Leicester where the side he managed were never out of the top half, made him a sought-after property. His thoughtful, measured replies and dry humour in response to the inane questions football managers are bombarded with were testimony to a sharp intellect. As a player, he benefitted from a trophy-laden career under the guidance of Brian Clough at Nottingham Forest.

At first there was something of the Midas touch from the Irishman. The first time he took charge, goals on 84 and 90 plus minutes from Vaughan and Larsson defeated Blackburn 2-1. Ten days later Wes Brown found an unlikely winner on 89 minutes at Loftus Road, given that QPR, having come from two behind, were in the ascendency. The crowning moment of the O'Neill honeymoon period arrived on New Year's Day. Manchester City, awash with new money from the Middle East, were in Premier League pole position having scored 53 goals in 18 games. When Wes Brown departed injured after only twenty minutes to be replaced by Matt Kilgallon, the home crowd feared the worst. City laid siege to a charmed Sunderland goalmouth. Three minutes into added time, South Korean forward Ji Dong-won, a late substitute, produced the only goal of the game in a moment that will forever be remembered as one of the stadium's greatest moments. 48 hours later Wigan were beaten 4-1 on their own turf.

There was a burgeoning FA Cup run; a strong Arsenal team were overcome before a live BBC audience as Sunderland marched into the quarter-finals. This was revenge of sorts for the previous Saturday, when after James McClean broke the deadlock at the Stadium of Light on 70 minutes, the Gunners took the points with goals from Aaron Ramsey and Thierry Henry, the latter in time added on. McClean, a direct left-sided attacker, hailed as one for the future when he signed from Derry over the summer, had been given his debut in O'Neill's first game in charge. Both he and the young midfielder Jack Colback, receiving approval from supporters, were regular fixtures during this run of form and both lined up at Goodison for the sixth round clash with Everton. Despite a somewhat unconvincing draw, Sunderland now with home advantage were nevertheless favourites to meet Liverpool in a Wembley semi-final. It was an unusually mild March evening. The novelty of only a third ever post-war sixth round replay on Wearside promised something out of the ordinary. David Moyes' patiently assembled side, featuring Baines, Cahill, Distin, Fellaini and Neville, may perennially have been on the outside looking in, chasing shadows of the big four Premier League clubs as they were numbered then, but on that abruptly sobering Wearside night they were a chasm apart from Sunderland. So too was their support; the Merseyside contingent of 6,034 who filled the South Stand outshouted and upstaged the subdued majority of a less than capacity 43,140 crowd. At the rear of the

Premier Concourse, there were rows of empty seats, almost unnoticed. For those of a certain generation, an old Roker Cup night it certainly was not. The colossus Fellaini assisted Jelavić for the opening goal before yet another of his forward charges instigated a mistake that forced Vaughan to put past his own goalkeeper. The squad's lack of depth was exposed; the absence of Brown and O'Shea through injury forced a Greek, bit-part, centre half, Sotirios Kyrgiakos to suffer a flawed appearance. Everton won 2-0. The Midas touch had deserted O'Neill.

In their next outing, Sunderland, defying logic, led Manchester City at the Etihad 3-1 with Larsson scoring twice before two very late goals allowed the home side to escape with a draw. The Everton game marked a watershed; the club failed to register a single win in their final eight matches. Only a head-to-head title clash of the two Manchester giants added spice to the closing weeks, with the Stadium of Light guaranteed a ringside seat as Sunderland hosted Ferguson's United on a climactic last Sunday. For United to win the Premier League they had to better City's result. On Wearside they accomplished an expected win. Over at the Etihad, with QPR guarding a 2-1 advantage in added time, it seemed a racing certainty that Manchester United, courtesy of the season's shock result, were heading for what had seemed a highly improbable title win. City, despite their firepower and 80% possession, were not igniting. When the final whistle sounded at the Stadium of Light, City had just equalised but they were now in the fourth minute of time added on. Seconds remained. Agüero found a winner on 93:20 to break the hearts of the United contingent, leaving players and management team transfixed in disbelief. The title had gone. Sunderland fans exploded in a joyous mood of schadenfreude. Backs turned to the pitch; they copied the Poznań, a celebration unique in England to Manchester City followers. For the long-suffering Sunderland fans, it had come down to this after five years of meagre rations in the Premier League. Surely now, in Martin O'Neill, the club possessed a man to take them forward and he would have all summer to fashion the side to meet the expectations of Short. But as a sixth consecutive Premier League season unwound, the American owner was further away than ever from rubbing shoulders with his fellow countrymen at the hallowed environs of Old Trafford and Anfield.

28

BLANK CHEQUES

2012-13 to 2013-14

Martin O'Neill signed forwards Adam Johnson and Steven Fletcher from Manchester City and Wolverhampton Wanderers respectively, for fees just into eight figures. The acquisition of locally-born Johnson, formerly an expensive signing for City from Middlesbrough and holder of 12 full England caps, was seen as an important step in Sunderland's progression to a top-half team. The manager said, 'He has terrific ability and great delivery. I am sure he is a player who will excite the fans. I couldn't be more delighted to have him at the club'. Danny Rose, an England under-21 international and another loan capture from Tottenham, temporarily solved the problem left back position. His impact led to speculation of Sunderland signing him but this was unlikely, given that the Spurs chairman Daniel Levy was a renowned hardball negotiator. So, as it transpired, the two best full backs at the Stadium of Light since Keane's promotion, namely Rose and Hutton, were loanees and pertinently, surplus to requirements at a club Sunderland were striving to emulate.

Visiting supporters were moved from the South Stand to the North Stand Upper. This was expected to improve match day atmosphere and avoid a mass of empty seats directly in line with camera angles. After a goalless draw at Arsenal, the first home game against Reading was postponed at short notice due to a sudden downpour.

Fletcher scored twice at Swansea on his league debut to earn a point. He was prolific in September finding the net in all of his five matches. Following four draws out of four, a second-half strike by Fletcher against Wigan earned a welcome first league success of the season. Apart from in the League Cup, no other player had scored for Sunderland up to that point. A 3-0 defeat at Manchester City ended the unbeaten start and only a fortuitous late own goal from Demba Ba prevented a further setback at the Stadium of Light Tyne-Wear derby. The early momentum faded. Despite the excellence of Sessègnon and goalkeeper Simon Mignolet, question marks persisted, as ever. Fletcher's purple patch was over, Johnson was having to readjust to a lesser calibre of player around him than at Manchester City and Connor Wickham, understandably, remained work-in-progress. Carlos Cuéllar, who had played under O'Neill at Aston Villa, signed on a free transfer. He proved an inadequate replacement for the long-term injured Wes Brown. Results were unpredictable at best: a 3-1 victory at Fulham was tarnished by a 4-2 home defeat by West Bromwich Albion. On Boxing Day, Manchester City, chasing rivals United at the top, were undone on Wearside for the third consecutive time by a 1-0 margin. Johnson returned a small portion of his £10 million fee in the 53rd minute of a contest in which the home side, for once, were not continually penned in their own half by light blue shirts.

Sunderland, having beaten Southampton 1-0 before the City game, were on the rise. Despite the minor affliction of an FA Cup exit, with only 17,000 attending the Bolton replay defeat, the club managed to put together a run of 15 points from eight games. The last of that sequence featured two excellent goals from Fletcher in a 3-2 victory at Wigan, which represented the first time since Keane's reign that the club had earned three points after going behind away from home. As is often the case, there seemed little explanation for those excellent results and the pendulum swung the other way with a vengeance. From a position of eleventh, Sunderland failed to win in seven matches. The January outlay of £10 million for Alfred N'Diaye and Danny Graham hindered rather than helped. Close season captures Louis Saha and James McFadden had seen negligible first team action. There was criticism that the manager was out of touch and that his playing style was defensive and overly reliant on the long ball. O'Neill's demeanour darkened, his characteristic deliberations in front of camera were lengthier and pained. Perhaps he was disadvantaged by the decision of his traditional sidekick and sounding board John Robertson not to become his right-hand man. Within six weeks Short had shifted his stance from acknowledging that 'this is Martin's first full season at the club and we are trying to build a team that will continue to improve our position', to commenting within very brief programme notes, 'Of course there is nobody that is happy with our current position and the way our season is going'. That latter statement was made before a game with Manchester United, lost 1-0 on the heels of an abject home draw against an untroubled Norwich, who played for an hour with 10 men. The end for O'Neill was no great surprise. It later came to light that his wife had been in ill health; one can only speculate as to the level of stress with which this had burdened him. With seven games remaining, Sunderland were sixteenth, only a point ahead of

Wigan and Aston Villa. The bottom two were adrift. The position was far from desperate but the next two fixtures were away at Chelsea and Newcastle.

Short moved quickly. The Italian Paolo Di Canio was prised from Swindon to become Sunderland's first continental manager. The appointment was controversial, not least because of his political allegiance to the far right and a fascination for Benito Mussolini, whom he named as the person he would most prefer to have a one-to-one with. David Miliband, a Labour MP, resigned his position as vice chairman when news broke. The baggage aside, Di Canio came with a reputation as a fiercely driven winner, a perfectionist, a straight talker and someone who Ron Atkinson, his former manager, described as a 'complete nutter'. Everything and everyone would be subject to change on his watch. He imposed his zero-tolerance ethos on what he perceived as a soft underbelly of indiscipline within the squad. Lax habits from highly-paid footballers was anathema to the principled Di Canio. Rather like Clough's 44-day tenure at Elland Road, Sunderland may not have realised who or what they were taking on. At first the shock therapy worked. Following an expected reverse at Chelsea, although a lead was established before succumbing 2-1, there was a sensational performance at St. James' Park. Goals without reply from Sessègnon, Johnson and Vaughan handed Sunderland a second success in seventeen derby encounters. It was incredible stuff. Di Canio's fine suit was mud-splattered as he knelt on the turf, punching his arms skywards in celebratory fashion, an image second, albeit a distant second, to that of Stokoe racing across the Wembley pitch to embrace Montgomery. David Maddock in the Daily Mirror sounded a cautionary note, 'He is as mad as a bag of baboons, and that will present its own problems in the coming years for this fine club'. There were 44,614 present to welcome him to Wearside against Everton, who were chasing Champions League qualification. A goal from Sessègnon overcame the side that had so comprehensively outplayed Sunderland in their previous visit. After claiming six points from two games, a crushing 6-1 defeat at Aston Villa failed to dampen spirits. In their next outing, despite being handicapped by the first-half dismissal of Craig Gardner and an early goal from Jonathan Walters, Sunderland tenaciously fought back against Stoke to earn a point, which may have been three had a post not thwarted Danny Rose. The Stadium rocked. Safety was all but assured.

In the summer of 2013 Short committed the club to a radical change in direction when he adopted a continental model of operation. Di Canio became the Chief Coach. Roberto De Fanti was appointed Director of Football. The devil makes work for idle hands. No less than 14 signings were made as De Fanti busied himself by scouring Europe and talking to agents. The new regime was full of noise. Chief Executive Margaret Byrne spoke enthusiastically of investing in a 'shadow squad' and said the team had been strengthened in many different positions. Yet the potent Sessègnon, who remained a great favourite, was sold to West Bromwich Albion as Sunderland adopted a similar pecuniary attitude to that which had led to Ferdinand's departure and the consequent centre back problems. There was further dismay with the departure of goalkeeper Simon Mignolet to Liverpool for £9 million. Incoming names such as Cabral, El-Hadji Ba, Diakité and Dossena had supporters scratching their heads. American Jozy Altidore from AZ Alkmaar and Emanuele Giaccherini from Juventus came for a combined £12 million; neither distinguished themselves, with Altidore's legacy being that of continual mentions within discussions to name the club's worst ever value for money signing. The farewells from Sessègnon and Mignolet, in addition to a swathe of free signings and loan arrivals, betrayed Sunderland's precarious financial situation.

Five league games into the 2013-14 season, with one point on the board after a shocking 3-0 defeat at the Hawthorns, Di Canio said that the players 'had rubbish in their brains'. After the final whistle he had bizarrely marched in front of the Sunderland fans only to receive obscene gestures. He would have remembered an end-of-season photograph in the Daily Mail regarding a squad outing that depicted a poleaxed Phil Bardsley stretched out on the floor of a casino, reputedly sober, covered in £50 notes. Ironically, Bardsley was one of those unfussy, underrated defenders whose value to a club is higher than any fee received in the event of a transfer. Following the West Bromwich Albion debacle, Di Canio became a victim of player power. A delegation led by Lee Cattermole complained to Margaret Byrne of his behaviour and derogatory comments. The short-lived adrenalin rush arising from his appointment had long abated; the hierarchy listened to the overpaid, underperforming players. It was all too easy to diabolize Di Canio. The sanitised, insular world of football was no place for his outspokenness or 'impossibly' high demands. When he played in the late nineties, he compared himself to Mussolini and by doing so acknowledged a weakness in himself. Di Canio, highlighting a striking contrast between himself and the sometimes politic Italian dictator, said he was unwilling to alter his beliefs, even when a failure to do so would prove detrimental. 'I couldn't (and haven't) compromised my ethics even to save myself. Too many times I've stood up for what I believe in, only to later pay the price.' The outcome for Sunderland was yet another round of expensive compensation payments for a discarded manager and only recently installed backroom staff. Short's actions were now resembling something said by Jack Nicholson. The actor, using language considered at the very least to be irreverent and inappropriate in today's world, referred to female company when he delivered his roguish one-liner, 'You don't pay them to be there, you pay them to leave'.

Uruguayan Gus Poyet was the new Chief Coach. He left his position at Brighton where he preached a possession game. His style of patiently building from the back, bringing every player into play before crossing the halfway line and denying the ball to the opposition, was a consequence of an increased overseas influence in the game and pitches of a bowling green standard. The method employed by Tony Pulis at Stoke to prevent the opposition from gaining possession, was to minimise the time the ball was in play and maximise set piece situations. Bob Paisley, the great Liverpool manager, claimed that only the right ball mattered, regardless of length. England manager Sir Alf Ramsey explained that he only picked the players who fitted the tactics he wished to use, whereas a club manager, lacking such luxury chose the tactics that best utilised the talent available. It remained to be seen whether Poyet already possessed or could attract the right players to suit his purpose, let alone be granted the time to impose his will. Although recruitment at Sunderland and Stoke was hampered by economic reality and a relatively unattractive location, the Pulis brand of football, although condemned by purists, kept an unfashionable club whose followers had moderate expectations in the top half of the Premier table. Poyet was acutely aware of the demands from a fervent Northeast public. Attendances had averaged 40,000 in the previous two seasons; Stoke in comparison were drawing 27,000. Poyet's smiling face reminisced about the first time he played at the Stadium of Light; the one-sided December afternoon when his Chelsea team were battered by Quinn and Phillips. He imagined what the original hotbed of soccer would be like with a hint of success. He quickly had an inkling. After a 4-0 defeat at Swansea in his inaugural game, the first experience of the home dugout was a derby against Newcastle on 19th October when Sunderland, with a late goal from substitute Fabio Borini, claimed their first league victory of the season. Borini, loaned from Liverpool, was a rare De Fanti signing who actually impressed. Despite the upheaval, despite the input of a coach leaving no stone unturned in his quest to provide that vital 1% improvement, there was no uplift in results. Another relegation battle was brewing. By January, with Sunderland bottom of the league, De Fanti was history and the majority of his signings on borrowed time. Left back Marcos Alonso, for whom Chelsea later paid £24 million, commenced a half-season loan period from Fiorentina. He became an important part of the side.

By then, paradoxically, the club had risen almost without trace to a two-legged last four League Cup tie with Manchester United. Home wins over Southampton and Chelsea were watched by 15,996 and 20,731. The competition, at first an unwelcome impediment to survival hopes, burst into life. 9,000 fans travelled to Old Trafford after Sunderland had beaten United 2-1 on Wearside. The return leg was remarkable. In the first half, former loanee Jonny Evans levelled the aggregate scores and as the clock ticked during extra time, a penalty shootout loomed. On 119 minutes Phil Bardsley hit a low, weak shot from 20 yards that de Gea unaccountably let slip.

Unbelievably, in the one minute added for the goal celebration, Javier Hernández levelled the aggregate, emerging unmarked to tap over the line from two yards despite the presence of eight defenders in the penalty box. The penalty shootout was nothing like any previous lottery. Only three from the ten were converted but crucially, it was Sunderland, with Alonso and Ki successful, who progressed to a Wembley final where they faced Manchester City. The Wearsiders, during their slew of poor results that autumn, had defeated City at home 1-0, for a fourth consecutive occasion. The richest club in the world regarded Sunderland as something of a bogey. It was in that game that Wes Brown reappeared after a 22-month layoff.

Between the United legs, four points were taken from two games including a 4-1 victory at Fulham. A hat-trick from Adam Johnson included a direct free kick and a penalty that Altidore won with an outrageous dive. The old guard were back in vogue with Poyet having culled the poor summer intake. O'Shea and Brown were together again, the pragmatic full back Bardsley complementing an adventurous Alonso on his opposite flank, whilst a fully-fit Cattermole linked defence and midfield. Jack Colback, the Academy graduate, had fought off competition to earn a regular place. Inevitably, weaknesses persisted. An out-of-form Fletcher meant there was no dependable goal threat although that problem was addressed later in the season with startling, sudden effect.

When the final came around, Sunderland were awaiting a quarter-final FA Cup tie at Hull City. In this competition, Southampton had again fallen victim when they were beaten in the fifth round, on this occasion watched by another paltry Wearside attendance of 16,777. Incredibly, in the league Sunderland achieved another 3-0 win at St. James' Park, set up by a Borini penalty with further goals coming from Johnson and Colback. A haul of 14 points from seven games that attained a heady fourteenth position seemed to suggest better days ahead. With Wembley in the offing and the derby win fresh, 43,000 were present for the visit of Hull in a league match that might have had some bearing on the relegation positions in May. The visitors, level with Sunderland on 24 points from 24 games and fielding Stephen Harper in goal, a month shy of his thirty-ninth birthday, were never troubled and departed with a comfortable three points.

Sunderland's biggest occasion for 29 years started like a dream. After ten minutes. Borini outpaced Vincent Kompany down the right flank before cutting in to fire Sunderland to a shock lead over Manchester City at new Wembley. The Italian almost scored again before the break. The rank outsiders returned to their dressing room in the ascendant. City followers harboured doubts. In the space of a hundred seconds the vocal Sunderland support suffered football's capricious nature. Yaya Touré, unmarked twenty-five yards out, swung his languid, calculating right foot and arched the ball into the top left corner of the goal, beyond the grasp of Mannone. Before Sunderland mobilised, Samir Nasri struck. With the second half only ten minutes old, the carnival that commenced the previous afternoon in Covent Garden was over. Navas added a third at the end. A sixth round FA Cup exit at Hull swiftly followed; the weakened eleven Poyet inexplicably fielded, for which he was heavily criticised, surrendered 3-0.

A 5-1 thrashing at Tottenham followed by an unlucky home defeat, gifted to Everton by an otherwise excellent Wes Brown who put through his own net, abruptly ended Sunderland's nascent revival. After the Spurs defeat, Poyet claimed it would take a 'miracle' for his team to stay up given that they were seven points behind fourth-bottom Norwich with two games fewer played. Current form of one point from eight games was ominous, only six fixtures remained and his next two opponents Manchester City and Chelsea, benefitting from home advantage, were in a three way title race alongside Liverpool. Suffering from an assortment of injuries to his players, in particular the forward Steven Fletcher, Poyet had recalled Connor Wickham from Leeds United where he had languished when Wearside prematurely partied at Wembley. Wickham, having already scored eight goals in eleven games at Sheffield Wednesday, a Championship staging post that welcomed underused Premier League players, had only made three league starts for Sunderland the previous season and overall shown little to warrant the excitement of his arrival from Ipswich. He was all but forgotten. The game in Manchester, following a handful of uneventful appearances after his recall from Elland Road, reminded those present why Steve Bruce had signed him. City claimed an early lead but were relieved to salvage a draw on 88 minutes after going behind through two Wickham goals. Sunderland's effort was admirable but in the cold light of day it was two points dropped. Unquestionably, it seemed mission impossible at a Stamford Bridge rendered impregnable by Jose Mourinho, the self-proclaimed 'special one', who had not suffered a league defeat there during 77 consecutive games, which spanned his two spells in charge. Chelsea, as expected, quickly led but Wickham capitalised on a fumble from their 41-year-old replacement goalkeeper Mark Schwarzer, who failed to hold an Alonso shot. Borini converted a late penalty to secure a 2-1 win. Sunderland's fate was no longer inevitable as they passed through West London's version of Venice's Bridge of Sighs. Cardiff's visit, ostensibly a six-pointer, attracted 46,000. Wickham delivered another two goals to dispatch the Welshmen 4-0. An encore might have seemed unlikely at Old Trafford, where Sunderland had failed to register a league victory in their last 22 attempts; this was surely a curtain call too far. Manchester United however were managerless and listless, out of contention for a Champions League place with Moyes, recently departed by mutual consent, having been unable to emerge from Alex Ferguson's shadow. Seb Larsson's strike ensured victory, offering the certainty that avoiding defeat in a rearranged home game with West Bromwich would render the last-game visit of Swansea academic. First half goals from Colback and Borini ensured the large crowd enjoyed the remainder of the evening. The future appeared bright but under the surface all was not well.

29

STAYING UP ... AGAIN

2014-15 to 2015-16

Despite healthy attendances, Sunderland had reported a financial loss in the seven seasons since returning to the Premier League. Over that period the club attained an average finish of fourteenth. There should be a reliable correlation between a club's wage bill and position within the league table; not so with Sunderland, their expenditure being consistently between the top eight to ten clubs in the country. Whilst this suggested an underachievement, the higher than average remuneration was probably an unavoidable incentive, offered to attract players to an area they perceived unattractive and to a club not capable of competing for honours. In a global Premier League, London is a magnet for footballers. The League Cup run helped to increase gate receipts from £12.6 million to £15.7 million but this had a minuscule effect on finances compared to previous Wembley visits. Sunderland's annual match day revenue was overshadowed for example, by Arsenal, who grossed around £100 million. The Gunners derived a disproportionate amount of this from no less than 146 private boxes, upmarket seats and, at the very highest level, an exclusive 'Diamond Club' that boasted a Michelin star restaurant. During the 2014-15 season the price of an adult, non-concessionary season ticket at the Emirates ranged from £1,014 to £2,013. They possessed 7,139 seats within a 'platinum membership' area and the revenue alone from this these, excluding ancillary spending on food and drink, amounted to a figure well in excess of Sunderland's annual season ticket sales.

The sport in general, through the increased gentrification of the game, had become attractive to a greater number of middle-class supporters, prepared to meet spiralling admission costs. Wages within the Northeast, in particular the old Durham coalfields that represented the traditional heartland of Sunderland support, had always been quite low, and now more so with the disappearance of highly skilled manufacturing work. This factor was not relevant in years gone by. A North-South wealth divide has always existed in the United Kingdom but in the era before the Premier League, football was essentially a spectator sport for the working-class masses; this was reflected by fairly uniform admission prices across all clubs. In 1981 the price of a Roker Park seat at £4.50 was marginally greater than that of Highbury. At all grounds in the then First Division, terracing made up most of capacity. Sunderland, by charging £1.90 to stand, were slightly above average. The economic football climate was undergoing radical change. The huge sums received from various broadcasting contracts were becoming less significant for a handful of elite clubs that were able to command mammoth revenue streams from sponsorship and merchandising. A gap between the haves and have nots was now a gulf.

The interest-free loans with which Short initially bankrolled Sunderland were represented on the balance sheet as an external creditor and therefore showed the club as heavily indebted. As this would have been a red flag deterring potential individual and corporate lenders, the Sunderland owner circumvented this between 2008 and 2010 by exchanging his £100 million debt for equity. This strategy was potentially risky for Short; in the event of an insolvency a shareholder ranks last in the pecking order and therefore there will usually be little if anything left with which to compensate a holder of equity. Over the same two-year period cumulative trading losses of £50.3 million were reported. Sunderland fared reasonably better vis-a-vis the Premier League norm concerning shirt sponsorship. An extension was agreed in July '14 with Bidvest, a Buckinghamshire food company, that was replaced the following year when Dafabet, a foreign betting company, agreed a £12 million deal over 2 years. This was a healthy increase on previous arrangements. It would for example, be better than that which Aston Villa and Everton commanded, although small beer compared to the £47 million per annum Manchester United were receiving from Chevrolet. Sunderland were unable to generate cash flow from trading activity and were increasingly dependent on television money and the generosity of a single individual. A desperation to maintain Premier League status was understandable. Included in the Sunderland annual report and financial statement dated 31 July '14 was a section entitled 'Strategic Report'. Amongst other things it said, 'The company is deemed to be a going concern due to the ongoing support of the immediate parent company, Sunderland Limited and the ultimate controlling party Mr. Ellis Short. The directors consider the major risk of the business to be a significant period of absence from the Premier League. Ongoing investment in the playing squad intends to reduce this risk'. Shortly after those cautious words, Sunderland signed Jack Rodwell from Manchester City and took Ricky Álvarez on loan from Inter Milan; both, in their different ways, were to hole the club's balance sheet.

In August '14, the club gave Rodwell a ground-breaking five-year contract at £70,000 per week whilst paying Manchester City £10 million for the out-of-favour midfielder. Although capped by England, his career had stalled at City through injuries, and in similar fashion to Adam Johnson, his former Etihad team-mate, he found competition for a regular first team place fierce. The tangle Sunderland found themselves in regarding Álvarez trumped everything for financial recklessness. He was a hasty afterthought after Borini, the prime summer target, reneged on a decision to sign from Liverpool. Álvarez only made 13 appearances and Sunderland backtracked on an agreement to convert his loan to a permanent transfer, whereby Milan would receive £10 million provided the Wearsiders avoided relegation. There was a wrangle between the clubs over the interpretation of a knee injury that the Argentinian received in a match with Swansea. Sunderland contended that as the injury was connected to a previous medical problem, it invalidated their agreement to sign him permanently. Milan appealed to the Court of Arbitration for Sport who ruled that Sunderland were liable to pay the transfer fee. The financial liability did not end there. In addition to wages already paid during the loan period, Álvarez was awarded an astonishing £4.8 million in compensation for the period of the following season when he was unable to play for either club. All told, it cost Short a numbing £20 million when the dust settled in 2017.

This figure though was less than that expended on Jack Rodwell. Over a four-year period, blighted by injury and a debilitating lack of confidence, he played fewer than seventy times. Rodwell was not part of a winning side on 39 consecutive occasions. Adam Johnson, on £60,000 per week, became an expensive luxury. His contributions, although often decisive against Newcastle, were marred too often in other games by inconsistency and a tendency to drop deep and assist overworked team-mates. Any debate around his effectiveness was soon rendered irrelevant by events off the field but despite this, Johnson was allowed to continue on the field.

Short, in his programme notes at the closure of the transfer window, acknowledged a lack of success in planning for the long term. He attributed this to a constant fight for survival under different managers that had forced the club to continually buy and release players on unfavourable terms. Perhaps in Poyet he presumed that he had found stability. He praised the acquisitions made by the new Director of Football, Lee Congerton, and commented that in taking Patrick van Aanholt from Chelsea the club had finally unearthed a specialist left back. On 24th August a £70 million loan was arranged with Security Benefit Corporation at an eye-watering interest rate of 7.5%. If all went pear-shaped and the club were unable to meet a repayment obligation after five years, the Stadium of Light and Academy would be at risk. Unsurprisingly, this enormous capital injection was not mentioned by Short within the notes.

Short may have ruefully mused that aside from upheavals in personnel, the other constant within the club was a scarcity of victories in the opening months of a new season. A noticeable change however was the higher number of away fans travelling to the stadium, a symptom of the growing popularity of the game. This was evidenced by the big three London clubs bringing 3,000 up to Wearside and even West Ham, in the depths of December, managing 1,771. By then Sunderland had suffered an eight-goal rout at Southampton with only two wins on the board. The visit to Newcastle a week before Christmas provided another chance to play their get-out-of-jail-free derby joker. In the final minute of normal time, Adam Johnson ensured a fourth consecutive win over the enemy to take his side four points clear of the bottom three. There was less hostility than usual. The St. James' contingent paid tribute to the support from Wearside given to the families of United fans Liam Sweeney and John Alder, both killed in the Malaysian Airlines tragedy in July, whilst the Sunderland fans countered with spontaneous applause on 17 minutes. The previous season on derby day, a United fan infamously punched a police horse.

The festive cheer was short-lived. Struggling Hull should have been put to the sword when Johnson scored in the first minute but 45,000 witnessed a 3-1 loss. The second half at the Etihad on New Year's Day 2015 produced a markedly different performance, unrecognisable from Poyet's usual cagey approach. Five goals were scored in 16 minutes. Manchester City scored twice in nine minutes before Sunderland replied with two goals in three minutes. Frank Lampard retaliated with a decisive third. Completely unexpected in January was the arrival of 32-year-old Jermain Defoe, distinguished as a clinical Premier League striker in a sparkling career that encompassed over 50 England appearances. Outside of London and south coast clubs, he had never previously played for anyone domestically. Put out to pasture at Major League Soccer club Toronto, he arrived in a direct exchange for Jozy Altidore. Nicknamed Dozy, his contribution in a Sunderland shirt of one goal from 42 league appearances was hardly surprising when judged against a haunting open-goal miss in a home game with West Ham weeks before his departure. Eleven games from the first 22 had been drawn when Defoe made his home league debut against Burnley. Both teams were in trouble. He made the first of his many vital interventions for Sunderland with a 34th minute goal that sealed a 2-0 win. Despite initial scepticism, Defoe endeared himself to everyone with his professionalism and personality, as he established a rapport with football and non-football follower alike. He was in his element with his back to goal, dancing along the eighteen-yard line surrounded by defenders, yet able to instinctively find the net with a sharp turn. He was capable of a venomous long-range shot and commanded a sense of the occasion, never more so than on Easter Sunday when his volley from 20 yards fashioned another win over Newcastle United.

Poyet had not witnessed Defoe's finest moment in a red and white shirt. In the previous home game against Aston Villa, following the concession of four first-half goals without reply, the South American deserted his post at the interval and within 48 hours Sunderland were looking again for a head figure. The Newcastle game was the first time on Wearside that the Dutchman Dick Advocaat appeared in the technical area. He stood unruffled in his trademark knotted scarf and warm woollen knee-length coat, comfortable in his own skin, exuding the appearance of a person almost past his time. Advocaat, 67, had been the Netherlands' national team manager and a championship winner in different countries. His appointment was supposedly purely a short-term, firefighting operation. His seen it all, done it all, careworn demeanour differed to the messianic Di Canio and bright-eyed, technocratic Poyet, although like his two predecessors, his first win was sampled in the region's big derby. Six days later, as if to tease Advocaat for his decision to come out of retirement, Sunderland shipped another four goals at the Stadium of Light on this occasion to Crystal Palace, all within 14 minutes of the second half. Yannick Bolasie only scored a dozen times in 133 appearances for Palace; on that afternoon he contrived an improbable hat-trick in 11 minutes. Adam Johnson did not feature in those games. On 2nd March he was arrested and charged with offences of a sexual nature against a girl fifteen years old. Johnson was initially suspended by the club before being allowed to return later in the season, although used mainly as a substitute, on the understanding that there would be no admission of guilt from him. After a draw at Stoke, Sunderland slipped into the bottom three with five games remaining.

There was no repeat of the heroics under Poyet, nor the emergence of a saviour such as Connor Wickham. Outrageous good fortune in May was responsible for the only back-to-back wins of the season. Jordi Gómez converted both his penalties against Southampton, the second of which was awarded when Defoe tumbled in an accidental collision with Ward-Prowse, who then received a harsh dismissal. Ten-man Saints pressed for an equaliser, only denied at the end by a wonder save from the 6'7" goalkeeper Costel Pantilimon. At Everton, who monopolised three-quarters of possession whilst taking 15 corners and having 22 goal attempts, escaping with a point would have been a minor miracle. Taking all three risked bringing the game into disrepute, especially when it was Danny Graham opening the scoring with his first for Sunderland in 28 games, before Defoe added a second. Advocaat, struggling to make sense of events, commented that Cattermole had been excellent but conceded that his team were plain lucky. John O'Shea missed out with injury but fortunately Wes Brown, following a short spell sidelined, had timed his return to perfection with a worthy performance to replace the Irishman. Leicester were the last opponents on Wearside before two final tough away games at Arsenal and Chelsea. By now Newcastle United were in trouble, a point behind Sunderland with only two matches left having taken one point from nine matches. Their poor form had commenced with the replacement of Alan Pardew by caretaker John Carver. The table revealed that QPR were doomed; with Burnley ready to join them, one relegation place remained between Leicester, Sunderland, Newcastle and Hull City. The Stadium of Light was almost at capacity for the visit of resurgent Leicester, who gained the required draw to guarantee safety. This left Advocaat with a midweek North London trip to earn salvation following news of Hull's crucial defeat at Tottenham. He was reduced to tears at the Emirates after a battling goalless draw gave the Wearsiders a reprieve for a third consecutive season. That was supposed to be his swansong but after failing to persuade Sam Allardyce to leave his Spanish holiday villa where he was enjoying a lengthy sabbatical from the pressure of management, Short tempted Advocaat to sign a one-year contract and promised him leeway in transfer policy.

A continual struggle at the wrong end of the table exposed Sunderland to rumours that they were a soft and lucrative destination for players without ambition. This was given credence in a series of books entitled 'The Secret Footballer', written by an established player who did not reveal his identity. His 'revelations' claimed to delve beneath the skin of the modern game by revealing locker-room gossip, the etiquette of contract negotiations, the type of characters the industry attracted and, amongst a myriad of other fascinating titbits, expose the blasé spending habits of obscenely wealthy and sometimes gauche young men with time to burn. Most of his disclosures, although entertaining, were hardly earth-shattering; no individuals were named and shamed. Sunderland as a club collectively were. In a publication entitled 'Access All Areas' they were hammered. After making the fairly obvious observation about paying a premium in order to attract players to a geographical outpost, the author commented that the club were 'totally chaotic'. From August to March the 'players of Sunderland football club have enjoyed a sort of prolonged stag party around the Northeast … the worry for fans is that one year soon the end of season miracle will fail to materialise and the club will end up in the Championship crippled with debt'. That at least proved prescient. Referencing the Adam Johnson saga, The Secret Footballer wrote damagingly, 'Johnson has pleaded not guilty and at the time of going to press he has yet to face trial, but all I can say is that if somebody had rung me up and told me the story without revealing the identity of the player, I could have named half-a-dozen Sunderland players before getting it right'. Criticism comes easily if results are poor. Win, lose or draw, John O'Shea and Seb

Larsson were rarely if ever on the booze; they were model professionals who exhibited exemplary off-field behaviour.

Advocaat unveiled a mixture of permanent and loan signings, of whom the two most expensive contributed the least. Jeremain Lens, at £11 million from Rennes, faded quickly and the eventual agreement of Borini to join permanently from Liverpool, a full year after he had withdrawn his word to sign, did not inspire confidence in his commitment. Not all were disappointments. The experienced Younes Kaboul from Tottenham enhanced the centre half position. The pick however was Yann M'Vila, an exceptionally talented defensive midfielder with the vision, tackling and passing ability to grace any European line-up. M'Vila seemed destined for greatness earlier in his career when he won a regular place within the France national team. Advocaat loaned him from the Russian side Rubin Kazan, who had previously farmed him out to Inter Milan. M'Vila came with caveats. His first run-out for Sunderland was a warm-up with the under-21 side against Norwich at Eppleton, where he was sent off for an alleged head-butt. Connor Wickham was sold to Crystal Palace and Sunderland counted their blessings when they recouped most of the fee they had paid Ipswich. Palace no doubt remembered his meteoric spell under Poyet that staved off relegation, earning him the transient recognition of a 'Premier League Player of the Month' award. Whatever Palace expected from the bulky forward rarely materialised at Selhurst Park. Steven Fletcher, signed the same time as Rodwell, had already left Wearside the previous season. A better goalscorer than Wickham, he was released on a free transfer after a four year contract expired. Few doubted that Sunderland were haemorrhaging money across a wide range of recruitment.

Sunderland started 2015-16 slothfully. After seven matches, Advocaat was already labelling West Ham's visit a must-win game. By highlighting a spirited display from Cattermole in a 3-0 defeat at Old Trafford, he cryptically drew attention to a general lack of commitment elsewhere. Energised by thinly-veiled criticism, Fletcher and Lens quickly put Sunderland 2-0 ahead before the Hammers retaliated on the stroke of half-time. Lens was then sent off and the afternoon darkened when Payet equalised. Short was relieved when the Dutchman's resignation spared him an unpleasant conversation. Furthermore, the honourable Advocaat, already in receipt of a £500,000 bonus for extending Sunderland's time in the Premier League, did not press for severance pay. There was a feeling that the club should have accepted his original decision to leave back in May. Sam Allardyce, his appetite restored after holidaymaking in Spain, Portugal and Dubai, judged this the right time to return. Less than eight years previously he had been pushed out of St. James' Park by Mike Ashley after only half a season when results merited otherwise. Before that he took unfashionable Bolton Wanderers into Europe and provided them with a permanent top-half position. He felt strongly that the wider football world did not appreciate his forte of using sports science and statistical analysis to evaluate players and tactics. He was returning to Wearside some years after Peter Reid had entrusted him with the running of the academy and, going back further, when he played for Sunderland under Ken Knighton. Allardyce and Reid were together in the Bolton team beaten at Roker Park in a 1976 promotion decider. Big Sam's induction as a manager at Sunderland was a reprise of Groundhog Day. A defeat at West Bromwich Albion dumped them to the bottom of the league before the now traditional unveiling in a Tyne-Wear derby of the new man to a Northeast public. Sunderland were chasing their sixth win in a row over Newcastle. United, also struggling, were only three points ahead with a goal difference four better.

Newcastle burst forward from the first minute. Mitrović continually sliced open the home defence. The game dramatically changed direction seconds from the interval. Cattermole, unnoticed, handled in his own box then quickly switched play to the far end where Coloccini, United's centre half, was dismissed from the field of play after accidentally colliding with Steven Fletcher in a race for possession. Johnson, awaiting his trial, tucked away the penalty. With a man short, United remained dangerous until defender Billy Jones and Fletcher intervened to give Sunderland yet another 3-0 derby win. The corner and shot count were lost 10-1 and 16-4 with possession at 40%. Newcastle committed fewer fouls yet were the only side to trouble the referee as he produced one red and two yellows. There was more mileage than before, in a saying doing the rounds, that the annual six points from their rivals was keeping Sunderland up. Furthermore, with an uncanny symmetry, Allardyce followed the precedent set by Di Canio, Poyet and Advocaat in securing his first win in a match against Newcastle; all four coincidentally had suffered defeat on opposition territory in their first game.

As usual, the feel-good derby factor only lingered a week. Sunderland lost at Everton 6-2. There was respite when a Defoe goal that earned three points at Crystal Palace was followed by victory over Stoke, through late van Aanholt and Duncan Watmore strikes. For Watmore, an educated young man possessing a first-class honours degree in economics and business management that he completed at Newcastle University, who Poyet had signed from Altrincham, his goal was an apt way to celebrate the award of a four-year contract. Five consecutive defeats however had Allardyce, and indeed other clubs with a less pressing need, impatiently eyeing the panacea of the January transfer window. Without immediate improvement, a seven-point gap from safety would soon become unbridgeable. Only New Year first-foots Aston Villa were below Sunderland. Two goals from the invaluable Defoe delivered his new manager breathing space.

The additions of Wahbi Khazri, Lamine Koné and Jan Kirchhoff in January transformed the season. Before this, there had been stirrings. Jermain

Defoe, now 33 years old but still youthful, scored a hat-trick in a 4-2 win at Swansea. At first, Kirchhoff, loaned from Bayern Munich, suffered a terrible debut at White Hart Lane when after leaving the bench to bolster a Sunderland defence that were holding Tottenham to a draw, he announced himself as error prone when three goals were conceded. In the next game he was switched to midfield, a move made permanent and ultimately so effective that the giant German was eventually voted PFA Fans' Player of the Month for April. Koné, signed from a French club for £5 million, formed a formidable back line with the resident Kaboul and his performances persuaded Everton, without success, to offer £16 million for him. The Frenchman, Khazri, was a £9 million arrival from Bordeaux as deadline day approached. All three joined forces in a narrow defeat by Manchester City, Kirchhoff unrecognisable in his new role. At Anfield on the 6th February a goal from Johnson, in the last game he ever played, and in the closing minutes Defoe, earned a point. Sunderland remained competitive in every game. They defeated Manchester United on Wearside, were edged out 1-0 at West Ham, then Borini managed a last-minute equaliser against Crystal Palace before a stoppage-time goal at Southampton prevented Defoe's earlier effort claiming all three points. M'Vila, marvellous as both creator and destroyer, had not missed a game since his introduction. Lee Cattermole, wearing the captain's armband, had added a degree of discipline to his usual robust presence.

Overshadowing events on the field were the devastating legal charges and impending trial hanging over 28-year-old Adam Johnson, the outcome of which in March '16 prematurely terminated his career and led to a six-year prison sentence. At Bradford Crown Court he pleaded guilty to one charge of sexual activity with a child and one charge of grooming. Alexandra Sims of the Independent newspaper reported, 'Speaking to the court the judge said: "This will be your first prison sentence; this is all entirely your fault." The former Sunderland and Manchester City winger was found guilty of sexual activity with the teenager following an incident in his Range Rover in County Durham last year.' The club's decision to allow Johnson to play after he had been charged, all of one year previously, directed opprobrium at the club and specifically at its 36-year-old chief executive Margaret Byrne. Days after the verdict was announced she resigned her £663,000-a-year role. Josh Halliday, writing for the Guardian, disclosed that Byrne was instrumental in introducing a barrister, Orlando Pownall QC, to act on Johnson's behalf. Damagingly club officials, despite having police access to no less than 834 WhatsApp messages between Johnson and the 15-year-old, supported the player when he said that he was pleading 'not guilty'. After the trial Byrne commented that it was a 'serious mistake' to allow Johnson to continue to play for the club and admitted that she made 'a serious error of judgement'. What had become of the club whose players in the 1950s received no more than a few occasional payments, albeit under the counter, a night at the Boldon Greyhound Stadium and a longing to perform in a Wembley final? What indeed had the glory game come to? The illegal payments' scandal of that era didn't harm anyone. Perhaps it is unfair to expect a sportsperson to assume the mantle of a role model. It is perfectly acceptable to like the art but not the artist. But this sordid episode reached far beyond the bounds of anything remotely acceptable; club and player were disgraced. Sunderland escaped without official censure.

When Sunderland met Newcastle on Tyneside they were aiming for a seventh straight derby win. Unlike the previous occasion, they were undoubtedly the better side and there should have been more between the sides than a goal from Defoe. When Mitrović equalised on 83 minutes to earn a reprieve for Rafa Benítez, his first game in charge, the draw meant both clubs remained in the bottom three. Aston Villa however, with seven games to play, were twelve points adrift. Leicester City, 5000-1 title outsiders before the season commenced, headed the table and the 3,040 supporters they brought to Wearside witnessed them take control of a tight match through a typical Vardy breakaway goal, before the former non-league striker wrapped up the points with a splendid solo effort. Although Sunderland's commitment since January had not validated the claims of the Secret Footballer, progress was stalling with too many draws and if Sunderland were to lose a crunch lunchtime match at fellow strugglers Norwich, the five games remaining allowed little wriggle room.

Allardyce need not have worried. On a day that confirmed Villa's relegation, Sunderland stormed to a 3-0 victory in East Anglia with Borini, Defoe and Watmore sending 2,000 fans home happy. Instead of a potential seven points behind Norwich they were one, and with a game fewer played. Jonathan Northcroft wrote in the Sunday Times of Lee Cattermole 'scrapping, snarling, scuffling, scraping clearances off the line'. He mentioned 'Lamine Koné and Jan Kirchhoff, the giant sentinels guarding the route to their goal' and acknowledged the quality of the visitors at the other end of the pitch, 'step forward Fabio Borini and that Peter Pan of Poaching, Jermain Defoe'. The Norwich manager was Alex Neil, a name Sunderland fans would be well acquainted with in the future. Pressure transferred to Newcastle, who by defeating Swansea hours later, remained two points behind the Wearsiders. In Rafa they believed.

On the penultimate weekend of the season Sunderland, a game fewer played and one point below fourth-bottom Newcastle, hosted reigning champions Chelsea at the Stadium of Light. Newcastle, an improved side under Benítez, faced Aston Villa at a ground where they suffered relegation six years previously. Villa, having lost eleven in a row, were marooned on 16 points and there for the taking. Before 47,050 on Wearside, Diego Costa gave Chelsea a lead he should have added to but for Mannone foiling him twice in short succession after the resumption. Without those saves, Sunderland stared into the abyss. Newcastle were unlikely to remain goalless. The average supporter in a lifetime of watching football will have only a handful of rare, special memories to treasure. This is an unfair trade off, considering the weighty accumulation of heartache, disappointment and plain mediocrity over the years. On that afternoon the balance was momentarily redressed. Chelsea were ahead 2-1 before an explosion of noise, rivalling the night Halom and Hughes tore apart City, rattled the Stadium to greet an equaliser from Borini on 67 minutes. Four minutes later Defoe scored a decisive third. The clamour in the closing stages forced the referee to use sign language. Amidst this maelstrom, almost unnoticed, the Chelsea captain John Terry received his marching orders. Against all expectations, Newcastle returned to Tyneside with an unwanted draw and this, allied to a defeat for Norwich, now gave Sunderland the opportunity to seize safety by beating Everton in their midweek game in hand. The Stadium of Light was full. Celebrations commenced from 38 minutes when van Aanholt fired his low free kick through a porous blue wall. Within minutes Koné had added a second and then on 55 minutes the big defender made it 3-0. Sunderland were in the clear, Newcastle and Norwich relegated alongside Aston Villa. Never had a home support cheered so loudly at a fourth consecutive liberation; never before had anyone been in a position to do so. The drama of relegating their neighbours temporarily silenced those dissenting voices who dared to suggest that the club would be better off in the championship and better off rebuilding at a lower level where they would be released from the constant scrape of a season-to-season survival. The majority, celebrating as football fans do, may have had some justification on this occasion in presuming better days lay ahead.

An opportunity presented itself to build on the best squad of players assembled since Peter Reid, provided Short was not compromised by a worsening financial state. In the European Championship, Iceland embarrassingly ousted England six weeks later. Allardyce, initially a 16-1 outsider to replace Roy Hodgson, had previously been overlooked by the FA. Impressed by his work on Wearside they wanted him and Sunderland were suddenly managerless, high and dry with a new season three weeks away. Within days, 53-year-old David Moyes was appointed with a glowing reference from Short, who enthused that the former Everton manager had been 'my number one managerial target for the last five appointments'. Moyes, his stock diminished after failing at Old Trafford, had since experienced a brief unsuccessful stint at Real Sociedad. Short's history of rebuffs should have provided a clue that the unemployed Moyes may have viewed his four-year contract as a marriage of convenience. His arrival added to a list of managers who had brought their own ideas to the club, accompanied by yet another set of different players, leaving those acquired by the previous incumbent to ponder an uncertain future.

The average attendance of 43,071 was the sixth best in the country. It was only slightly less than the numbers thronging Wearside when Keane promised a new, fearless era but it was apparent that something had been lost in translation when the annual accounts were published. Gate receipts of £10.4 million were significantly down on the £13.6 million generated then. The extra discounts available for family areas did not fully account for an average admission price per head of only £12. It was clear that Sunderland had expanded their policy of distributing free tickets and that the public in general had tired of nine consecutive seasons of mediocrity and were gradually, imperceptibly, losing interest. Significantly more worrying were the other figures. On a turnover of £104.1 million a loss on ordinary activities of £33.8 million was disclosed, an increase from £26.7 million on the previous year. The interest paid on debt was a staggering £6.9 million, equating to £132,692 per week, the majority arising from the Security Benefit Corporation (SBC) transaction in 2014. In addition, two figures shown as 'amounts owed to group undertakings' (falling due within one year and after one year) presumably represented the escalating interest-free loans Sunderland owed Short. They amounted to £69.4 million.

30

ALL OUR YESTERDAYS

2016-17 to 2017-18

As the summer days of 2016 shortened, Sunderland reeled from the abrupt departure of Allardyce. The permanent signing of Yann M'Vila was not pursued because he would be a free agent half way through the season. The reluctance to arrange a relatively small fee with Rubin Kazan and pay M'Vila a premium in recognition of his strong bargaining position, owing to a mere six months remaining on his contract, was a mistake. The money saved was squandered on inferior fare. A club record £13 million purchased Didier Ndong, a little-known Gabon international, who had spent a season with an anonymous French side FC Lorient. An energetic midfield player, he offered little more than perspiration topped with distinctive, dyed, pineapple-styled hair. It can be risky taking a player from the French league, especially if unproven in top European competition. Papy Djilobodji was problematically bought for £8 million from Chelsea to replace Kaboul, who strangely, was allowed a return south, where he joined Watford. Chelsea had signed Djilobodji from Nantes, primarily as cover, and judged him not ready for selection. Instead, they loaned him to a German club and Sunderland, having lost M'Vila and Kaboul, were grateful for crumbs from the Premier League's high table. The £21 million pair struggled from the off. David Moyes was further disadvantaged by a return of Kirchhoff's injury problems and the distraction of Koné by Everton's persistent interest.

It could be said however that Moyes was the architect of his own downfall. The outlay of £5.5 million on the Manchester United second-string defensive pair McNair and Love were for players Moyes had managed previously. They disappointingly accumulated less than twenty starts between them in a campaign that started with nine defeats and two draws. Following a defeat by Middlesbrough in the second game, Moyes unwisely set a negative tone when he replied in the affirmative to a question whether he thought Sunderland would find themselves in another relegation battle. It was a comment he bitterly regretted. Apart from the relatively prolific Jermain Defoe, named Northeast Football Writers' Player of the Year, the bright spot was goalkeeper Jordan Pickford from Washington, who emerged from the Academy. Pickford scooped the Young Player of the Year award. Such was his brilliance, Everton parted with £25 million for him at the end of the season, the third highest amount ever for a goalkeeper. Finally, at Bournemouth, came a league victory at the eleventh attempt after Nigerian Victor Anichebe, a former Moyes player signed out of contract, equalised on his debut. In the next fixture, two goals earned him a man-of-the-match accolade when Hull were vanquished 3-0 on an afternoon marred by darkness during a 10-minute stoppage through a power failure. Defoe's opener for Sunderland was his 150th Premier League goal. An immense Pickford continued his heroics against Leicester, when the Anichebe-Defoe partnership raised hope of another great escape. With Defoe on the scoresheet, a 2-1 win that made it nine points from twelve took Sunderland off the bottom but alas, the respite was premature. In the closing minutes, the burgeoning career of Watmore was curtailed when he snapped his left knee ligaments in a challenge with Christian Fuchs. Events conspired at Turf Moor on New Year's Eve. A pulled hamstring forced Koné to leave proceedings early and Anichebe sustained an injury that markedly reduced his effectiveness when he eventually returned to first team action. Sunderland comprehensively lost 4-1. The forthcoming Africa Cup of Nations further depleted numbers. There was no magic remedy in the winter window. More former Moyes' men in Bryan Oviedo, Darron Gibson and Joleon Lescott arrived and likewise failed to impress; 34-year-old centre half Lescott hardly kicked a ball in anger. Gibson's contract was ingloriously terminated the following year when he was banned from driving for forty months when found to be three times over the legal limit. This was not the only controversy during his time at Sunderland.

As if to taunt, a 4-0 win at Crystal Palace that featured two Defoe goals was followed by a 4-0 home defeat by Southampton. By Easter Sunderland were nine points adrift from the fourth-bottom club; by the end it was sixteen points. Counting all four divisions, Sunderland, over a decade of continual struggle, lost more games than anyone. Their expertise in escapology, an unerring knack of staving off the inevitable, only served to bury the club in a deeper financial hole. Whereas Chelsea recycled their coaching staff each year to win a trophy, Short's constant regime changes perpetuated a crisis that threatened the very existence of Sunderland.

Despite relegation, £93.5 million was received from an upgraded Sky deal, an increase of a third on previous figures. However the financial accounts for that season showed a loss before tax of £9.5 million. This figure would have been zero if the £9,721,000 paid to Inter Milan for Álvarez had been ignored. In accounting jargon, this was classed as an exceptional item, a 'one-off' event unlikely to occur again. Worryingly however, the relatively small bottom-line loss failed to convey the true picture of a club hurtling towards financial oblivion. Shirt sponsorship and match day revenue was to drop in the Championship. There was an immediate £13 million balance sheet reduction in the value of existing players. The normal practice was to write off a transfer fee in equal instalments over the length of a player's contract but the figure of £13 million represented an accounting write-down to anticipate the release of those players who were likely to be sold at a loss before the end of their contracts. Overall debt had increased by another £24 million, Short contributing the bulk of the lending. The accounting figures were unlikely to be inflated by another cash windfall similar to that accruing from Pickford's departure. A reduction in broadcasting revenue dwarfed all concerns. Sunderland were eligible for parachute payments on a sliding scale over three years to compensate for this eventuality. The first such payment of £41 million was already spoken for in order to terminate contracts and meet heavy interest payments on borrowings. A famous quote from the American stock market guru Warren Buffett, 'only when the tide goes out do you discover who has been swimming naked', was highly relevant and darkly ironic, considering the financial services expertise of the owner. David Moyes with his reputation as one of the leading managers in the game irredeemably tarnished, agreed to part company and made a rare, correct decision when he commendably refused a £3 million compensation package.

The day-to-day practicalities remained. Simon Grayson, steeped in Football League experience, replaced Moyes. Jermain Defoe, after scoring 29 Premier League goals over two seasons, left for Bournemouth in the summer. Borini, Lens, Djilobodji and Khazri were financial liabilities and unsaleable because of their high wages. Sunderland were over a barrel. They had no alternative other than to loan those players out to predatory clubs, at the same time subsidising part of their wages. The ageless John O'Shea, as ever a credit to the game, was pressed into action on forty occasions during the Championship season of 2017-18. Tyias Browning and Brendan Galloway were hurriedly borrowed from Everton. Within a few games it was obvious that Galloway, a left back of coltish enthusiasm, was out of his depth. Browning, persevered with alongside O'Shea, rarely looked comfortable. The pound shop transfer budget available to Grayson was all a club on the edge of administration could afford. Goalkeeper Jason Steele from Blackburn and forward James Vaughan from Bury both cost £500,000 whilst £250,000 secured the veteran Irish winger Aiden McGeady from Everton. Vaughan neither made nor scored goals and soon ended up at Wigan. Steele survived slightly longer. The mistakes of Lee Camp, his replacement, commenced a further search for someone reliable between the sticks.

Grayson was dismissed within minutes of a 3-3 home draw with basement club Bolton at the end of October. Chief Executive Martin Bain, who the previous year's accounts revealed had earned £1.25 million, delivered the usual platitudes that only served to damn Grayson with faint praise. Sunderland, with one win from fifteen matches, were third from bottom. Well-versed by now in unearthing a new manager, Sunderland handed Chris Coleman the task of warding off third-tier football. Before he took over, a draw against Millwall gave the club an unwanted English record of 20 consecutive home games in all competitions without a victory. The arrival of loanee Jake Clarke-Salter from Chelsea suggested recruitment remained flawed. The defender suffered red cards in consecutive appearances. A stirring fightback from three down to earn a point at Bristol City proved a false dawn. A week later Sunderland unravelled against a Brentford side benefitting from the presence of their progressive Assistant Coach Thomas Frank. A Stadium of Light crowd of 28,000 witnessed the unfashionable West London club, resembling Brazil with their slick movement and one-touch passing, outshining a sterile home team. Two in arrears after 28 minutes, Sunderland did not recover. By March they were rock bottom and easy pickings for Aston Villa, who cantered without duress to a 3-0 victory against a backdrop of bleached, empty, pink seats. There was a silent acceptance, anger extinguished by anguish, a throwback to the dark days of Brown and, dare his name be mentioned in the same breath as the Bomber, Lawrie McMenemy – all our yesterdays without undisturbed pigeons, Bovril, the pall of tobacco smoke and a sparse Roker End.

Coleman, whose international and Premier League managerial background prompted the impression that he was employed beneath his station, failed to stave off relegation. With games running out, Sunderland missed an opportunity to leapfrog over Burton Albion when former player Darren Bent equalised in the 86th minute and his side scored again in additional time. Burton were averaging less than 5,000. They had enjoyed a rapid rise through the soccer pyramid; when Peter Reid was at Sunderland in the Premier League, Burton were Northern Premier League champions, a competition that included Bishop Auckland, Burscough and Colwyn Bay. The game is less respectful of tradition than ever before. As remains of the revered Archibald Leitch wrought-iron lattice balcony sat abandoned and decaying in a car park at the back of the West Stand, boos echoed around a rapidly emptying stadium as the inevitability of third-tier football drew closer. No missed penalties or last-match drama, merely a sobering realisation that Sunderland's world had tilted on its axis. Only seven wins were mustered in 46 matches.

Louise Taylor is a highly regarded football journalist, primarily a Northeast correspondent for the Guardian. Back in September '84 as a law graduate from Durham University, she compiled an emotive, heart-rending article for The Observer newspaper about her favourite team Sunderland. She mentioned 'the pursuit of fading stars … giving away Gary Rowell, the club's leading scorer for six out of the past seven seasons … Roker Park was built for better things … mismanagement of resources'. Thirty or so years on, with the exception of three major domestic Cup final defeats and two consecutive seventh-placed Premier League finishes, nothing much had changed.

31

PURGATORY

2018-19 to 2020-21

Ellis Short, who had received little in return for his philanthropy, either in the way of esteem, appreciation, or silverware, was no longer prepared to pour cash into a bottomless pit. He had tried without success to sell the club over the previous two years and with the situation worsening, now realised that in order to find a suitable buyer he would have to clear any debt, which would also involve writing off a personal loan. In May '18 Oxfordshire-based Stewart Donald stepped forward to agree a £37 million purchase alongside his legal and financial advisor Charlie Methven, who took a minority interest. Donald, formerly owner of an insurance company, was reckoned to be worth somewhat less than £10 million. There was a question mark regarding his track record in football, with a six-year failure to meet his stated aim of taking Eastleigh into the Football League. Furthermore Donald, by stretching himself to take a controlling 94% stake, was unable or unwilling to meet the majority of the purchase price by the conventional method of leveraging either himself or the club with debt. He therefore struck a novel arrangement with Short. The American waved goodbye to the £80 million Sunderland owed him and in addition to this, agreed to settle the SBC loan of £70 million, leaving Donald's purchase with minimal debt. In return, Short clawed back the second year's parachute payment of £33.5 million therefore depriving Sunderland of this windfall and neatly providing the cash-strapped Donald the means to finalise the takeover. This financial alchemy exposed the club to the risk of being undercapitalised. Cue the arrival within weeks of the Monaco-based, Uruguayan businessman Juan Sartori, who bought a 20% stake. Observers wondered if the new regime had the substance to take the club forward or if their venture was purely that of a speculative short-term buy and flip operation.

When Rodwell finally agreed to leave he squeezed every penny from his employer. Despite a clause in his contract reducing his wages in the event of relegation, Sunderland who were in hock for £40,000 per week, had no alternative but to pay up the remaining part of his contract. As for the disenchanted, incognito Koné, he commenced a one-year temporary arrangement with Strasbourg, eventually settling there permanently, leaving Sunderland with the regret of not acquiescing to Everton's interest. Chris Coleman was never likely to hang around in League One; he was replaced as manager by Jack Ross, who left Scottish First Division side St. Mirren.

A value for money 'Basics' range was introduced. Sunderland signed a clutch of lower-league players. Flanagan, Baldwin, Maguire, Power, O'Nien and Wyke were persuaded by the prospect of performing at the Stadium of Light in a team expected to regain Championship status quickly. In only a year Manchester United had been replaced by Accrington Stanley on Sunderland's fixture list. Donald needed to look no further than the Stanley owner Andy Holt if he required a role model. Holt had just propelled his club, representing an obscure former cotton town, to the same status as the one-time 'Bank of England' outfit, on average gates of 1,979 and an annual wages budget of £670,000 during their League Two promotion campaign. Against the backdrop of a mothballed Premier Concourse, over 30,000 saw Sunderland eclipse Charlton 2-1 on an opening day crowned with a 90th minute Josh Maja winner. There were pastures new for Wearside away fans to explore; likewise, the Stadium was a magnet to visitors from the far-flung outposts away from the madding crowd of the Premier League.

Chris Maguire, after a few crowd-pleasing cameos, was christened 'The King'. In the land of the blind the one-eyed man is king. When Hurley played in the sixties, 60,000 pairs of eyes witnessed a living legend. Hopes were pinned on the experienced Charlie Wyke from Bradford City, who although hardly a Ford, Clough or Phillips, was expected to produce at this level. It was Maja however, possessing an instinctive radar for goal, who outshone his expensive, £500,000 partner. The public were prepared to forgive a lower standard of football if it was spiced with blood and sweat. What George Honeyman and Lynden Gooch may have lacked in ability they made up for in endeavour and heart. The deceptively frail looking Luke O'Nien traded more knocks than a flyweight and climbed from the canvas quicker. McGeady, a class above, was two passes ahead in thought and action; in this type of football his creativity was unequalled. There was a bright, confident air about Ross. By the middle of November five straight wins took the club to second place before a noticeably physical Wycombe Wanderers, streetwise in taking time out of the ninety minutes and managed by the astute Gareth Ainsworth, were only denied by a late Maja equaliser. Perhaps Ainsworth had discovered a way to stop Sunderland.

Outside the ground before kick-off, the smoothly attired, charismatic Charlie Methven, proved an accommodating magnet for well-wishers seeking selfies, that tedious scourge of social collisions. Easily recognisable in a brightly coloured pair of chinos and with his distinctive Old Etonian accent, the photogenic Methven, owning a 6% share in the club, milked the publicity and put a smile on the face of anyone he encountered. On Boxing Day he appeared on the pitch at half-time in a bizarre public relations stunt announcing that Sunderland, with an attendance of 46,039, had established a League One record figure. Overlooked were the larger attendances Aston Villa and Hull City achieved back in the days of the Third Division and Third Division North but then, of course, proper football had not been invented. The story of the eventual 1-0 victory over Bradford City was a side issue.

A six-part fly on the wall Netflix documentary entitled 'Sunderland 'Til I Die' was being filmed. Due for release after the campaign finished, it featured supporter fanaticism, stilted snippets of games and the daily politics infecting the inner sanctum of the stadium. The fourth episode, aptly named 'Playing Poker', exposed the inexperience of Donald by revealing a crazy few days at the end of the January transfer window when promotion ambitions were unwittingly blown apart. Josh Maja, despite 15 goals and with an existing contract due to expire in the summer, had not been offered realistically improved new terms. With Cattermole, McGeady and Oviedo benefitting from barely unaltered Premier League contracts, signed when Short was spending with irrational exuberance, Maja was offered little more than £7,000 per week following protracted negotiations, a figure similar to the misfiring Charlie Wyke. Sunderland therefore allowed Bordeaux to buy Maja for a cut-price £1.5 million rather than receive the £500,000 compensation they were entitled to if he left on a free transfer at the season's end. With time ticking, a replacement was desperately sought. Will Grigg, scoring at a decent rate for Wigan, caught the eye with the only goal of the match when Manchester City were knocked out of the FA Cup. The Sunderland manager valued him at £1.25 million and as the Netflix cameras rolled, the car crash of Donald ignoring the advice of Ross and other senior figures was compulsive viewing. As the deadline transfer window hour approached, Wigan continually upped the ante before the Sunderland owner reluctantly agreed to pay an inflated £3 million, no less than three times his opening offer. Grigg's agent was now in a strong position when it came to discussing terms for his client. The forward did not set the Stadium of Light on fire; he scored five times in forty-seven appearances before taking the familiar loan path out of Wearside leading to the inevitable contract termination.

Batches of three consecutive home games in February and April should have provided momentum but only nine points were taken from the eighteen on offer. The feel-good factor of the new regime faded. In the earlier set of home fixtures, Grigg missed a host of chances as only a point was taken from Blackpool and Accrington Stanley. At some stage Stanley were two ahead.

The lure of a weekend in London and the prospect of a massed gathering of the clans in Trafalgar Square produced a record attendance of 85,021 for the comparatively meaningless final of the EFL Trophy against Portsmouth. The competition comprised League One and League Two clubs plus sixteen invitations to Premier League and Championship academies. Aiden McGeady's second goal with a minute remaining of extra time had levelled the scores. Lee Cattermole missed the only penalty from the ten taken to stretch the club's losing Wembley sequence to seven visits. Despite an unbeaten league run that stretched to all of nineteen matches, supporters were unconvinced. They were displeased with time-wasting tactics of visiting players and second-rate officialdom. Coventry ended the long sequence when they won a Keystone Cops game 5-4 in front of 36,000 on Wearside. A gate of 41,129 witnessed the closing home game against Portsmouth but yet another drawn Stadium of Light encounter, the tenth of the campaign, left those magnificent supporters with the potential bogey prize of a play-off.

That end of season lottery had never been kind. Only 26,000 witnessed the first-leg victory against Portsmouth, well down on the season's impressive average of 32,157 that only eleven clubs in the country had exceeded. Chris Maguire scored the only goal over 180 minutes of football and a resolute Sunderland played the last half hour on Wearside without the sent-off centre back Alim Öztürk. The play-off final was against Charlton Athletic. Despite an early gift of a freakish own goal, there was little drama to compare with the other Charlton Wembley experience in 1998, although for the Sunderland fans, comprising a majority of the 76,155 crowd, the outcome was no different. The lead was conceded before half-time and then with extra time looking inevitable, the game was lost in the 90th minute.

The policy of scouring the free transfer market and buying from lower divisions did not inspire confidence. As the 2019-20 season commenced with a flat draw at home to Oxford, George Dobson, a modestly priced midfielder from Walsall made his debut. His three-year contract at a rumoured £4,000 per week underlined the straitened circumstances on Wearside. In October after some poor results, Jack Ross, almost as a matter of routine, was replaced by Phil Parkinson who had a proven promotion-winning record outside the top two divisions. An expected upturn did not happen. When Sunderland failed to overcome Bolton on Boxing Day, a return of nine points from the previous ten games saw them languish in fifteenth position. McGeady was banished from the first team squad following a dispute with Parkinson and sent to Charlton on loan. Sunderland sometimes sank to the standard of their opposition. Only when defensive caution was abandoned were calls for Parkinson's sacking muted. The club climbed to a play-off position but a stoppage-time goal conceded against Gillingham on 7th March would have repercussions. Another free-transfer man Kyle Lafferty scored twice but the two dropped points and a following 2-0 defeat at Bristol Rovers came at the worst possible time. The Covid pandemic abruptly stopped league football; after this 36th game at the Memorial Stadium, Sunderland were on 59 points, eighth in the table, only one point behind the third-placed team but having played more games than anyone else. The play-off places were decided on a points-per-game ratio. That late Gillingham equaliser prevented a ranking of seventh and condemned Sunderland to a third season in the doldrums. Donald's suspected aim of promotion and then selling on to make a quick profit was in tatters. Supporters felt he had outstayed his welcome. Furthermore, Wyke and Grigg were not justifying their transfer fees. Lynden Gooch, primarily a bustling wide man, was top scorer with eleven goals. Maguire, an unpredictable bag of tricks, also reached double figures. Gabbiadini and Gates they were not.

With the country in a series of Covid-induced lockdowns, the 2020-21 season kicked off behind closed doors. The doom-mongers who predicted a wholesale collapse of long-established clubs were miles off the mark. The government provided financial assistance but the survival probability of even a cash-strapped, heavily indebted, and poorly supported lower division member is similar to that of a cockroach in a nuclear war. The prolific striker that Sunderland desperately needed and the conduit to maximise his worth were already at the club. Wyke in truth, handicapped with a knee injury when signed from Wigan, had struggled to regain full fitness. He was used as a target man; his style of play at Wigan indicated that his game was all about scoring rather than making goals. Parkinson failed to utilise his strengths. McGeady, having spent loan time at Charlton, was in limbo. Results over Parkinson's watch were not even matching the low bar Ross had set. With uncertainty again surrounding future ownership, as Donald explored ways to offload his shareholding, another change was made. Sunderland were eighth after thirteen games.

Lee Johnson, formerly at Bristol City, was appointed head coach. Of greater importance was the installation of Kristjaan Speakman as Sporting Director. The arrival of Speakman, responsible for player recruitment and development, suggested that Sunderland were contemplating a radical long-term strategy that placed an emphasis on nurturing young talent. This represented a wholesale change from the haphazard transfer policy that characterised their time in the Premier League. Johnson had a habit of saying the same thing four or five different ways whilst spicing his language with jargon. He was however sharp enough in recalling McGeady from loan to mark his first game in charge, a defeat at Wigan. At promotion chasing Lincoln on 12th December, Johnson selected Charlie Wyke to start with McGeady, instructing the forward to go directly for goal as opposed to playing as a target man. He scored twice in a stunning 4-0 victory. In February, Wyke headed all four goals against Doncaster Rovers, benefitting each time from a McGeady cross.

A week later, immeasurably important news broke. Supporters were delighted to discover that Sunderland had a new majority shareholder. It was initially reported in newspapers that a 23-year-old Frenchman, Kyril Louis-Dreyfus, had bought more than half of Donald's shares to secure a 51% controlling majority and become chairman of the club. Louis-Dreyfus is the son of former Marseilles owner, the late Robert Louis-Dreyfus. It is his mother who currently has responsibility for running the family's extensive multinational enterprises. Kyril Louis-Dreyfus has a trust fund reportedly estimated at £2 billion, although the extent of his access is not known.

However, to the understandable annoyance of supporters who no longer wanted the old guard involved, it later emerged that the Frenchman had acquired 41% of the shares and not the previously presumed 51%, whilst Donald, Sartori and Methven retained the remaining 59%. Although it was reported that the other three would back any decision Louis-Dreyfus made, doubt existed over the level of financial commitment they could afford, given that it was rational to assume that any costs incurred would be met in equal proportion to their holdings.

After Sunderland finally buried their Wembley jinx by defeating Tranmere 1-0 through a Lynden Gooch goal in the EFL Trophy Final, they lapped a stark, empty bowl on a surreal Sunday afternoon whilst housebound supporters were glued to their flat screens. A born-again Wyke, without the advantage of taking penalties, scored 26 league goals to finish second behind the 31 strikes of Jonson Clarke-Harris of Peterborough who converted 7 penalties. The play-offs place disappointed again. In the second leg semi-final against Lincoln City, the authorities allowed the public into the stadium for the only time of the season, albeit in vastly reduced numbers, as a cautious return to normality commenced in response to a weakening Covid threat. A 2-1 victory in front of 9,971 on Wearside was insufficient to overcome a 2-0 deficit at Sincil Bank.

There was a sense of regeneration as fans throughout the country looked forward to attending matches in unrestricted numbers. At Sunderland, the inevitability of a regime change in addition to a proposed reopening of the ground, notwithstanding the continued closure of the Premier Concourse, softened the defeat by Lincoln. Although a fourth season in League One beckoned the mood was upbeat.

32

A NEW MODEL ARMY

2021-22 to 2023-24

Optimism abounded. New investment, a realistic wage bill and excellent attendances in a league where gate receipts contributed the major source of income, maintained Sunderland debt-free therefore allowing leeway in the 2021 transfer market. It was hoped that a self-sustainability model would avoid the previous mistakes that resulted in being saddled with nothing to show for a decade of profligacy except consecutive relegations. In any event, UEFA-imposed Financial Fair Play regulations now broadly meant that clubs were unable to spend more on wages and players than that which they could generate from gate receipts, broadcasting, sponsorship, and commercial activities.

Kristjaan Speakman appeared to have a network of contacts that opened doors. Promising talent was targeted. This comprised players released from Premier League clubs that Sunderland were confident they could improve, or young foreign players under the radar of the elite clubs. There was an aim to transform the whole ethos of Sunderland football club. It was anticipated that an enhanced reputation for developing and educating players would ensure that the Stadium of Light became an attractive destination for leading clubs wishing to provide their loanees with game time to fulfil potential. The Premier League-standard Academy at Cleadon would remain an important centrepiece, despite annual operating costs of £4 million. It was imperative that Sunderland developed a conveyor belt of talented players. A massive imbalance of wealth within the game prevented them from realistically competing in the transfer market with a number of middle-ranking provincial clubs, let alone clubs owned by a Saudi Arabia Public Investment Fund or by an Abu Dhabi United Group headed by Sheikh Mansour.

The close season arrivals bore the stamp of Speakman. Callum Doyle, a highly rated Manchester City Academy prospect, joined on loan. Left back Dennis Cirkin, signed from Tottenham for £1 million, was subject to a £6 million buy-back clause. Both had appeared for England under-19 and under-20 teams. Winger Jack Clarke, also from White Hart Lane, had cost the London club £10 million when they signed him from Leeds and Sunderland, hoping to make a temporary arrangement permanent, were confident they could revitalise his career. Competition was fought off to attract the slight but skilful Alex Pritchard on a free transfer, for whom Spurs had once paid Norwich £8 million. There was a massive clear out. Surprisingly, Wyke was not awarded a new contract. This was puzzling and drew criticism. Ross Stewart, a tall, gangling forward had joined halfway through the previous season for a nominal fee from Scottish Premier side Ross County. His appearances during the remainder of the term on Wearside were mainly from the bench and there was some doubt if he could replace the Renaissance man Wyke.

Methven disposed of his shares, perhaps at profit, whilst Sartori, at the expense of reducing Donald's influence, increased his stake from 20% to 30%. The Frenchman, Louis-Dreyfus, finally established a majority of 51%, thereby further diluting Donald's holding to 19%. Speculation that other investors would come on board has not yet materialised. Donald later admitted that he did not realise the size of the job he had taken on. He oversaw a massive upheaval in personnel, including staff redundancies. He made incremental improvements to the stadium such as replacing faded, worn-out seating and strived through various initiatives to reconnect a disillusioned public with the club. He joined the Board of Trustees at the Foundation of Light charity and was initially, at least, always available for podcasts and group discussions with supporters. The pandemic, with a lack of paying customers and uncertainty over government help, proved a challenging period. There is, however, no certainty that history may view him less unkindly; a vast number of supporters rejoiced as his importance waned.

The 2021-22 season was a rollercoaster. One of the darkest winters of Sunderland's history was replaced by a wonderful Wembley occasion. The encouraging early season form was complemented by the blossoming of teenager Dan Neil and the unexpected emergence of Ross Stewart, his 'Loch Ness Drogba' nickname a nod to the former Chelsea man-mountain Didier Drogba. Callum Doyle even had supporters marking his card as a future England captain. Perhaps the pernicious influence of the lockdown had altered the perceptions of some of the most knowledgeable fans in football. Unquestionably, there was a slickness and quickness in Sunderland's passing game that suggested better days ahead. A 4-0 win at Crewe in October placed the club two points behind leaders Plymouth with two games fewer played.

Sheffield Wednesday were summarily dispatched 5-0 in the last game of the calendar year as Sunderland climbed to the top of the table, reaching 49 points from 24 games. Stewart contributed a hat-trick. There had been two heavy defeats by 4-0 and 5-1 margins at Portsmouth and Rotherham respectively. If the first of those was a freak result on a day of biblical rainstorms, no such excuse could be advanced for the capitulation in South Yorkshire. During the January window a talented winger, Patrick Roberts, was initially loaned from Manchester City for six months, for a prospective fee of £3 million. City had signed the then 'mini-Messi' from Fulham in 2015 for a consideration of £6 million. With an obscene surfeit of wealth enabling them to buy and hoard players on a whim, they farmed Roberts out to a variety of destinations including Scotland, Spain and France; therefore he was unable to add to the substitute appearances made when first joining City. Eclipsed by the arrival of Roberts was that of Trai Hume from the Northern Irish club Linfield.

Maguire returned with Lincoln in January '22 and inspired his new club with a hat-trick. That defeat was bad but paled against a shocking 6-0 thrashing at Bolton. The team were jaded. The insistence of Johnson in persevering with the youth of Neil and Doyle ran counter to the growing voices who implored him to rest them. The decision was taken from him when he was dismissed within hours of the Bolton debacle. Sunderland were no longer in an automatic promotion place. With Johnson removed, the new ownership were able to indulge in a little fantasy football during the slack period before a replacement was announced. They bowed to popular demand. Jermain Defoe, now 38, short of match fitness and perhaps against his better judgement, was persuaded to return. He attracted 38,395 to the stadium. With the game against Doncaster in progress, every twist, every turn near the touchline from Defoe was cheered by young supporters, craning forward from rows of normally empty seats. He was merely staying supple during his occupation of the substitutes' bench. He finally entered the fray after 70 minutes. An unfit Defoe failed to match the hype. Sunderland already two down, were en route to another home defeat.

Alex Neil, formerly manager of Premier League Norwich, was appointed to save the season. A one-year rolling contract implied a lack of commitment on both sides. Neil fashioned his new team in similar vein to his straight-talking, no-nonsense self. Dan Neil and Callum Doyle, both jaded, were dropped. Danny Batth, an experienced stopper that the club had signed from Championship Stoke just before Johnson's departure, was drafted into the defence. A rejuvenated Lynden Gooch was a revelation with his width and crossing ability, whilst Patrick Roberts left no one in doubt that he was a class beyond the level he was playing at. On 26th February Sunderland travelled to Wigan, all of ten points behind the second-placed Lancashire club and having played three games more. One solitary win from ten matches did not augur well. The large travelling support were agitating to voice disapproval. Instead, Sunderland prevailed 3-0 with Stewart converting two penalties. This game heralded a remarkable upturn. The club did not taste defeat in any of their remaining eleven league games and entered the play-offs as the form team. Ross Stewart emerged as a formidable leader of the line who could find the net and hold the ball up. There was an uncanny series of late, late goals and a momentum ensuring the stadium was full when Sheffield Wednesday entered a febrile atmosphere for the first leg of the semi-final. Stewart's 25th goal of the season gave a narrow advantage for the Hillsborough game. The night was heading for extra time after the home side equalised deep into the second half but with seconds of normal time remaining, Patrick Roberts secured a dramatic winner.

The clamour for Wembley tickets did not abate. More were released, until the number of the red and white invasion was finally capped at a little over 47,000. The 2-0 scoreline over Wycombe Wanderers, courtesy of goals from Embleton and Stewart in front of 72,332, was a modest translation of Sunderland's supremacy. There was enough emotion and excitement on the warm North London afternoon for that not to matter.

Corry Evans walked up the steps to collect the trophy. Such was the outpouring of joy, the noise was equal to that famous day when HRH The Duchess of Kent presented Bobby Kerr with a red and white ribboned FA Cup but on this occasion, the moment was shaken by a cacophony of bland music and disfigured by fireworks. New Wembley despite, or perhaps because of, its rude commercialism, is a stunningly suitable temple to permit that vast majority of the population, now in thrall to the vacuous values of the modern game, to worship their false gods. There was no ghost of Stokoe bounding across damp turf to his goalkeeper, no ghost of Baxter tormenting England's finest, and no ghost of the South Shields-born Stanley Mortensen, the only player with a hat-trick in an FA Cup final, whose performance is forever overshadowed by the 1953 game being known as the Matthews final. Nevertheless, the experience of that play-off Saturday was of some consolation after four years in the wilderness.

In readiness for a new campaign there were signings; all in line with Speakman's blueprint of future development. Dan Ballard, who from the age of eight had been in Arsenal's academy and been successful on loan with Millwall, arrived for a fee of £2 million. Islington-born Aji Alese left West Ham for £500,000 having represented England at five different age levels. Jack Clarke's move from Tottenham was made permanent, whilst goalkeeper Anthony Patterson was given a four-year contract, in recognition of being the best prospect between the posts since Pickford. The financial results covering the year to July '22 and released the following April would include a statement illustrating the club's direction of travel: 'Since Kyril Louis-Dreyfus acquired control of the football club the average age of the squad has reduced from over 29 to under 24 … This is consistent with the strategy to grow and develop talent in the first team.' The accounts stated that the two shareholders, Louis-Dreyfus and Sartori, put £10.4 million into Sunderland during that accounting period. The former was presumed to be the sole investor. Over the following year to July '23 an additional £5.5 million of funding increased the cumulative amount of shareholder commitment to £18.05 million. Although it was anticipated that those funds would be 'converted to equity in due course', they represented a modest commitment compared with the excesses of Ellis Short.

For clubs graduating from League One to the Championship the financial demands were greater than for those ascending from the Championship to the Premier League. No minimum guaranteed broadcasting money of £100 million existed. Second-tier clubs, some with a sense of entitlement, greedily eyed the riches above them. Ambition often outstripped reality. Freshly relegated clubs benefitted from high parachute payments. At the end of Sunderland's first season in higher company a relatively modest loss of £9.68 million was disclosed, despite revenue from broadcasting tripling to beyond £10 million. This windfall was soaked up, and more, by an inevitable increase in wages. No less than 20 fellow Championship clubs sustained greater losses; that fact alone underlined either a realistic caution from Louis-Dreyfus or, as some supporters suspected, a lack of ambition. The Coates family of Bet 365 fame that controlled Stoke City, possessed personal wealth of £8 billion. When they called, Alex Neil marched to their beat. Sunderland had just beaten City in the Potteries through a Ross Stewart goal to attain an eighth point from five matches. Presumably, Neil had thrashed out terms after the game with the Stoke hierarchy in cloak-and-dagger fashion. There were calls of 'Judas' but Neil considered a modest pay award an unsuitable recognition for his achievement of promotion, particularly as he had vented concern at the playing squad.

Within 72 hours, Tony Mowbray was named head coach. Teesside-born, he captained Middlesbrough at 22, later managing them. His appointment induced more opprobrium than any other of Sunderland's 30 previous permanent post-war appointments. The long-standing Boro club fanzine is named 'Fly Me To The Moon' in recognition of a comment by Mowbray's former manager Bruce Rioch, who said that if he had to fly to the moon he would take Mowbray with him. The 58-year-old's homely manner and unfashionable dress sense belied his innate knowledge of the game; he would eventually win over a moaning majority. Mowbray wanted Sunderland to play attractive football but was initially disadvantaged by the loss through injury of Ross Stewart and on-loan Ellis Simms. Particularly disappointing was Stewart's absence, sidelined after two goals against Rotherham, on the very day Mowbray took a watching brief on commencing a two-year contract.

As in a previous job at Blackburn, Mowbray preferred working with young players. His first signing arose when he persuaded Manchester United that Sunderland were capable of progressing the development of Amad Diallo, their exciting £27 million purchase, who had spent the previous season on loan to Glasgow Rangers. Mowbray's first notable public utterance was to express surprise that there had been no regular place for Patrick Roberts, a player whose talent he described as 'scary'. Reading were defeated 3-0 away in mid-September. Roberts, bristling with confidence, scored two wonderful first-half goals. Sunderland's third, from Clarke, the culmination of a breathtaking, brilliant bout of passing, would have graced the Etihad and perhaps gained Raich Carter's approval as a suitable enhancement to a mid-thirties Roker Park afternoon.

The joy of a 2-1 Boxing Day victory over Blackburn before 43,921, was tempered when leading scorer Stewart, having just recovered from an earlier injury, ruptured an Achilles tendon. He was ruled out for the remainder of the season and growing speculation around the future of the player, said to be on a modest £5,000 a week, was conveniently suspended. Despite Stewart's absence, Sunderland won 4-1 at Wigan in their last outing of the calendar year and moved to fourth in a league where at least half the sides harboured legitimate play-off hopes. Centre half Dan Ballard returned from an injury that he had received in the season's third match.

Diallo, eased into action, was linked with Roberts to form a potent right-side pair. At 15 years and 203 days, Chris Rigg became the youngest ever outfield player for the club when he appeared as a substitute at Shrewsbury in a third round FA Cup tie. When the fourth round Fulham game finished, the average age of the Sunderland eleven was under 22. The performance was a ringing endorsement of the new direction taken. A late goal denied them victory and the replay encouraged a healthy 30,000 crowd. A spirited performance ended with a 3-2 defeat. Pierre Ekwah, unable to force himself into West Ham's side, joined in January on a four-and-a-half year contract after Alese recommended Sunderland to him as an appropriate environment for his development. Left-footed, he settled into midfield with a nice range of passing.

However, when Alex Neil brought Stoke to the Stadium of Light at the beginning of March Sunderland had taken one point from three games and lost heavily 5-1. Ballard was then injured again, shortly afterwards to be joined by Danny Batth, his vastly experienced partner and bedrock of the defence. Three fixtures remained. A bereft Sunderland rallied. They stormed from behind at West Bromwich Albion through two Dennis Cirkin goals, against opponents also in contention for a top-six place.

The 45,000 attending the last home league game raised the average to 39,326, a figure bettered by only nine clubs. The three points required to advance play-off hopes looked remote when Watford opened a 2-0 lead on 69 minutes and although O'Nien, playing out of position to cover the stricken pair absent in the heart of defence, retaliated within seconds, it wasn't until the final moments when Roberts, cutting in from the right on his left foot as was his manner, curled a prodigious effort into the corner of the net to equalise. The play-off challenge was over barring an unusual set of results during the next week. On the final day, closest challengers Millwall with two goals from Duncan Watmore at the New Den, were 3-1 ahead of Blackburn at half-time and at that juncture Sunderland, drawing at Preston, seemed out of contention. Not so. In the space of 15 minutes Millwall lost their lead and Sunderland, through Diallo, Pritchard and Clarke, earned a scarcely believable 3-0 advantage. Millwall threw everyone forward but their desperate attempt to score a vital fourth goal to move back into sixth place rebounded when Blackburn claimed a fourth themselves. Wearside fans at Deepdale recovered their breath.

Semi-final play-off opponents Luton presented a formidable, physical barrier to a side without a recognisable spine. They took an early lead but failed to capitalise on their height advantage leaving a welcome absence of high balls for Sunderland to counter. A splendid Diallo equaliser prefaced a stirring second period that was crowned by a diving Hume header. The stadium shook, sending a message that a famous club were alive and kicking. For the return at Kenilworth Road, Luton reverted to type. Sunderland's makeshift side were unable to withstand constant aerial bombardment and were beaten 2-0, 3-2 on aggregate.

When Luton defeated Coventry City in the final, the narrative centred on their meteoric climb from the National League and an anachronistic 10,000-capacity ground that would disfigure the pristine landscape of the Premier League. Brentford's achievement, finishing England's ninth-highest club, including a league double over serial trophy collectors Manchester City, suggested it was possible for anyone, provided they possessed the right management and infrastructure, to carve a suitable niche in the game. Sunderland, with Speakman on board and Louis-Dreyfus a majority shareholder, were hopeful of progress. Stoke City, who poached Neil, ironically finished only sixteenth, and reported a loss of £26.7 million. The new figures of influence within Sunderland were striving to forge a different path to the repeated failures of the past, which in 1958 had brought to an end an unbroken run in the top tier, to be followed by ten further relegations and at least two occasions when the very existence of the club was threatened.

A second season in the Championship beckoned with the ownership issue resolved; Kyril Louis-Dreyfus and Juan Sartori held 64% and 36% of shares respectively. Season ticket sales numbered 35,000, a figure never previously attained, with some sold for a reopened Premier Concourse. Diallo returned to Manchester United as expected. Although missing most of the previous campaign injured, Ross Stewart's sale to newly relegated Southampton was met with surprise. Stewart was a commanding presence up front when fit and the £10 million fee received, minus a sell-on clause to Ross County, was perhaps inadequate compensation. Other departures were ill-received. Although the consistency of 33-year-old Danny Batth in central defence was recognised by the Supporters' Player of the Year award, he was disappointingly not granted a second full season. Lynden Gooch, the longest serving of the current players, like Batth an experienced performer, was released. Sporting Director Kristjaan Speakman's quest for a new model army gathered pace. As Birmingham City's Academy manager he had nurtured the gifted Jude Bellingham. Speakman, referring to then fifteen-year-old Bellingham, is quoted in Micheal Calvin's revered book No Hunger In Paradise, 'When, in say five years' time, he is in the first team he has got to have all the component parts. He has to have the clear head to play as a four, the box-to-box qualities of an eight, and the cleverness and creativity of a ten. He needs the challenge of taking on substantially different roles. Combine those qualities, and you have the project, to produce a world-class player'. At twenty, he became a valuable part of Real Madrid and the England team; he was the parade horse of Speakman's career. His younger brother Jobe, also developed at Birmingham, was amongst a further raft of youngsters he attracted to Sunderland. The average age of the squad was reduced further. A number of unproven forwards arrived, including Mason Burstow a Chelsea academy loanee, Luis Hemir, handed a five-year contract after impressing for Benfica reserves and Abdoullah Ba, signed from Le Havre. Nazariy Rusyn, a 25-year-old Ukrainian centre forward, in comparison a veteran and two inches short of six feet, came from Dynamo Kiev for a fee of £2 million. Not so much a team in transition, Sunderland resembled a team in a test tube. Mowbray's work was cut out.

Despite a marked lack of goals from front players, Sunderland unexpectedly enjoyed September. The rapidly improving Jack Clarke, whom defenders often found unplayable, both scored and created openings as he cut in from the left wing on his right foot. The month commenced with a 5-0 home win over Southampton and included three away wins, each featuring three goals. Five matches produced twelve points with six of the fourteen strikes attributed to Clarke. Tony Mowbray constantly reshuffled his forward line but goals would not come from Speakman's neophytes. Winter approached; optimism faded. Pierre Ekwah and the highly regarded Dan Neil struggled whilst Bellingham, who started the season as a 17-year-old and hardly missed a game, unsurprisingly became tired. Without Diallo to complement him, the ersatz Roberts was reduced to the level of a somewhat unpredictable ball-player. Alese, Cirkin and the particularly unlucky Huggins suffered a series of injuries. Through Batth's departure O'Nien had become a permanent, rather than stopgap centre back alongside Ballard. After a Neil penalty rescued a point at Millwall, Tony Mowbray vented his increasing frustration at not having a recognised forward, 'But we're still lacking a real goal threat. We didn't look like we were going to score loads of goals. That's not meant to be a criticism – these are young players who need the game time to learn the job. They're learning on the job and we have to keep showing them.' Those 'off message' utterances were his last. Within days he was replaced by Michael Beale, an unexceptional former manager of Queens Park Rangers and Glasgow Rangers. Supporters, although divided in their reaction to Mowbray's abrupt departure, were unanimously critical at Beale's appointment, clamouring for his removal after the first game, a 3-0 home defeat by Coventry days before Christmas.

The welcome distraction of a first FA Cup derby since 1956 with Newcastle United backfired spectacularly. Through the auspices of the Football Association it was inevitable that the travelling United support would receive a large allocation, leading to anger from season ticket holders forced to relocate from the North Stand. The unnecessary concession of the Black Cat corporate facility to away fans was compounded when Sunderland rebranded this area with United colours and slogans. Facing a public relations backlash, the branding was hastily removed but the saga spoke of a Stadium of Light hierarchy not in tune with their public. On the pitch, Sunderland proved just as accommodating to their Tyneside visitors in a 3-0 third round defeat. They played a tedious game passing out from the back instead of launching the ball into the Newcastle half, a tactic that would have at least reduced the gulf in ability between the sides. Ballard put through his own goal and as the second half began, a culpable Ekwah was robbed of possession on the 18-yard line allowing Alexander Isak to score the first of his two goals, the latter of which was a penalty arising from a rash Ballard challenge. Clarke, normally Sunderland's standout player, hardly featured.

In January '24 the departure to Birmingham of the vastly accomplished Alex Pritchard left Beale in the unenviable position of managing a squad shorn of experience. Results worsened. Beale, after only 12 matches, was offered up as a sacrificial lamb on the 19th February, to become the shortest managerial appointment in Sunderland's history. Mike Dodds again resumed the role of interim head coach. Sunderland were out of play-off contention having suffered six consecutive defeats, which equalled their two worst historical runs of losses in the second tier. A goalless draw in mid-March on Wearside against lowly QPR stopped the rot, despite a failure to land a single effort on target. Jack Clarke's continued absence with an ankle ligament injury contributed to the poor results, in addition to underlining Sunderland's reliance on him.

A day of miserable, unrelenting drizzle marred Easter Monday. The response to Blackburn's fourth goal on 54 minutes was a cascade towards the exits. As the match wound to its torturous conclusion, the few thousand die-hards remaining from an official attendance of 42,019 were silhouetted against acres of shiny, bright seats. Long before the final whistle signalled a 5-1 defeat, traffic inched west on a congested Wessington Way towards the A19. It was ever thus, or so it seemed. An unsatisfactory campaign of boom and bust meandered to a humdrum close. None of the last seven home matches were won. All told, Sunderland finished sixteenth and suffered no less than 22 defeats from a 46-match programme. The sad passing of Charlie Hurley on 22nd April, at the fine old age of eighty-seven, was commemorated on the final match day. His last appearance at the Stadium of Light in 2016 featured an emotional pitch appearance before the commencement of a fixture against Hull City. It marked the relocation of the newly refurbished original training ground gates to a visible location behind the West Stand; gates that honoured his name and were previously installed in a quiet part of South Tyneside that is now subsumed by the club's Academy. The great man is not forgotten.

33

AN ECHO OF 1973

2024-25

The Frenchman Régis Le Bris, possessing a reputation for nurturing young talent, was appointed head coach and signed a three-year contract at the beginning of July '24. The 48-year-old had completed two seasons in that position at FC Lorient, the last of which saw the club relegated to Ligue 2. Kristjaan Speakman's decision was made after Will Still, his main target, joined Lens despite initially agreeing to a Wearside move. The arrival of Le Bris, unknown in England, seemed symptomatic of the reduced circumstances of a club who in recent years had experienced the household names of Keane, Bruce, O'Neill, Allardyce and Moyes. He was the twentieth permanent holder of the role in the twenty-two years since Peter Reid departed. Perhaps it was too much to presume he might change the fortunes of Sunderland, albeit on a smaller scale, in similar fashion to that of his fellow countryman Arsène Wenger, who had revolutionised Arsenal and like Le Bris possessed a background so modest that hardly any supporters were aware of him.

Before the 2024-25 campaign commenced, Sunderland lost Jack Clarke to newly promoted Ipswich, a fee of £15 million simply too much to refuse. With 12 points from 5 games in August, Sunderland led the division. Then, injuries to both central defenders Dan Ballard and Aji Alese, forced the loan of Chris Mepham from Bournemouth. Mepham was outstanding and yet, the fact he was unable to get a regular game for an ordinary Premier League outfit, highlighted the gap between the two leagues; little wonder some supporters feared promotion. Sunderland remained top until dislodged by a series of five draws and a defeat in November. Despite attendances regularly topping 40,000 and the emergence of exciting forwards, Eliezer Mayenda and Romaine Mundle, a predominantly young team seemed edgy, unable to press home an advantage or hold a winning position. Bellingham, having added a noticeable physicality to his game whilst impressing in midfield, attracted interest from other clubs. Chris Rigg, his junior, hardly missed a game. Dan Neil, entrusted with the captain's armband at the age of 22, seemed a veteran in comparison. Throughout, Luke O'Nien remained stellar. He has made more appearances at the Monkwearmouth stadium than anyone else, earning a cult following for his commitment on the pitch and likeable presence off it.

Tommy Watson was a highly regarded academy graduate. He was brought up in nearby Horden, the same former pit village that supplied Stan Anderson. The refulgent forward, mostly positioned out wide, lit up a gloomy, winter's afternoon that was assailed by Storm Darragh. He scored twice, the first quickly cancelling out an early Stoke goal, and also had an effort pushed against a post as he led Sunderland to a 2-1 victory. Less than 20 minutes into the next game, also on Wearside, Watson's tall but slender frame crumpled against a challenge from a Bristol City defender. The 18-year-old did not start another game for Sunderland. When he regained his fitness Brighton agreed to buy him for £10 million, the transaction not due to be completed until June. He had only made 11 full appearances. In the meantime, his first team appearances were as a substitute; an inauspicious ending on Wearside seemed likely for Watson, who had joined his favourite club when he was a junior schoolboy.

The major contenders for an automatic promotion place were Sheffield United and Burnley, both relegated the previous season, alongside Leeds United who were relegated the year before that. The common denominator was the advantage of parachute payments, a lucrative source of revenue unavailable to Sunderland. Nevertheless, when the Wearsiders defeated both Sheffield United on New Years Day, through goals by Mayenda and Wilson Isidor, and then Portsmouth the following Sunday at the Stadium of Light, only three points separated them from table-topping Leeds. The next Championship away outing was at Burnley who were in second position. Enzo Le Fée, a creative Frenchman from Roma, made his debut. An agreement was struck for Roma to receive £19 million if Sunderland were promoted. It was a cruel Friday night at Turf Moor. With the game deadlocked on 87 minutes Isidor, the forward Sunderland had spent £6 million on in the summer, and who supporters remained divided about, had a penalty saved by James Trafford. Worse followed. He took a second penalty in the seventh minute of added time and was denied by Trafford again. The goalkeeper was booked for his gamesmanship in delaying the kick. Exactly a month later, Le Bris suffered another night containing a bitter ending for his young team. In Elland Road's bear-baiting pit of venom, Sunderland scored through Isidor and then sitting back, defended stoutly. On 78 minutes, Leeds United's substitute Pascal

Struijk equalised and five minutes into added time scored a second headed goal.

Sunderland drifted, too far behind the three clubs jostling for automatic promotion and too far ahead of the chasing pack. Little urgency came from the players or crowd. Le Bris shuffled his pack, remaining calm, impervious to a growing unrest. This was either a phoney war from the Frenchman or an attempt to revive a spent force. Sunderland slumbered as others scrapped like alley cats for a coveted play-off place. The last five games were lost. It was common knowledge that Jobe Bellingham was set to join the German club, Borussia Dortmund, for their record fee of £27.8 million. Frank Lampard's Coventry were semi-final opponents. The Sky Blues were unbeaten in 10 previous games against Sunderland, stretching back to 2018. None of this mattered as the Wearsiders, transformed and displaying a fervour to match their travelling support, tore into Coventry. After 20 minutes a wild tackle from Dennis Cirkin, on their danger man Tatsuhiro Sakamoto, left the full-back fortunate to escape with only a booking. Isidor, without a goal in three months, received a pass from Le Fée to put Sunderland ahead on 68 minutes but within two minutes Jack Rudoni had equalised. With the match evenly poised, the football gods smiled on Sunderland. Eliezer Mayenda seized on a bad back pass and dribbled calmly around the goalkeeper, to secure a 2-1 advantage for the return leg. The bedlam back home in the pubs and private gatherings was a mere appetiser.

On the following mild Tuesday night, the Sunderland team bus was greeted by a cordon of chanting fans as it inched forward to the ground, some holding aloft torch flares that spewed forth a red haze of smoke, contaminating the air with sulphur. Not one single person of the 46,530 heading to the Stadium of Light, even in their wildest imagination, foresaw the drama to follow. At first, little separated the sides. A cagey contest then swung almost imperceptibly in Coventry's direction and it was hardly a surprise when Ephron Mason-Clark scored on 76 minutes. The Stadium of Light for once held its collective breath as the visitors pressed strongly but Sunderland, displaying a tenacity that belied their tender years, held firm and in the 30 minutes of extra time seized the initiative as a constant roar infected the arena. When Le Fée walked to the corner flag, readying himself to launch the ball into a crowded penalty box, the clock behind him on the South Stand revealed that less than 30 seconds remained of added time. The electronic advertising boards displayed the Sunderland play-off slogan of, 'TIL THE END. The shoulder of Dan Ballard's giant frame made contact and as the ball thudded off the underside of the bar, bouncing over the line, a microsecond of disbelief froze time. The noise that jolted everyone back into their world was intense and prolonged. Even Roker Park, famed for its Roker Roar, did not experience such commotion. Only those who remembered the Tottenham FA Cup tie in 1961 may beg to differ.

Sheffield United summarily dispatched Bristol City 6-0 over two legs. They finished third in the table, ten points behind both Leeds and Burnley and, despite having had two points deducted for irregularities, no less than fourteen above Sunderland. United's play-off record was shocking. All nine previous attempts had ended in failure, including four Wembley visits. They were, however, clear favourites to beat Sunderland. Le Bris fielded the following eleven: Patterson, Hume, Cirkin, Neil, Ballard, O'Nien, Rigg, Bellingham, Mayenda, Le Fée, Mundle. Finishing behind United meant they wore a change strip of mainly white, a contrast to the traditional red and white stripes of the opposition. United's Gustavo Hamer had recently been voted EFL Championship Player of the Season. The Wembley final was dubbed the £200 million game, as the winners were guaranteed a minimum of £120 million the following year from a new television deal and if relegated, substantial parachute payments.

The drama that unfolded eclipsed that of the second Coventry game. Events came thick and fast. Anthony Patterson produced the best save of his career in the second minute. In the blink of an eye, he threw himself at a short-range header from Kieffer Moore, palming it around a post. A lengthy delay then followed when O'Nien, in considerable pain with a dislocated shoulder from his attempt to stop Moore, was substituted by Mepham. With Hamer dictating proceedings and his side the more robust it was no surprise when Tyrese Campbell, capitalising on a quick break after a corner was cleared, opened the scoring. The pivotal moment of the afternoon came in the 33rd minute. Harrison Burrows' shot from the edge of the box evaded a posse of bodies and fizzed past Patterson. The lifeline of the Video Assistant Referee, commonly known as VAR, came to Sunderland's rescue. Exclusive to the Premier League each week, the authorities had permitted its use in the play-off final. A panel of three independent assessors surveyed video coverage of the incident and concluded that Patterson was partially unsighted by an offside Sheffield player. In an instant everything changed as thousands of Yorkshire voices were silenced. Sunderland, freed from their tentativeness, enjoyed more possession. Nevertheless, in the second half another tense moment arose. Cirkin, caught in two minds, allowed United to steal possession but Patterson again rescued the situation by sticking out his leg to block the goal-bound ball. VAR would probably have intervened as on close inspection it was apparent that the ball was handled to gain an advantage over the full-back. On 73 minutes Le Bris, realising his team hadn't threatened despite an improvement, made a brave double substitution by replacing Neil and Mundle with Watson and Isidor. Coincidentally, Sheffield United's influential Hamer was forced to retire through an injury. A mere three minutes later, Sunderland equalised.

Patrick Roberts, introduced much earlier as a replacement for Rigg, received a superb pass from Le Fée and returned an even better pass to Mayenda, who took only two touches to transfer the ball from his weaker left to stronger right foot and smash a shot into the roof of the net. He had been bought from the lowly French club Sochaux for £1 million in 2023. Mayenda looked a steal in that magical moment. The final twist of the 2024-25 Championship season, even if scripted for a Paramount Pictures blockbuster, would have seemed far-fetched. United were disadvantaged when having used all five substitutes, their defender Anel Ahmedhodžić was taken off with concussion. When play resumed, with United still reduced to ten men, five minutes of the seven added on had elapsed. The name of Tommy Watson was missing from the team line-up in the Wembley programme. Le Bris had used Watson sparingly since announcing his transfer and the youngster, marking time before uprooting to Brighton, was a mere shadow of the rampaging force who burst to prominence before Christmas. Indeed, even allowing him to train with the first team squad, let alone play a few cameos here and there, was regarded as questionable. Truth is stranger than fiction. Extra time looked inevitable with little danger apparent when Watson picked up a loose ball. He drove forward and from 22 yards struck a low, sweetly placed right-footed shot into the extreme corner of the goal. 'TIL THE END!

There were cheers and tears of joy, an inability to take it all in, an inability to process the significance. Sunderland were again a Premier League club. Unlike the joyous League One Wembley game with Wycombe Wanderers, this was visceral, close to the bone and laden with a heavy now or never vibe. The events of 1973 will never be repeated but those supporters present experienced an echo of it. The Sunderland players, many in the flower of their youth, cavorted around the Wembley pitch without a care in the world. Their future however was uncertain. A majority have so far failed to clear the high bar of Premier League football.

Over the last two seasons, the six promoted clubs have been relegated immediately. Throughout 2022-23, Nottingham Forest spent £143 million net, a record for a club leaving the Championship, and although to many this represented a profligate gamble, it was enough for them to survive, albeit by the skin of their teeth. It seemed likely that Sunderland's major shareholders, Robert Louis-Dreyfus and Juan Sartori, would hedge their bets, and in similar fashion to some promoted clubs, accept the likelihood of relegation in exchange for keeping some of the Premier League windfall, therefore guaranteeing long-term financial security. Then, if another promotion were achieved fairly quickly, the chances of staying in the world's richest league for longer than one season would be enhanced.

Two hours before the beginning of the 2025-26 season, a bright sun warmed Wearside. Thousands milled around the Stadium of Light, the turnstiles already admitting those eager to see a Sunderland team newly promoted to the top-flight. It was back in 2007, a period featuring Roy Keane, Niall Quinn and the Drumaville consortium, since that last happened. Football supporters and logic are not compatible. Judging from their smiles and air of expectancy, it was easy to deduce that the years of struggle had been consigned to the past. Of course, the younger followers, unsullied by failure and with the noise from Ballard's goal still renting their senses, could be excused. Yet, it had been only a little earlier in the previous season when a number of supporters were of the opinion that it might be better if Sunderland remained in the Championship a little longer, in order to maximise the 'model' of buying cheap and selling dear. Now, their champagne corks were popping, the glasses no longer half empty. 38,000 season tickets had been sold. The play-off experience might have softened their stance but it has been the remarkable splashes in the transfer market since then that have changed expectations. Not since the Bank of England era has a Sunderland boardroom been so ambitious in a close-season; with Kristjaan Speakman remaining as Sporting Director there was every confidence that the right players had been recruited, unlike previous decades. Sunderland marked their first game of the season by defeating West Ham United 3-0; the scorers were Mayenda, Ballard and Isidor. The former showcased his potential with a wonderful, glancing header. Eight players made their debut, including seven who lined up for the kick off, a record for a Premier League match. The prize capture was none other than Granit Xhaka, signed from Bayer Leverkusen, who proved a major influence during seven years at Arsenal. A month short of his thirty-third birthday, he led Sunderland out and his presence throughout a nervy, goalless first half was invaluable. Habib Diarra, a club record £30 million buy from Strasbourg featured, as did Simon Adingra, an exciting left-winger who Brighton were reluctant to part with. Anthony Patterson, despite concerns around his distribution, had excelled in the play-off games but was replaced by Robin Roefs, a young Dutch goalkeeper. Roefs, purchased for £10 million, was not first choice for NEC Nijmegen but on the early evidence he looked an inspired signing. The £140 million Sunderland spent on twelve players, which included a loanee and two free transfers, was only slightly offset by the fee received for Bellingham. Within hours of going on sale, all tickets were snapped up for the second league match at the stadium against Brentford. Perhaps it is not the hope that kills, perhaps it is the hope that regenerates.

When Sunderland relocated to Monkwearmouth, the Stadium of Light became the largest football arena built in England since Wembley. Immediately, the club caught or overtook many of its rivals, if not at first on the pitch, then certainly off it. For a few heady years they remained box-office. A couple of decades on, the climate had changed unimaginably. Sunderland, a provincial powerhouse for so many periods in their history, faced an uncertain future and even though they had climbed out of League One, the Premier League seemed tantalisingly out of reach. Sunderland's traditional strengths, that have served them in so many different ways, were no longer relevant. As an example, the 'Team of All The Talents', champions of England three times in four seasons, benefitted from a proximity to enormously gifted Scottish players. Conveniently, those Anglo-Scottish pioneers were able to earn extra income as they were suited to the very type of heavy industrial work that was unavailable further south. Furthermore, where there was muck, there was brass. Self-made businessmen, resident in a thriving large town such as Sunderland, poured wealth into their favourite local team. An incentive existed because the football clubs of the North enjoyed a monopoly of the working man's leisure time. Alternative entertainment was scarce and there was a thirst for the game.

Now, after a 33-year, relentless, ingenious marketing onslaught, that owes its origins to pay-per-view live broadcasting arising from the formation of the Premier League, most of the population is captive. This is despite the leading players enjoying different lives to those who watch them on the field; millionaires rarely socialise with anyone but their own type. When Sunderland defeated Arsenal in the 1973 FA Cup semi-final both sets of players raced off the pitch within thirty seconds without acknowledging their supporters. That was perfectly normal then and not thought of as disrespectful. Although this was some years after the abolition of the maximum wage, players and supporters remained in the same communities as each other, their lifestyles not markedly different. The Premier League, worried that a growing disconnect between both parties would damage the integrity of their brand, altered the immediate moments that followed the referee's final whistle, therefore creating an illusion that nothing had really changed since those relatively innocent days. There is now a communal, convoluted stage-managed ten minutes or so, when players, management, media and supporters enmesh in celebration or commiseration. This public relations masterclass, copied throughout the lower leagues, also introduces a veneer of entertainment to what may otherwise have been an ordinary ninety minutes.

Football, far removed from its origins of twenty-two blokes kicking a ball around an unenclosed field, now replicates the design of the gory 'bread and circuses' entertainment once dispensed inside the colosseums of the Roman Empire. The basic sustenance of the bread is increasingly supplied by food banks; the round ball provides the metaphorical circus side of the bargain to distract and placate the populace. Sunderland, despite returning to the Premier League, are unable to benefit fully from the modern mania for the game unlike the glamorous, elite clubs that are able to charge exorbitant ticket prices. For that gilded minority match day revenue, apart from the actual price of tickets, is a lucrative source of revenue and also handy in mitigating the effect of Financial Fair Play or whatever similar legislation may evolve. When they were striving to leave the Championship, Sunderland were bound by legislation to restrict any losses over a three-year period to within a strictly defined limit; this restriction could only be increased by permitting an owner to inject cash but crucially, only in regulated, modest amounts. Similar restrictions exist in the Premier League. The era of a Roman Abramovich or even an Ellis Short, able to bankroll anyone, is over. For now, at least.

The Stadium of Light, despite cosmetic improvements in readiness for the return of Premier League football, remains disadvantaged by tight concourses, limited catering facilities and a dearth of upmarket viewing areas. It is no longer ahead of its time and even if it were, its catchment area, which includes a disproportionate number of food banks, is relatively impoverished. Tottenham Hotspur took residence of a state-of-the-art 62,000 capacity stadium in 2019. The public are in situ hours before and after kick-off, whilst their pockets are emptied by a range of diversions. The stadium expenditure is comfortably over a million pounds every match day. Even little old Fulham, at a once dated, twee Craven Cottage, have rebranded. Their nondescript, bland Riverside Stand built on the cheap in the seventies, which replaced a popular open side, has been superseded by a shimmering temple of conspicuous consumption. The rain and wind that once swept in from the Thames, intermingled with the common reek of Bovril and convenience food, has been supplanted by a rooftop swimming pool, two Michelin star restaurants and a health club. The most expensive of the season tickets within the 8,000-seater stand are priced at around £3,000. Despite an overall capacity of 28,500, Fulham's ticket sales and ancillary revenue outstrip those of a sold-out Stadium of Light. Everton inhabit a futuristic waterside setting in a city completely changed from the monochrome drabness that prevailed before it was awarded 'European Capital of Culture' status. The facilities available within their new home attract worldwide interest from 'football tourists', whose growing numbers underline the game's popularity. If, in the 1950s, Sunderland were behind the curve through an overreliance on expensive imports, now it could be argued that compared to the global superpowers in English football, they are no more than a mere smudge on the graph. Yet, their achievement in returning to the Premier League is exceptional. Sunderland have succeeded by developing their own academy players, a judicious recruitment policy and establishing a first-class relationship with the local community. How far can this enlightened self-sustainability model take the club? The journey so far has proved an unqualified success.

Whatever the future holds, there will be little triumphs along the way, battles won and battles lost. The 50th anniversary of the 1973 FA Cup win has come and gone. Bob Stokoe said 'I didn't bring the magic; it's always been here. I just came back to find it'. In an ever-changing world, the fanaticism of those who turn up at the Stadium of Light endures. Those supporters were rewarded in 2025. The magic returned.

BIBLIOGRAPHY

Books

Allison, Malcolm	Colours of My Life (Everest Books 1975)
Anderson, Stan	Captain of the North (Sports Books 2010)
Appleton, Arthur	Hotbed of Soccer (Rupert Hart-Davis 1960)
Ashurst, Len	Left Back In Time (Know the Score 2009)
Bagchi & Rogerson	The Unforgiven (Aurum 2002)
Baxter, Jim	The Party's Over (Hutchinson 1984)
Best, George	Where do I go from here? (Queen Anne 1981)
Bingham, Billy	Soccer With The Stars (Stanley Paul 1962)
Bower, Tom	Broken Dreams (Pocket Books 2003)
Bowler, Dave	Danny Blanchflower (Victor Gollancz 1997)
Buchan, Charles	A Lifetime In Football (Phoenix House 1955)
Canio, Paolo Di	The Autobiography (Collins Willow 2002)
Carter, Raich	Footballer's Progress (Sporting Handbooks 1950)
Chapman, Lee	More Than A Match (Arrow Books 1993)
Clough, Brian	Clough, The Autobiography (Partridge Press 1994)
Curran, Terry	Regrets of a Football Maverick (Vertical 2012)
Davies, Barry	Interesting, very interesting (Headline 2007)
Docherty, Tommy	My Story The Doc (Headline 2006)
Ford, Trevor	I Lead The Attack (Stanley Paul 1957)
Keating, Frank	The Highlights (Guardian Books 2014)
Gallacher, Ken	Slim Jim Baxter (Virgin Books 2002)
Gibson, John	Wor Jackie (Sportsprint 1990)
Giles, John	A Football Man (Hodder and Stoughton 2010)
Giller, Norman	Football And All That (Hodder and Stoughton 2004)
Glasper, Harry	Middlesbrough A Complete Record(Breedon 1989)
Greaves, Jimmy	The Heart of the Game (Time Warner Books 2005)
Green, Geoffrey	Soccer In The Fifties (Ian Allan 1974)
Hardwick, George	Gentleman George (Juniper 1998)
Hill, Jimmy	Striking for Soccer (Peter Davies 1961)
Hill, Jimmy	Jimmy Hill Story (Hodder and Stoughton 1998)
Hodgkinson, Alan	Between the Sticks (Harper Sport 2013)
Hopcraft, Arthur	The Football Man (Collins 1968)
Hunter, Norman	Biting Talk (Hodder and Stoughton 2004)
Inglis, Simon	Soccer in the dock (William Collins 1985)
Jones, Vinnie	Vinnie The Autobiography (Headline 1998)

Keane, Roy	The Second Half (Weidenfeld and Nicolson 2014)
Lawton, Tommy	My Twenty Years of Soccer (Heirloom Library 1955)
Malam, Colin	The Len Shackleton Story (Highdown 2004)
Mason, Rob	Sunderland: The Complete Record (Breedon 2005)
Macadam, John	The Macadam Road (Jarrolds 1955)
McMenemy, Lawrie	The Diary of a Season (Arthur Barker 1979)
McNeill, Billy	Hail Cesar (Headline 2004)
Moore, Brian	The Final Score (Hodder and Stoughton 1999)
Moynihan, John	The Soccer Syndrome (MacGibbon & Kee 1966)
Parlour, Ray	The Romford Pelé (Century 2016)
Peacock, Keith	No Substitute (Charlton Athletic Press 2004)
Quinn, Niall	The Autobiography (Headline 2002)
Reid, Peter	Cheer Up (Sport Media 2017)
Rothmans Yearbook	Editions 1 to 27 (Macdonald & Jane, Queen Anne)
Smith, Denis	Just One Of Seven (Know the Score 2008)
Smith, Tommy	Anfield Iron (Bantam Press 2008)
Stock, Alec	A Little Thing called Pride (Pelham Books 1982)
Tabner, Brian	Football Through the Turnstiles - Again (Yore 2002)
The Secret Footballer	Access All Areas (Guardian Books, Faber 2016)
Thomas, Dave	Jimmy Adamson (Pitch Publishing 2013)
Tueart, Dennis	My Football Journey (VSP 2011)
Varley, Nick	Golden Boy (Arum Press 1997)

Newspapers

Daily Express
Daily Mirror
Daily Sketch
Liverpool Echo
Manchester Evening News
Nottingham Evening Post
Sunday Express
Sunday Sun
Sunderland Echo
The Evening Chronicle
The Guardian
The Independent
The Journal
The Observer
The Sunday Times

Companies House
Sunderland AFC Financial Statements

Sunderland Match Day Programme
Chairman & Manager notes
Everton 26/08/1980
Arsenal 13/12/1980
Notts County 01/09/1982
Queens Park Rangers 07/03/1984
Everton 24/08/2002
Arsenal 09/02/2013
Manchester United 30/03/2013
Tottenham Hotspur 13/09/2014

Websites
BBC
British Newspaper Archive (for Liverpool Echo, Manchester Evening News and Nottingham Evening Post)
Historic League Table Generator